5/94

Wanderings of an
Environmental Journalist

≺   ≻

Wanderings of an Environmental Journalist

In Alaska and the American West

PHILIP L. FRADKIN

University of New Mexico Press
Albuquerque

Designed by Joanna V. Hill
Illustrations by Michael Taylor
© 1993 by the University of New Mexico Press
All rights reserved.

Library of Congress Cataloging-in-Publication Data

Fradkin, Philip L.
Wanderings of an environmental journalist:
In Alaska and the American West / Philip L. Fradkin.—1st ed.
p. cm.
ISBN 0–8263–1416–3
1. Man—Influence on nature—Alaska.
2. Man—Influence on nature—West (U.S.)
3. Fradkin, Philip L.—Journeys—Alaska.
4. Fradkin, Philip L.—Journeys—West (U.S.)
I. Title.
GF504.A4F73 1993
304.2'0978—dc20
92–34821
CIP

For *Justin Roberts* and *Jack Bliler*,
my first editors.
They passed on their knowledge
with patience and understanding.

Contents

Preface

For a period of ten years following Earth Day, with fourteen months off to play bureaucrat in Sacramento, I roamed Alaska and the American West as an environmental journalist. I worked for the *Los Angeles Times* and *Audubon* magazine. The *Times,* under its ambitious publisher, Otis Chandler, was accumulating one Pulitzer Prize after another. *Audubon,* guided by its talented editor, Les Line, was racking up one National Magazine Award after another. These were the golden years for those two publications, and I was fortunate to work for both of them: for the *Times* from 1964 to 1975, the latter five years as the paper's first environmental writer, and for *Audubon* from 1976 to 1981 as its first western editor.

I was fortunate for a number of reasons, not the least of which was that I was allowed to practice deep journalism. The editors on those two publications gave me virtual carte blanche to write about whatever I wished. They did not hesitate to allot sufficient amounts of time and money to research stories. The articles ran at great length, were well displayed, and had national exposure either through the *Los Angeles Times-Washington Post News Service* or the membership of the National Audubon Society. Thus, I had an opportunity unmatched by any other journalist to document the Southwest, West, and Northwest during the decade of the 1970s.

Besides being adequately paid, there was an additional bonus. Those articles gave me the ideas for the books that I would write in the following decades. As I attempted to free myself from the constraints of format, length, institutional biases, and deadline pressures by traveling the road from newspapers to magazines to books, I increasingly indulged my primary interest in history. What I write is history with an environmental twist, envirohistory if you will. I am fascinated by the repetitive cycles of history. Names change, memories fade, a set of circumstances arises again, past responses are repeated, and life rumbles on with some continuity.

This sense of elongated time gives me great comfort. Most of us in the American West are recent arrivals—transients who know little about what went on before. We live in the present. I needed to find my place within a context, so I have discovered the past through the exploration of present-day issues. I went backwards into time as far as I was allowed to as a journalist.

I believe that my written time line in these stories extends further back into the past and forward into the future than the artificial boundaries of any single decade. The power of a wild place, oil pipelines in the North, energy production in the West, war, a father's relationship with his son, Indian lands, forestry practices, wildfire, drought, grazing, overcrowding, and the dryland fantasies of humans are subjects that will always be relevant north and west of the one hundredth meridian.

For me, writing is a personal quest. I write to learn what is around me, what I think, and who I am. Hopefully, some good will come of what I have documented. I document. I don't spin ethereal webs of piety, theory, or description. Unlike many nature writers, if that is what I am, I like people. As with most nature writers, I am greatly interested in place, but perhaps not in the same manner. I am fascinated by the effect of place upon human behavior, the result of that particular concoction being history. Folly in decision making also attracts me, as does the intense competition for what is mistaken as the empty spaces of Alaska and the American West. Given all the demands being imposed upon these lands, and their inherent limits, they are very crowded lands, indeed. I keep asking myself, and hopefully others, how is this great land north and west of the Rocky Mountains being used; and is it being used wisely?

If these be unifying themes, so be it. All that I know with certainty is that these subjects were sufficiently interesting to compel me to write about them.

I have edited these articles to read better in a book format. I did not alter any material or interpretations in order to make myself seem more prescient. What has transpired since these stories were published is dealt with in the "Epilogue" under the same heading as the article. The reader can wait until he or she reads all of the articles; or upon finishing one, skip immediately to the end of the book to find out what has happened, if anything, during the intervening years.

PHILIP L. FRADKIN
Pt. Reyes Station, California
February 28, 1992

‹ I ›

Alaska

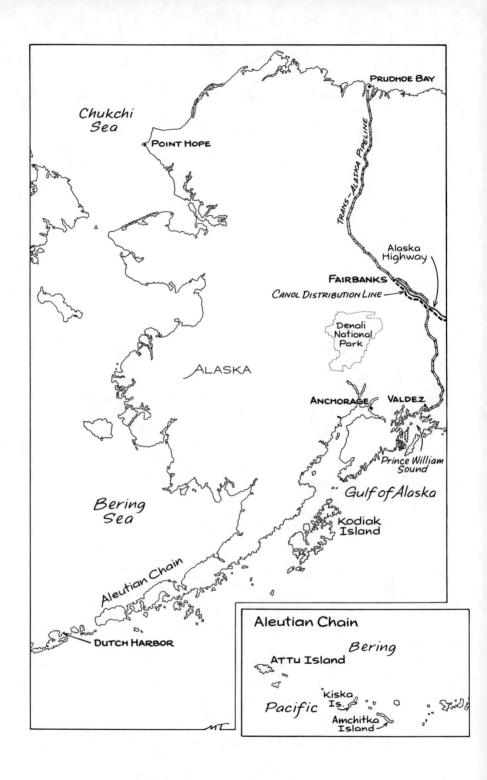

Chukchi
Sea

PRUDHOE BAY

POINT HOPE

TRANS-ALASKA PIPELINE

Alaska
Highway

FAIRBANKS

CANOL DISTRIBUTION LINE

Denali
National
Park

ALASKA

ANCHORAGE   VALDEZ

Prince William
Sound

Gulf of Alaska

Bering
Sea

Kodiak
Island

Aleutian Chain

DUTCH HARBOR

MT

Aleutian Chain

Bering

ATTU Island

Kiska
Is.

Pacific

Amchitka
Island

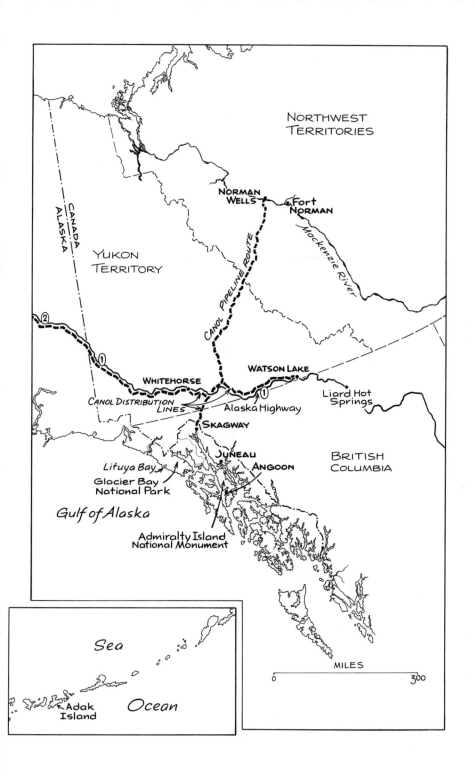

NORTHWEST TERRITORIES

NORMAN WELLS

Fort NORMAN

Mackenzie River

CANADA
ALASKA

YUKON TERRITORY

Canol Pipeline Route

②

①

WATSON LAKE

WHITEHORSE

Liard Hot Springs

Canol Distribution Lines

①

Alaska Highway

SKAGWAY

BRITISH COLUMBIA

JUNEAU

ANGOON

Lituya Bay

Glacier Bay National Park

Gulf of Alaska

Admiralty Island National Monument

Sea

Ocean

Adak Island

MILES

0   300

Lituya Bay

I first heard of Lituya Bay when I visited Glacier Bay National Monument in 1976.* While Glacier Bay is inland and reachable by commercial airlines and comfortable cruise ships, Lituya Bay is on the outer coast of southeast Alaska—a different place, entirely. I returned four years later and spent ten days at Lituya Bay. When I departed, I felt as though I had passed through the dark side of nature and been spared, for the time being.

Lituya Bay is compelling for its power. It is a wildly beautiful, volatile landscape whose history has been punctuated by the

*See "A Summer With Alex."

grinding action of glacial ice that rapidly advances and retreats across its surface, destructive earthquakes, volcanic eruptions, giant waves that move with blinding speed from the mountains to the sea, and other deadly waves that unexpectedly burst upon its entrance. The glaciers have scraped the landscape to its bone, the earthquakes have toppled mountains, and the waves have periodically decimated the vegetation and the few people who, from the time of the Tlingit Indians, have infrequently visited the bay. The Indians thought it was a bad place.

Lituya Bay is a separate place. It is walled off from the outside world. The only access is by small boat or seaplane; and when it storms or when the fog closes in tightly and the waves build up at the entrance, that place is locked up tighter than a vault. To the west is the Gulf of Alaska, one of the wildest bodies of water in the world. Cutting off access on the north is the Fairweather Glacier and on the south is the Lapérouse Glacier, whose ice calves directly into the gulf. To the east, towards the populated areas in southeastern Alaska, there are three barriers. First there is the three-thousand-foot Coastal Range. Then there is the rubble- and glacier-strewn gutter of Desolation Valley, the surface manifestation of the Fairweather Fault, which is the northern extension of the San Andreas Fault. Towering above all are the frozen wastelands of the fifteen-thousand-foot Fairweather Range.

The depth of the glacially scoured bay reaches a maximum of 470 feet, enough for the occasional gray whale seen swimming within it. There is a maximum tidal range of fifteen feet. With such a tremendous volume of water pouring in and out twice during a twenty-four–hour period, currents at the constricted entrance reach speeds of nearly fifteen miles per hour and treacherous waves can form with blinding speed on an ebb tide, particularly when an opposing wind blows from the gulf.

Indians and whites have drowned in these waves. An island in the center of the bay is named Cenotaph Island for the memorial that was erected there in 1786 when twenty-one French sailors perished in the waves at the entrance. On the average, one fishing boat a year is now lost in those waves. Others have been sunk by the giant waves that careen down the bay from the direction of the mountains.

Over the years animal and human activity has centered along the edges of the bay and the coarse black sand beaches that extend along the coast for fifteen miles in both directions. The dark-green interior is virtually impenetrable. It is guarded by a dense, wet rain forest consisting of interlocking trees, thick shrubs, and the spikes of devil's club plants. The vegetation, swamps, and coastal streams are fed by more than one hundred inches of annual rainfall.

It is an outsized land dominated by water in all its forms: glacial ice, snow, and rain; rivulets, streams, creeks, and rivers; and fogs, mists, vapors, and low clouds. There are bogs, swamps, ponds, peatlands, heaths, and muskeg. In the dark fall and winter months there are frequent gales. Snow drifts pile up in the lowland forests of Sitka spruce and western hemlock that shade into Alaska yellow cedar and mountain hemlock on the hillsides. The Tlingit Indians had no expression to describe blue skies, but plenty of words covered bad weather. People hung on only intermittently to the edges of this hostile land, where the magnetic compass variations are extreme.

On June 6, 1952, a young geologist, who was working for the U.S. Geological Survey's oil investigation program in the gulf, arrived in Lituya Bay. Don J. Miller poked around for a few days. He found the cabin of a hermit who had lived on Cenotaph Island before World War II, and made it his base camp. Miller noticed a difference in the tree lines surrounding the bay. He talked to the fishermen who were anchored there. They told him of the giant waves that had periodically swept the bay. The geologist was immediately caught by that place.

Don Miller graduated with a master's degree in geology from the University of Illinois and went to work in Alaska for the U.S. Geological Survey in 1942. He was a serious person dedicated to his work. A loner who was close to nobody except his family, Miller lived in San Francisco when he was not on one of his frequent Alaska trips. He was short, extremely strong, and quite capable in a wilderness situation. A photograph showed Miller with round, wire-rimmed spectacles and a face that was cast down, seemingly in an introspective mood.

The geologist returned the next summer for a three-week stay and camped on the island and at the mouth of Topsy Creek, a few miles south of the bay. Miller resumed his work, which was to map the oil-bearing strata. At the same time he pursued the matter of the giant waves. Miller cut sections from trees and gave them to the Forest Service Research Center in Juneau. A tree-ring count disclosed that there had been a disruption in 1936 and another in the 1853–1854 growing season. Miller reported his preliminary findings at the Seattle section meeting of the Geological Society of America in March 1954. He asked his fellow scientists what they thought the cause of the giant waves might be. He guessed it was earthquakes, but he had no proof.

The region in and around Lituya Bay is one of the most seismically active in the world. In the first eighty years of this century there have been eight major earthquakes within a three-hundred-mile radius of the bay. The Fairweather Fault is part of the interlocking fault system that forms the boundary between the North American and Pacific tectonic plates. At such places as Lituya Bay and, say, along the San Andreas Fault in northern California, those two huge masses are constantly straining against each other. Once in a while the land snaps.

Don Miller was on a geological survey vessel in Glacier Bay on July 9, 1958 when a strong earthquake rocked the bay. Since earthquakes were not that unusual in Glacier Bay and the damage did not seem extensive, Miller did not think much of it until he heard on the radio early the next morning that some boats were swamped and people had drowned in Lituya Bay. He also heard that the earthquake measured 7.9 on the Richter Scale, a rating that approached the 1906 San Francisco quake. He chartered a small plane and departed at 9:15 A.M. for Lituya Bay.

Five miles south of the bay large rafts of severed tree trunks were floating on the surface of the gulf. The freshly denuded trees had been completely stripped of branches and bark. As Miller and the pilot approached the bay, they could not believe what they saw.

"The bay is a shambles, the destruction is unbelievable," Miller jotted hurriedly in his journal.

Flying at the same altitude and using the altimeter, they judged that the maximum height of the surge was 1,800 feet, a figure that was later adjusted to 1,740 feet—still enough for the wave to qualify as being the highest ever recorded in the world.

Miller marveled at the force and power of the wave. He noted: "Cut a channel across the top of Cenotaph Island, washed away the cabin there, stripped entire La Chaussee Spit bare, removed lighthouse and several hundred feet of trees adjacent to it at Harbor Point. Washed into Fish Lake to north and across to sea east of The Paps."

They flew back and forth along the length of the bay looking for a possible cause, but found none. Back at Glacier Bay Miller heard a radio interview with Bill Swanson, one of the surviving fishermen, and accounts by others of one of the world's most unusual cataclysmic events.

It began inauspiciously. An oily swell undulated across the surface of the gulf as three fishing boats headed toward the calm entrance of the bay to anchor for the night. The thirty-eight–foot *Edrie* was first into the bay at 8 P.M. On board were Howard Ulrich and his son, Howard Jr., who was nicknamed Sonny. They were tired after a long, unsuccessful day trolling for salmon. Ulrich was tempted to anchor in the lee of Cenotaph Island but instead selected a cove on the south shore about two miles from the entrance. He was in a contemplative mood; and the black-legged kittiwakes on the south end of the island were unusually raucous, filling the bay's empty spaces with their piercing cries of *kittiwake, kittiwake*. Father and son ate dinner, washed the dishes, and then settled down in their bunks. Another long day of fishing lay ahead of them, or so they thought.

Just before falling asleep at 9 P.M., they heard a boat's engine. It was the *Badger* with Bill and Vivian Swanson on board entering the bay. The Swansons headed toward the island and then reversed course and put their hook down in Anchorage Cove. At about the same time the *Sunmore* entered the bay and anchored just behind the spit, about half way between the *Badger* and the entrance. Orville and Mickey Wagner, a young couple who had just purchased the *Sunmore* a few months ago, were friends of the Swansons. The couples exchanged waves. The fishing community was a tight-knit family that looked out for each other.

While these three boats entered the bay, others were preparing to leave it. A dozen members of a Canadian mountain-climbing expedition were quickly breaking camp. They had reached their goal, the summit of Mount Fairweather, and descended to their base camp on a sandy beach by the bay. They were to depart the next day, but the pilot of their plane arrived at 6 P.M. and told them to pack up immediately. He was worried about the possibility of fog and wanted to get the climbers safely back to Juneau that night. The climbers cursed the pilot's nervousness. They missed dinner in the hurry to pack and left at 9 P.M., just as the last two boats entered the bay.

As the Canadian climbers flew away, so did the nervous black-and-white kittiwakes. The gulls ascended like so much confetti blown upward. The high intensity alarm call of thousands of birds echoed throughout the still bay. As they passed over the *Badger,* they splattered the deck with droppings and some gulls crashed into the vessel's rigging and plummeted to the deck. The Swansons were frightened. Just before the earthquake another fisherman noticed the birds squatting on the black-sand beach to the north of the bay, as if they were waiting for something.

The gulls of Lituya Bay were not the only wildlife exhibiting strange behavior that evening. Some Yakutat families were fishing in the Situk River and picking berries nearby when they noticed the terns and other small birds suddenly taking flight. The birds circled in the air and made frantic cries. The fish became excited. Each cast hooked a fish.

The earth shook and the land was torn apart at 10:16 P.M. Mountains swelled, one peak rising fifty feet in an instant. The tip of an island in Yakutat Bay surged twenty feet into the air and then slipped one hundred feet underwater, sucking three berry pickers to their deaths. All that was left of their outing were the paper plates that floated upon the roiled water. When it was over three minutes later, the earth had moved 21.5 feet horizontally along the faultline.

Ulrich was awakened by a deafening roar. The water around the *Edrie* began to vibrate. He looked toward the mountains in the waning light and saw them smoking from avalanches. Then he saw the huge wave.

"Christ, it looks like the end of the world in here," he yelled into the radio microphone.

Other fishermen heard him and stopped their aimless chatter.

"The noise is terrible and it looks like there's a fifty foot tidal wave heading towards me. It's a solid wall of water coming at me. I'm going to try to head into it and see if I can ride up over the top of it."

Then another hurried transmission: "Mayday. Mayday. This is the *Edrie* in Lituya Bay. All hell has busted loose in here. I think we've had it. Goodbye."

Silence.

In the photograph of father and son that I have seen, Ulrich, a solidly built man in his thirties, has one large hand on the shoulder of a smiling Sonny, who has both of his hands in his pockets. Father and son look like true partners. Their boat was strong yet graceful. The three seemed like a unit that functioned together smoothly. They would need all the solidarity they could summon.

When Ulrich first saw the wave, he remained rooted to the deck for a moment. Then he moved fast. He threw a life jacket on Sonny and started the engine while putting out his call for help. He tried to haul in the anchor with the power winch. It would not budge, so he let the anchor chain out to its 210-foot limit and maneuvered the boat so that it was pointing into the oncoming wall of water.

The wave was cresting as it sped by the north end of the island, but on the south side it had a rounded face some fifty or seventy-five feet high. It pushed the boat back and lifted it up high. The anchor chain snapped. Ulrich looked down and saw trees underneath the boat. The wave carried the craft over the shore then back into the bay where Ulrich turned it about to face the back-wash that rebounded from the shoreline. A confused sea buffeted the *Edrie* as Ulrich made for the center of the bay.

Other fishermen heard him say, "It's awful."

Silence.

"Well we rode to the top of it. We got over the top okay."

Gradually the bay calmed.

The fishing boat *Lumen* arrived off the entrance to the bay and Stutz Graham, Ulrich's radio partner, asked if he should come in and help.

"No, for Christ's sake don't come in here. Stay out."

Silence.

"There's big trees, branches, leaves, roots, and everything everywhere I look. All around me. I've got to get out of here. I never saw anything like it. I've got to get out of here."

Another fisherman pointed out that the current in the entrance was at its most dangerous stage, and the boat could be swamped by the waves. On the other hand huge logs were threatening to puncture the thin skin of the boat.

Instinct told Ulrich to flee.

"The big timbers are closing in all around me. I have to get out. I'm heading toward the entrance. This looks like the end of everything. I don't know if I can make it, but I can't stay here. I have to get out. I'm heading toward the entrance."

Silence.

"We're right in the middle of the entrance."

Silence.

"We made it. We're on the outside."

The Wagners were not as fortunate. The *Sunmore* was last seen by Swanson, heading toward the entrance. It was picked up by the giant wave and hurled over Harbor Point, and disappeared from sight. An oil slick marked the young couple's watery grave.

Swanson's time was not up, yet.

Like Ulrich, the Swansons felt their boat vibrating. They looked out the door and saw the side of a mountain collapse into the upper end of the bay. Then they saw the cresting wall of water heading toward them. "As it came up out of the deep water and hit the shallow water, then it just piled sky high. It just seemed like it grew about fifty feet right there near the entrance. And it was just a matter of seconds later that the base of the wave hit us, and that popped the cable," said Swanson in the radio interview.

The boat rose and kept rising and was hurled, like so much flotsam, into the gulf. It was propelled stern-first eighty feet over the trees on the 150-foot wide spit. There was a horrible crash at the end of the wild descent, and the boat started to sink. Huge trees were landing all about like so many spears. One came through the door and hit Swanson in the chest, driving him toward the stove. The tree exited the mortally wounded boat the same way it entered, leaving Swanson with four broken ribs.

The couple clambered into their skiff with only their underclothes on. It was a cold night, and when the wind came up, it became chillier. They were seized with cramps. They heard an engine. A searchlight swept the water but missed them. The searchers disappeared, reappeared, then disappeared again. The couple cried for help. Mrs. Swanson, clutching a Bible, passed out. Her husband was nearly gone.

It was now about 11 P.M. Graham and an exhausted Ulrich searched for survivors in their separate boats. About a half hour later Graham and his son, Ken, decided to make one more swing through the area on the *Lumen*. The Grahams saw a light on shore and headed toward it. They described it as "a small flickering light." Diane Olson monitored the radio transmissions and took notes that night on board the fishing vessel *White Light* located some thirty-five miles from Lituya Bay.

The Swansons were found huddled in their half-sunken skiff in a direct line between the *Lumen* and that light on shore where nobody was known to have been that night. They were taken to a Juneau hospital, where Swanson was interviewed.

Mrs. Olson, who lived in Ketchikan, typed up her notes of the radio transmissions and sent a copy to the Park Service in Juneau. That is where I read them. Mrs. Swanson mentioned the light in an *Alaska* magazine article, and I talked to her about it in her Seattle-area home. She said the light was definitely there, but nobody knew its source. It was the last time that Vivian Swanson went fishing with her husband. In a new boat, purchased with the contributions of fellow fishermen, Swanson and his brother-in-law reentered Lituya Bay on May 26, 1962. It was the first time he had been in the bay since the night of the giant wave. Swanson died of a heart attack shortly after passing through the entrance to the bay. He was fifty years old, had been fishing for nearly thirty years, and had no known health problems.

I found Ulrich's addendum to that night in a 1960 *Reader's Digest* article. One year after the earthquake and giant wave Ulrich ran the *Edrie* aground on a moonless night. He plugged the hole in the starboard side of the vessel and refloated it on the incoming tide.

Don Miller returned to Lituya Bay for a brief visit one month after the earthquake and then came back for a longer stay later that August. He took no chances and located his campsite at the peak of a 290-foot hill on Cenotaph Island. With him was Don

Tocher, a seismologist from the University of California at Berkeley. They heard rumbles from the head of the bay and subsequently small waves lapped at the shoreline, but Miller was disappointed. "Nothing unusual," he noted in his journal.

On September 2 the two geologists flew back to the San Francisco Bay Area and began to reconstruct what happened on that previous July 9 from the accounts of eyewitnesses and the scientific evidence that was writ so large upon the landscape.

Beginning at 10:16 P.M., the west side and most of the bottom of Gilbert Inlet moved northward in a series of violent lurches. Rockslides and avalanches tore down the mountains. Clouds of rock dust and snow rose into the air—the smoke that Ulrich saw. The noise was deafening. Not less than one minute nor more than two and one-half minutes after the first shock, the flank of an unnamed 5,616-foot peak on the east side of the inlet was shaken loose and plunged into the head of the bay—the earthfall that Swanson saw.

The violent impact of forty million cubic yards of rock, ice, and coarse soil weighing ninety million tons was heard fifty miles to the north. The splash wave had tremendous force, a conservative estimate being twenty-five million foot pounds of pressure. The surge of water rose 1,740 feet and instantaneously snapped and flayed the trees on the granite spur of the opposite ridge like so many matchsticks.

A giant gravity wave with a steep front surged outward and, supplemented by the splash wave that washed over the spur, slammed into the steep cliffs near Mudslide Creek on the south side of the bay, causing a two-thousand-foot landslide that added to the chaos. The giant wave, rebounding from shore to shore and diminishing in size, sped down the bay at one hundred miles per hour.

Nature was turned upside down. Four square miles around the bay's shoreline were stripped of all vegetation, leaving the bedrock exposed and glistening. Fissures were cut in the land. Sand geysers and sheets of water gushed into the air like ruptured arteries. Rivers ran upstream. Coyotes howled. Grizzly bears fled. Bull moose broke their antlers in panic-stricken flight through the forest. Shellfish and barnacles were swept from their rocky perches, their attachment plates neatly severed in the process. Fish rotted on shore and bloated mammals floated in the water. Marine plants withered on land and fresh-water plants atrophied in salt water. The smell of rot mixed with the fog to form a miasmic stew that hovered over the bay.

After the 1958 wave, the Park Service abandoned plans to establish a permanent ranger station in the bay. Although Miller, calculating that a giant wave occurred about every quarter century, estimated that the odds of it taking place on any single day were nine thousand to one. Captain Eliot Roberts of the U.S. Coast and Geodetic Survey, writing in the May 1960 issue of the *U.S. Naval Institute Proceedings*, termed it the highest wave known to oceanographers, the previous record being a 112-foot sea wave encountered by a U.S. naval ship in the North Pacific. Miller published his findings about the 1958 wave and four earlier such waves in a Geological Survey professional paper entitled "Giant Waves in Lituya Bay Alaska."

There is a postscript. Don Miller drowned one year later while on a field trip with a young assistant in southcentral Alaska. Their bodies were found not far from their overturned yellow raft on the Kiagna River by the bush pilot who had dropped them off a few days earlier and had flown back over the area to check their progress. They were lying below a canyon on separate sand bars.

When I returned from Lituya Bay, I drove to San Francisco and talked with Miller's wife, Carmen. She thought that her husband was flirting with death in Alaska and cited his attraction to all that moving water. I recognized similarities between Miller and myself, and I thought that Mrs. Miller did too. I left her home with a deep feeling of dread, remnants of which wash over me to this day.

Written on assignment for *Audubon* but not previously published.

War on the Refuge

The Coast Guard plane, a lumbering C-130 transport, made its approach over Murder Point, banked sharply to the right, then burst out of the fog that was hovering less than one hundred feet above the runway. The plane plopped down smoothly without the help of any guidance system and with a lot of prayers from this anxious passenger. The landing and subsequent take-off were not much different from those I had experienced in South Vietnam in the same type of aircraft. There was a minimum of preliminaries in each case.

On hand to greet us was a coastguardsman dressed in the colorful finery of a horny bird, the mascot of the isolated loran station on Attu, the westernmost island in the Aleutian chain.

19

Word had preceded the plane that there was a woman on board, but when she turned out to be rather obese, enthusiasm dampened. The thirty-man Coast Guard detachment (the length of duty is one year and no dependents are allowed) is the linear descendant of a once large military presence on Attu. Priorities on this austere island have changed little in the intervening forty years.

The movie that night in the recreation lounge used H. G. Wells's time machine, which resembled an aged helicopter bubble, as the device for shuttling characters from late nineteenth-century Victorian England to the libertine atmosphere of present-day San Francisco. On Attu, however, one's feet are a time machine. They take you back to a forgotten, bloody battle—the only battle of World War II that was fought on North American soil—and the subsequent boredom of the military occupation of an exceedingly hostile piece of terrain that is a national wildlife refuge.

The time machine works this way:

Adorning the walls of the two-man rooms at the loran station are the sexually explicit posters of the present era. Walk a couple of miles to Casco Cove and enter a Quonset hut. There on the arched walls are the pinups of the 1940s, which seem so innocent by comparison. Marilyn Maxwell, fully clothed in fading colors, is taking a bite out of an apple. She is the epitome of exuberant health, and if an allusion to Eve was intended, it is very obscure. Metro-Goldwyn-Mayer labeled Maxwell "the dynamite blonde." Another blonde MM (Marilyn Monroe) was to come along and replace Maxwell on such walls for the next generation of servicemen.

It was in such places that I fleetingly touched that remote war. There were others. Pews are scattered about the interior of a church on Hogback Ridge, while outside the plywood pulpit is exposed to the elements. Fog swirls through the chapel and around the pulpit, which is no longer the chief prop of a man of God. At the large gymnasium a few sport artifacts remain, such as a climbing rope and the support for a basketball backboard. It is not too difficult to imagine bare feet padding across the concrete floor of the shower room and its easy camaraderie.

There are no bears on Attu, but this does not mean one can walk in complete safety. There is always danger involved in travel by time machine. Scattered across the tundra are live shells whose explosive charges have become increasingly unstable with the passing years. Nor would I want to bet that all the land mines laid by Japanese and American troops have been removed. A small boy picked up what he thought was a mess kit at Cold Bay at the eastern end of the Aleutians, and got his hand blown off by a mine. There are shell holes, disguised by thick vegetation, to stumble into and rusted stakes used to anchor strands of barbed wire protruding just above the ground.

Despite the battlefield mementos, which dot only a small portion of the fifteen square miles that were fought over and an even smaller percentage of the whole island, the feeling of tranquillity, of peacefulness in an exceedingly verdant land, pervades Attu. At least this is what I experienced during the brief summer when the steep volcanic mountain slopes and the wide glaciated valleys are covered with a profusion of wildflowers and grasses. Curiously, the flowers seem to grow best in shell holes where they are sheltered from the violent winds, called williwaws, that sweep down from the mountains. And as I walked up Peaceful Valley, a snowy owl rose in startled flight from a rusted metal roof; it landed across the valley on a utility pole devoid of wires.

War is the most intensely destructive of human activities. It is reassuring to see that its impact, too, passes with time. In a sense, war is just another quick boom to be forgotten and absorbed by the land when the subsequent bust comes, much like the gold rush towns of the old West and the energy boomtowns of the new West, both of which can also be found in Alaska. Rusted scraps of metal, a landing barge here and oil drums there, and the weathered gray wood, brought so far to this treeless island to be used for the construction of buildings and bridges, no longer dominate the landscape; they are just so much litter that is melting back into the earth.

There are some thirty military sites of World War II vintage in the Aleutians. Scattered about the islands are 8,200 metal or wood-frame buildings, 20,000 barrels of petroleum products, 23 aircraft, an unknown quantity of ordnance ranging from .30-caliber carbine to 14-inch naval shells, and other assorted military paraphernalia. It would cost far in excess of $100 million to clean it all up, obviously too high a cost for only slight benefits. So it rots.

But once it was life, a teeming life on Attu for fifteen thousand servicemen, and a place of death for some three thousand Japanese and American troops. Weather and terrain were the principal environmental factors with which the combatants had to contend. It shaped their lives, and their deaths, to an extent rarely encountered before in a major armed conflict. In an attempt to understand this dominance, to feel it vicariously, I walked across Attu in the footsteps of a Japanese medical officer and a correspondent for *Time* magazine.

The walk from Massacre Bay to Chichagof Harbor is not too taxing, mainly because the old road system is still intact enough for foot traffic. The raised roadway keeps the hiker off the spongy hillsides and out of the bogs and thick vegetation along the valley floors. The road up Hogback climbs past the chapel and then the Air Force seismic facility used to detect nuclear tests in Russia. Near the crest of Engineer Hill the track spirals down into Siddens Valley and crosses Bassett Creek on a wooden bridge. There is a slight incline into Jim Fish Valley, then a pleasant amble past Lake Cories where the road, now washed out in spots, climbs to a slight rise and the compact, sheltered harbor unfolds below. It is a very pleasant way to spend five or six hours.

The names on the map for the natural features on Attu's eastern end are mostly American, bestowed during or after the war. The interior of the island was not mapped before the conflict. Most of the natural features on the western two-thirds of the island are still unnamed, and there are places, it is said, where no humans have ever trod. The most accurate map shows a blank space over Attu's west side, with the notation "obscured by clouds." The map has not been field-checked for accuracy.

Despite the American names, Attu is really a bit of Asia set adrift between the Bering Sea and the North Pacific. Russia's Commander Islands are just to the west, and beyond lies the Kamchatka Peninsula jutting south from Siberia. Bird, plant, and animal species found on Attu are native to the Russian islands and mainland. This is where the international date line makes a special jog to include the Near Islands (near to Russia) in the same day as the rest of the United States.

Life in the Near Islands, of which Attu is one, has always been clustered along the coast. The Aleuts lived there, as do the coastguardsmen. Olaus J. Murie noted that the blue foxes of Attu fed on the shorebirds that found their main source of food in the rich intertidal zone. The foxes are native to Attu and the Russian islands to the west, but not the Aleutian Islands to the east, where they were raised for commercial purposes. There are rocky points, islets, and deep bays, all ringed by the blackness of rock and sand found in a volcanic landscape. Inland the peaks rise to three thousand feet. There are a few glaciers high up in cirque valleys. The U-shaped low valleys are wide and wet, the meandering rivers chock full of salmon. It is a difficult landscape to comprehend, since there is no one distinctive feature trending in a specific direction, like a Sierra Nevada or a Yukon River. It feels like a labyrinth, even with a semiaccurate map in hand.

Forty miles long and fifteen miles wide, Attu is covered by a thick carpet of tundra to the one-thousand-foot level; above that the alpine vegetative zone begins. The higher one goes, the firmer the footing and the stronger the wind. The climate is not as extreme as that of the Arctic, but the fierce winds, when combined with snow or rain, can make survival precarious, and did so for the American troops, who had been trained and equipped for desert warfare. They were from the Southwest, and more than half their casualties were related to the cold and dampness.

In the Aleutians the weather was the great equalizer and the primary enemy. Military historian Samuel Eliot Morison wrote, "The hazards of surface and air navigation are greater there than in any other part of the world." Brigadier General William O. Butler of Alaska's Eleventh Air Force told his superior, "The weather out on these Aleutian Islands is about the world's worst. . . . It is about the worst place I can imagine for air operations." Army major general Simon Bolivar Buckner, Jr., impatient with the Navy's lack of aggressiveness, composed for Rear Admiral Robert A. Theobold a poem that concluded:

> The Bering Sea is not for me nor for my fleet headquarters.
> In mortal dread I look ahead in wild Aleutian waters,

Where hidden reefs and williwaws and terrifying critters,
Unnerve me quite with woeful fright and give me fits and
    jitters.

Tales of bad weather are legion throughout the Aleutian chain. A Russian priest at Unalaska counted 53 clear days, 1,263 cloudy days, and 1,230 days when there was either rain, snow, or hail. At Shemya, near Attu, there is an average of six clear days a year. At Cold Bay it rains about two hundred days a year. Corporal Dashiell Hammett wrote a short history of the Aleutian campaign in which he recounted that the wind gauge on Adak had a limit of 110 miles per hour, which was sometimes exceeded. When I camped at Chichagof, violent gusts coming down from the mountains caused the sea quite literally to smoke. The Coast Guard station at Massacre Bay recorded winds of 74 miles per hour that same night. In the summer it is dense fog. The supply and mail plane could not get into Attu for six weeks the summer prior to my visit. In the winter it is intense storms. The Aleutian low is a well-known fixture on weather maps. All things considered, there were better places to fight an unnecessary battle.

Neither the occupation of Attu by the Japanese, nor its recapture by the Americans, was necessary to the main thrust of the war in the Pacific. The Japanese first bombed Dutch Harbor on Amaknak Island on June 3, 1942; four days later they invaded Kiska and Attu in order to divert American forces from Midway. They also feared that the Aleutians might be used to launch bombing raids on Japan. The Americans retaliated massively to get foreign troops off domestic soil (basically a political decision) and to protect the Alaskan lend-lease route to Russia (more a strategic consideration). There also were fears the Aleutians would be used by the Japanese as a staging area to invade the Pacific Northwest. The invasion gave a boost to the plans to construct an oil pipeline in neighboring Canada.*

Morison termed the Aleutian campaign "the Theater of Military Frustration." He wrote, "None of the operations accomplished anything of great importance or had any appreciable effect on the outcome of the war . . . . Both sides would have done well to have left the Aleutians to the Aleuts for the course of the war." The natives on Attu would have greatly appreciated that, since they were interned in Japan for the duration of the war. Only half their number returned to be relocated elsewhere in the Aleutians.

Murder Point stands at the western end of Massacre Bay, so named for the killing of fifteen Aleuts in 1745 by the first Russian fur traders to come to the islands. It was a name that spooked American troops who landed in the bay nearly two hundred years later. In the intervening years the Aleuts had not fared well at the hands of white men who stopped at the islands for furs, fish, and women. Their numbers had dropped from perhaps fifteen thousand when the Russians first came to about two thousand. No full-blooded Aleuts remain today.

When the Japanese invaded Attu on June 7 they found about forty Aleuts plus a white schoolteacher and his wife. It was Sunday morning when the foreign troops descended from the hills above Chichagof Harbor after landing elsewhere on the island. The small native village was spread along the black-sand beach at the head of the protected harbor. The Japanese were ill-prepared and nervous. They had little knowledge of the island, outside of the fact that it had a rocky shoreline, and no accurate

* See "The First Pipeline."

maps. They had gotten lost on their way to Chichagof, where they mistakenly thought there was a detachment of American soldiers. The village was surrounded. There was shooting. An Aleut woman was hit in the leg, and the soldiers shot some of their comrades, a not uncommon fate in those fog-shrouded islands. The elderly white couple cut their wrists the next day; the husband died and the wife was taken to Japan. And so, events were set in motion.

≺ ≻

On May 11, 1943, when American troops landed on Attu, the snow line extended almost to the valley floors. An easy three-day battle was envisioned. Instead it took an embarrassing nineteen days. Some of the fiercest fighting occurred around Buffalo Ridge, Holtz-Sarana Pass, and Fish Hook Ridge. The route from Chichagof Harbor to Holtz Bay leads past these battlegrounds, identifiable now only by the intermittent remains of a trail (probably first used by Aleuts), scattered bits of rusted shrapnel, grenade pins, an unexploded shell or two, shell holes, and shallow pits that were once foxholes.

I soon began to sweat on the climb toward the pass because the day was balmy. It was one of those extremely rare clear summer days in the Aleutians. Only a remnant of fog lay behind Engineer Hill, and the vistas were of a land at rest. A decayed telephone line, laid on the ground, marked my route. Upon gaining the pass I lay down in its lee for a snack and a nap in the warm sunshine before tackling the steep descent to the East Arm of Holtz Bay.

It was this same route, only in reverse, that Nebu Tatsuguchi followed during the Japanese retreat from Holtz Bay to Chichagof Harbor. Tatsuguchi, who had obtained a medical education and wife in California before returning to Japan in 1940, accompanied some wounded soldiers over the pass. Here are extracts from his diary:

May 17: At night under cover of darkness I left the cave. The stretchers went over the muddy roads and steep hills of no man's land. No matter how long we went, it seemed we would not get to the pass. I was rather irritated by the thought of getting lost in the fog. Sat down after every twenty or thirty steps. Would sleep, dream, and wake up again. The patient on the stretcher who does not move is frostbitten. Sitting on my rear and lifting my feet, I slid down the other side of the pass very smoothly, using my sword to change directions. The time it took to get to Chichagof was nine hours without leaving any patients.

May 20: The hard fighting of our 303rd Battalion in Massacre Bay is fierce, and it is to our advantage. Have captured enemy weapons and used them to fight. Mowed down ten enemy coming in under the fog. Five of our men and one medical NCO died. Hear enemy. Pilots' faces can be seen.

May 23: Day's ration, a pound and one half. Nothing else. Officers and men alike in cold. Everybody looked around for food and stole everything they could find.

May 24: It sleeted and was extremely cold. Stayed at the barracks alone. A great amount of shells were dropped by naval gunfire, and rocks and mud flew all around. In a foxhole about five yards away, Hayeaka, a medical orderly, died instantly by a piece of shrapnel which pierced his heart.

May 25: Battalion commander died. I am suffering from diarrhea and feel dizzy.

May 26: Naval guns firing. It felt like the barracks blew up, and things were tremendously shaken. Consciousness becomes vague. The last line was broken through. There is no hope for reinforcements. There was a ceremony granting the Imperial Edict. Will die for the cause of the Imperial Diet.

May 27: There are two days of rations remaining. Other companies have been completely annihilated, except for one or two. Many cases of suicide. Heard that they gave 400 shots of morphine to the badly wounded and killed them. Ate a half-dried thistle. It is the first time I have eaten something fresh in six months. It is a delicacy.

May 29: Assembled in front of headquarters. The last assault is to be carried out. All patients in the hospital were to commit suicide. Only thirty-three years of living, and I am to die here. I have no regrets. Banzai to Emperor. I am grateful that I have kept the peace in my soul which Christ bestowed upon me. At 6 P.M. took care of all the patients with grenades. Goodbye to my beloved wife, who loved me to the last. Until we meet again, Miseka, who just became four years old. I feel sorry for you, Tokiki, born this year and never having seen your father. The number participating in the attack is 1,000. We are to take the enemy artillery position. It seems the enemy is expecting an all-out attack tomorrow.

The diary ends at that point. Tatsuguchi was correct. The Americans were expecting some kind of counterattack, but they were poorly prepared. The Japanese had been pushed back to Chichagof. If they were not going to surrender, if there were no ships to rescue them, then the only way out was a concerted rush through Jim Fish Valley, across Siddens Valley, and up Engineer Hill, where an artillery battery could be captured. The guns would then be turned on the Americans and used to pin them down while the Japanese raided the supply depot in Massacre Valley. Colonel Yasuya Yamasaki's plan, which depended on speed, was bold and simple. It almost succeeded.

In the first gray light shortly after 3 A.M. on May 29 the Japanese attacked. The fog added to the confusion, which was described by participants in *The Infantry Journal,* a War Department publication: "Then hell broke loose. Grenades began to burst in the valley ahead of them, and machine guns opened up. Japs, lots of them, began appearing through the fog in the strange glow of the red flares. They charged through the disorganized company, reducing it to little pockets of fiercely resisting men who shot down column after column, and still they came. The scattered pockets of men began falling back." They were running in terror, according to another account.

An advance aid station at the foot of Engineer Hill, from which the wounded were winched up the sharp incline, was overrun by the Japanese. "Shots were flying fast now. The stovepipe was hit with a crash. Bryce was on his stomach crawling over to [a still-sleeping] Captain Buehler. The two aid men woke up, startled, full of questions. One moved toward the door. Thud! A bullet hit him, and he dropped with a gasp. The shouting was all around now, and a stream of running feet pounding the tundra passed the door. Bryce was shaking Buehler, 'Wake up, the Japs are here!' Buehler mumbled, 'Too early to pull that stuff, Bryce.'" Twelve men, including Captain George S. Buehler, who finally woke up, played dead inside the tent for thirty-eight hours, and survived.

The Japanese swept up Engineer Hill. On the crest was a ragtag assortment of troops—engineers, artillerymen, cooks, stretcher-bearers, medics, clerks, and staff officers. They were hastily organized by Brigadier General Archibald V. Arnold, who held an M-1 rifle in his hand. The Japanese reached the crest. "It began to be light finally, and some of the men tried to get organized. We discovered seven Japs in Company D's kitchen. They were eating anything they could find. We threw some grenades, which broke up the meal, and a BAR [Browning Automatic Rifle] man finished the Japs off—and also some of Company D's kitchen equipment that was left." It was hand-to-hand combat.

The Japanese were close, so close to the 105-millimeter howitzers. They faltered, then fell back and regrouped at the bottom of the hill, charging again in reduced numbers against strengthened American defenses. Colonel Yamasaki, sword in hand, led the last attack and was killed by a .30-caliber bullet.

Those Japanese who survived the night and early morning, perhaps 500, committed suicide later in the day. Of the 2,600 Japanese troops on Attu when the Americans landed, only 28 surrendered. None were officers. There were no wounded. American burial parties counted 2,351 Japanese bodies. American losses were 549. There were 1,200 severe cold casualties (more suffered from exposure) and 1,148 wounded. The landing force had numbered about 11,000.

Not long after the Japanese attack on Engineer Hill, *Time* correspondent Robert Sherrod walked from Massacre Bay to Chichagof Harbor. Here is a portion of his dispatch: "The results of the Jap fanaticism stagger the imagination. The very violence of the scene is incomprehensible to the Western mind. Here groups of men had met their self-imposed obligation, to die rather than accept capture, by blowing themselves to bits. I saw one Jap sitting impaled on a bayonet which was stuck through his back, evidently by a friend. All the other suicides had chosen the grenade. Most of them simply held grenades against their stomachs or chests. The explosive charge blasted away their vital organs. Probably one in four held a grenade against his head. There were many headless Jap bodies between Massacre and Chichagof. Sometimes the grenade split the head in half, leaving the right face on one shoulder, the left face on the other."

Sherrod was troubled by that scene. He noted the Japanese sought companionship in death. He thought the suicides were not necessary, that the Japanese could have fought longer. He found sake bottles among the dead. And beside a stream that fell from Engineer Hill was the body of a captain, whose white hand-kerchief bore a bawdy ink drawing. Not far away was the body of another officer, who carried a photograph of his wife and children. Was it Tatsuguchi? Sherrod wrote, "It had rained the previous night, so the officer's open mouth was half filled with water." Tatsuguchi's family was to join him soon. His wife and two children died on August 6, 1945. They lived in Hiroshima.

There are no memorials for American fighting men on Attu. The U.S. Navy placed a marker for Colonel Yamasaki on Hogback Ridge in 1950. A few years ago, relatives of the Japanese soldiers visited Attu and erected three memorials within a small cleared space atop Engineer Hill. One is a black stone, another a metal plaque; both are anchored to the ground. Two live shells and three white plastic flowers lie at the head of the third memorial, which bears a lengthy inscription and the formal portrait of a Japanese soldier holding his sword. The lightweight rectangle rests upon the ground. Underneath is an unlined hole just large enough to hold a water-soaked, mud-encrusted book. A plastic packet containing a steel-gray lock of hair is inserted in the book. The fog hugs the hill tightly, partially disperses, then descends again on this early August day.

As a war front, the Aleutians were not only perpetually obscured by fog but also by the military's management of the news. The Japanese invasion, not reported until five days after the fact in a minimal three-paragraph news release that did not even mention the simultaneous invasion of Kiska, was an embarrassment. It would be two weeks before there was a full explanation of the enemy occupation of an American outpost following repeated broadcasts of the news by Radio Tokyo.

The American invasion of Attu was also an embarrassment. Morison wrote of Attu, "The landing and unloading of transports was done badly, naval bombardments were delivered from unnecessarily long ranges, and the 7th Division, owing to initial training for desert warfare and poor top leadership, showed little dash and initiative." After Attu, American forces stormed Kiska, only to find that the Japanese had quietly departed.

However, the remote campaign did have its chroniclers, and some famous ones at that. In addition to a short history, Dashiell Hammett wrote the introduction to a collection of GI cartoons, which centered on sex and the weather. John Huston made a film for the Signal Corps. Gore Vidal wrote a novel titled *Williwaw*.

But memories began to erode, as did the military works erected on the islands. Attu, Kiska, and most of the other islands in the chain became what they had been before the war, the Aleutian Islands National Wildlife Refuge (now known as the Alaska Maritime National Wildlife Refuge)—2.7 million acres encompassing nearly seventy named islands. The refuge, established in 1913, stretches eleven hundred miles from the tip of the Alaska Peninsula to within five hundred miles of the Kamchatka Peninsula. Among other distinctions of the Aleutians campaign was the fact that the only battle within a national wildlife refuge was fought on Attu.

Of course, no one got a special-use permit, wrote an environmental impact statement, or conducted public hearings on a proposal to wage war on the refuge. But warfare and the subsequent military occupation of the islands, which ended in most places by 1950, caused little lasting environmental damage. Yes, there are the crumbling structures and rusting oil drums, some of them still full. But there are plenty of salmon in the streams, and the snowy owl I saw on Attu used the military debris for a perch in an otherwise unrelieved terrain. The marks of tracked vehicles are still visible in some places, but the land has a remarkable recuperative ability.

Robert D. Jones, Jr., an officer on Amchitka Island and for twenty-seven years after the war the refuge manager, believes that exotic species introduced to the islands created more havoc with the balance of nature than the war. Rats were found on the islands before the war, but came in greatly increased numbers on ships and airplanes during the conflict. Fox farming reached its height between the two world wars. Together, foxes and rats nearly caused the extinction of the Aleutian Canada goose. Another exotic, the black fly, arrived on board aircraft used by the Atomic Energy Commission, which conducted nuclear tests on Amchitka.

There is one final irony. Although the Japanese lost the war, they won the peace in the Aleutian Islands, at least economically. Dutch Harbor and neighboring Unalaska, the only sizable settlements, are booming mostly because of the investment of Japanese money in the fishing industry. Verne Robinson, who remembers shooting at Japanese Zeros with his hunting rifle, now sits in his Unalaska grocery and liquor store and complains about a new competitor across the harbor who is being financed by Japanese capital.

Audubon, November 1980.

The First Pipeline

It took only a one-page memo and little more than a day to decide to build the first oil pipeline in the North, and therein lies a tale never before told in its entirety. Canol (short for Canadian oil) was conceived in the early, bleak days of World War II when the United States and its allies were losing. It was a time for desperate measures. Between December 7, 1941, when the Japanese bombed Pearl Harbor, and the end of April 1942, when Canol was authorized, Guam, Wake Island, Manila, Singapore, Rangoon, Java, Bataan, and the Battle of Java Sea were all lost. Oil tankers were being sunk in the Atlantic Ocean at an alarming rate, and the U.S. Navy could not guarantee the safety of these vessels on the West Coast. The Aleutian Islands were threatened—and, indeed, later invaded. Airplanes had to be ferried to Alaska for defense and to Russia for lend-lease purposes.

A route was selected for the Alaska Highway, conceived primarily as a link between landing strips, and military planners cast about for an energy source. Crude oil sources in Edmonton, Alberta, and southern Alaska were discussed. The Arctic explorer, Vilhjalmur Stefansson, called the War Department's attention to the availability of crude oil at Norman Wells, ninety miles south of the Arctic Circle on the Mackenzie River in Canada. Sir Alexander Mackenzie, who explored the area in 1789, first noticed oil seeps along the riverbank. A successful oil well was sunk in 1920, but it was not until 1933 that the continent's most northerly oilfield was put into commercial operation by Imperial Oil, a subsidiary of Standard Oil of New Jersey (now the Exxon Corporation). The informal discussions within the War Department soon centered on Norman Wells, as it was the only producing oilfield of those considered.

Wanting to get some specifics on Norman Wells, the military planners invited two representatives of Standard Oil to meet with them on April 29, 1942. Three generals, a representative of the Board of Economic Warfare, and James H. Graham, dean of the engineering school at the University of Kentucky, attended the morning meeting. After the meeting, Graham, a part-time, dollar-a-year aide to Lieutenant General Brehon B. Somervell, wrote a one-page memo to Somervell advising the construction of a four-inch pipeline from Norman Wells to Whitehorse and placement of a refinery at Whitehorse to serve truck and air traffic on the Alaska Highway. (Graham mistakenly placed Whitehorse in Alaska instead of Canada.) The pipeline and refinery were to be operating in five months.

The next day Somervell addressed to the head of the Army Corps of Engineers a memo stating, "The recommendations made by Dean Graham have been approved by me. You are requested to take the necessary steps to carry out these recommendations at the earliest practicable date."

And so was born a project that was to spawn unparalleled bitterness and controversy within the administration of President Franklin D. Roosevelt. It was to help one man, Harry Truman, become president, and it was to mar the otherwise brilliant career of Somervell, at one time considered a candidate for army chief of staff and president. Two presidents, Roosevelt and Truman, had to intervene to straighten out squabbles pertaining to Canol. It was to produce a strain in U.S.–Canadian relations during the war.

Canol diverted men and equipment when they were needed with greater urgency elsewhere. The project, conceived in panic and carried out in pride, was to end an expensive failure. The cover-up of that failure evokes images of a slapstick comedy and Watergate. The Joint Chiefs of Staff (JCS) spent an inordinate amount of time trying to circumvent a congressional investigation of their role in Canol. That time was expended at the expense of more pressing matters.

Seventy-seven years after the end of the Civil War, the project was to show that blacks—in this case a black engineer battalion—had progressed little beyond a state of slavery.

Also, Canol was carried out with almost utter disregard for the environment; bulldozers and trucks sank into the muddied earth when the permafrost layer was ripped apart, and crude oil by the tens of thousands of barrels was spilled into rivers. Surprisingly enough, Canol has left few significant, harmful environmental effects, a heritage that can be attributed more to the resiliency of sub-Arctic lands than to any wisdom of the builders.

Some have seen the virtue of Canol as demonstrating the North could be "conquered" and put to good economic use. Others would learn of it and follow, it was argued. Except for a few hunters and prospectors who used a portion of the old Canol Road, it is difficult to see who benefited in the long run from the project. Certainly Alaska and northern Canada are overrun now with those searching for and producing crude oil and natural gas. But not because of Canol. As a lesson in history, Canol has been lacking, since few know of it.

I see Canol as the best possible example of how not to make a decision and carry it out. Conversely, it demonstrates the need for such decisions to be made after all the available information is at hand and all factors have been carefully weighed. Canol proves that decision-makers—in this case the U.S. military, but it could just as well have been an oil company or a president or Congress—need to be protected from themselves by some neutral, fact-finding process.

◄ ➤

Doubts arose even before the project was authorized. One of the generals who attended the meeting on April 29, 1942 noted that he had talked with a vice-president of Standard Oil Company of New Jersey four days previously "who is not too optimistic about the whole proposition." According to a later army report, on the day Somervell approved Canol the assistant chief of the Army Corps of Engineers "expressed the opinion that it would be more expeditious and economical to deliver petroleum products from the United States by barges already available on U.S. rivers than to construct the project as proposed, but that he was prepared to carry out the orders to the best of his ability."

Things began to move with lightninglike speed. On May 1, the Canadian government was informally asked for its approval. On May 8, the formal request was made. The State Department, in forwarding instructions to its Ottawa legation, "pointedly noted that it had made no examination of the merits of the Canol project," wrote one historian. The Canadians were prodded for a reply on May 15, since the summer construction season was fast approaching. The government had serious doubts about the feasibility of the project. The Canadians suggested the Americans look at it in greater detail. But after the initial hesitation, the Canadian government informally approved the project on May 16, and all subsequent approvals were routinely given. Formal sanction was rendered on June 29, after U.S. military and civilian construction crews had already arrived in Canada.

A Canadian military historian, C. P. Stacey, later wrote, "Canadian officials were haunted by a tendency on the part of Americans to disregard Canadian sovereignty. American officers and officials . . . acted as if they were on their own soil." Referring to Canol, Prime Minister Mackenzie King, who otherwise had a close working relationship with President Roosevelt, commented, "We ought to get Americans out of the further development there and keep control in our own hands."

It did not help matters that the Americans failed to ask Canadian permission to construct a string of landing strips not covered by any specific agreement. Unknown to the Canadians, a key U.S. general on Somervell's staff wrote a memo stating that "under no circumstances" would the Canadians be given information on the results of oil drilling at Norman Wells. Secretary of War Henry L. Stimson told Secretary of State Cordell Hull such information would be classified, and "there was no question the Canadian government should be informed."

The Permanent Joint Board on Defense consisted of U.S. and Canadian officials. It was formed to consider the defense of the northern half of the Western Hemisphere. Historian Stacey noted the U.S. secretary to the board "thought the Canol project to be such a fool idea that he did not have the heart to route it through the board, which he held in such warm regard." The secretary was New York mayor Fiorello H. La Guardia. Thomas Riggs, a former territorial governor of Alaska and U.S. member of the International Boundary Commission, wrote Somervell: "In my opinion the idea of the pipeline from Fort Norman to White-horse is completely cockeyed." (Riggs had the location wrong. Norman Wells is about fifty miles northwest of Fort Norman. Nobody was sure where anything was at this stage of the project.)

Doubts continued to mount as the army's commitment solidi-fied. On May 2, Imperial Oil wrote the War Department that there was no assurance the goal of three thousand barrels a day could be met since "we have no knowledge of the extent of this pool." The letter continued, "The feasibility of constructing a pipeline from Norman Wells to Whitehorse over unknown coun-try, a considerable part of which is known to be mountainous, and a great deal of which is reported to be muskeg, is a matter which we have not attempted to investigate, either with regard to such feasibility or the expedition with which it might be ac-complished, or its year-round operation."

Only a few trappers, Indians, and gold seekers had traversed the Yukon–Mackenzie River divide. No airplanes had ever flown the projected route. Nevertheless, Imperial Oil signed a lucrative contract that month to drill at least nine new wells, operate them, and construct additional storage tanks. Also in May, a contract was signed with a consortium of three construction companies to build the pipeline and refinery by December 31, 1942. The firms were W. A. Bechtel Company of San Francisco, H. C. Price Company of Oklahoma, and W. E. Callahan Con-struction Company of Dallas. The consortium became known as B-P-C, or "Bull-Promises-Confusion," by the civilian construc-tion workers. A souvenir book published in 1945 by the contrac-tors and distributed to libraries as a public relations gesture termed Canol "an epic of the North." It went on to claim, "In respect to area covered, time of accomplishment, and sheer pioneering, the pipeline and refinery project, combined with the Alaska Highway, was destined to become the biggest construction program in the history of the world." The book mentioned nothing about the violent controversy swirling around the project.

Standard Oil Company of California was hired that same month as a consultant and to operate the refinery and pipeline after they were completed. Standard of California warned Secretary of War Stimson it would be close to two years (as it turned out, an accurate guess) before the Whitehorse refinery would be operating and suggested a pipeline from Prince Rupert, British Columbia, to Whitehorse would get fuel to the Alaska Highway quicker. Prince Rupert could be served by rail from interior Canada and Montana, or by ship from California. But there was no stopping Canol.

One of Interior Secretary Harold L. Ickes's aides bumped into a Canol contractor in a Washington hotel lobby in May and learned about the project. Ickes, petroleum administrator for war, exploded. He had not been informed, and his turf had been violated. On May 29, Ickes wrote President Roosevelt. It was Ickes's opinion that tankers could bring the fuel from California to Skagway, Alaska; and from there the fuel could be transported to the Alaska Highway. Stimson conferred with Roosevelt, and the military won the day. On June 10, the President wrote Ickes, "The Secretary of War informs me that this project is being undertaken in an effort to supply aviation and motor gasoline for use in Alaska in the event that transportation by sea should become dangerous or uncertain through enemy action. It is fully recognized that the project is not commercially feasible. The recent enemy attack on Dutch Harbor [and Attu] discloses the possibility of great military need for this additional source of supply . . . . In view of the military needs of Alaska, the project has my full approval."

To a lesser man, this would have meant the end of the matter. But not to Ickes, a self-described curmudgeon. As Robert P. Patterson wrote after World War II when he succeeded Stimson as secretary of war, "The agitation against the project can be traced to the opposition of Mr. Ickes, who was tireless in stirring up protests against it." Patterson, who as undersecretary of war during World War II was the principal public defender of Canol, wondered why the project aroused such bitter criticism. But in a 1947 letter to a Scripps-Howard newspaper reporter, he pronounced the ultimate judgment on the project. He confided to Jim G. Lucas, "I suppose that we must bow to the verdict, that the project was useless and a waste of public funds."

Who were Ickes, Stimson, and Somervell, these giant ghosts from the past? It has been my experience that public decision making is as much a case of personalities and the quirks of the moment as the constituted process, which serves as a check on personalities. In this case the check was Truman's Special Committee to Investigate the National Defense Program. But the committee entered the scene late and, because it was wartime, had only a peripheral effect on Canol. Two other basic laws were at work here: Success gives rise to the illusion of infallibility; and there is always someone waiting to chop down a powerful person. All that is needed is a pretext. Somervell's enemies were gathering.

Somervell is the central character of the Canol drama. His name has virtually sunk into oblivion today; but in the early days of World War II he was being spoken of as a successor to Army

Chief of Staff George Marshall and even President Roosevelt. Other speculation had Somervell running for vice-president with Roosevelt in 1944 to offset the effect General Douglas MacArthur might have as a possible Republican nominee.

Somervell's roots were in the South. His grandfather, who voted for Tennessee to secede from the Union, had declined President James K. Polk's invitation to join his cabinet. Born in Little Rock, Arkansas, Somervell moved with his family to Washington, D.C. His father was a doctor. His mother founded Belcourt Seminary, a fashionable girls's school in Washington. He graduated sixth in the 1914 class at West Point, where the yearbook noted, "If you could take his mind and examine it, you would find it pigeon-holed and arranged like a card index." He was a builder, an unhesitant doer. "Dynamite in a Tiffany box" was one description of Somervell current at the time of Canol.

The young officer, who was commissioned in the then prestigious Corps of Engineers, rose in rank rapidly. He was in charge of building the Florida Ship Canal when he was tapped to head the Works Progress Administration (WPA) in New York City. There had been seven predecessors in that job; none had lasted a year. The colonel lasted four years and was credited by the *New York World Telegram* with transforming the WPA "from a sprawling, boondoggling enterprise that specialized in internal office intrigue and Red-baiting . . . into a quietly efficient business organization able to spend nearly a billion dollars with nary a scandal or critic of greater than trifling proportions."

Somervell's trademarks emerged during his WPA days. They were hard work, the aura of effectiveness, a violent temper he had difficulty controlling, and the shrewd accumulation of power. *The New Yorker* described him thusly: "Colonel Somervell is a military man, thin and lanky, with slicked-back graying hair and a close-cropped mustache. He wears bow ties and rather dapper mufti, speaks with a slight southern drawl, and seldom raises his voice. His manner is pleasant and shrewd, and there is a touch of Will Rogers in his public personality; he frequently refers to himself as 'just a country boy from Arkansas trying to get along in the big city.' "

Somervell worked closely with Mayor La Guardia (one of his WPA projects was La Guardia Airport), and his performance in the sensitive post caught the eye of President Roosevelt and Harry L. Hopkins, the president's close aide. Hopkins later backed Somervell for army chief of staff, but Marshall was appointed instead. Back in Washington in 1940, Somervell headed the army's camp building program.

World War II broke out; and in March 1942, Somervell was put in charge of the army's Services of Supply. In this post the lieutenant general was second in command under Marshall and was in charge of everything the army did except the actual fighting. Somervell traveled with Roosevelt to all the high-level Allied conferences during World War II and was photographed with the president's half-dozen top advisors. He had the logistics of a second front in Europe to plan at the time he made the Canol decision. With three stars on his shoulder and in the midst of a brilliant career, Somervell had the attention of the national media. *Time* ran a cover story on the general in June 1942. *Newsweek* and *Life* magazines followed with generous inside spreads. Meanwhile, Canol was being built, and Somervell's enemies were sharpening their knives.

Where the general was cool and controlled, Interior Secretary Ickes was impetuous. He offered Roosevelt his resignation countless times, but the president valued Ickes's honesty and never accepted it. He went on to serve thirteen years in the cabinet post. Ickes, who had a reputation for frugality in government spending, fiercely guarded his bureaucratic turf but made frequent forays into others's territories. He vainly tried to steal the Forest Service from the Department of Agriculture. Ickes, an early New Dealer, thought he, not the Republican Stimson, should have been named secretary of war in 1940. It was the most powerful cabinet post. Ickes played a key role in Roosevelt's early years as president, but as the war approached, he was less involved in the major decisions. He thought his appointment as petroleum administrator gave him control over all the oil aspects of defense. Somervell and Stimson thought that Ickes was restricted to domestic oil considerations.

Somervell was the protagonist; Ickes, the antagonist. Stimson, the elder statesman, stood aside and entered the fray only from Olympian heights. Stimson had served two Republican presidents; he was secretary of war under Taft and secretary of state under Hoover. In 1932, after the Japanese invasion of Manchuria, he issued the disastrous Stimson Doctrine. When Roosevelt joked with Stimson on the telephone about his "Manchurian policy," the secretary of war hung up. He felt like an outsider in the Roosevelt administration and was a stranger to all its fierce bureaucratic infighting. Stimson finally resigned in 1945 after making the recommendation to President Truman to drop the atomic bomb.

These three strong men and others circled around the centrifugal force—Roosevelt. It was the president's style of governing to make the major decisions himself after consulting all parties, but to delegate almost everything else. A student of Roosevelt's administrative policies wrote that the agencies and the persons who headed them "were on a survival of the fittest basis." To Stimson, who worshiped thoroughness, Roosevelt was "the poorest administrator I have ever worked under in respect to the orderly procedure and routine of his performance."

Around the time Canol was starting and Ickes was taking

potshots at it, the president addressed this memo to his cabinet officers: "Too often in recent months, responsible officials of government have made public criticism of other agencies of the government; and have made public statements based either on inadequate information or on failure to appreciate all the aspects of a complex subject which is only partly within their jurisdiction."

Against this backdrop, it is not hard to imagine how Canol originated and became the morass it did for those on both sides.

It was cold and raining in early June 1942, when the troops of Task Force 2600 got off the train at the end of the tracks in Waterways, Alberta, and began the job of transporting thousands of tons of equipment and supplies eleven hundred miles north into a land they knew nothing about and were somewhat terrified of. Task Force 2600 was the strangest military group to land in the North.

The task force consisted of the 388th Engineer Battalion (Separate) and the 89th and 90th Engineer Heavy Pontoon Battalions, together with signal, quartermaster, finance, and medical units. Altogether, there were twenty-five hundred soldiers, half of whom were from the 388th. This engineer battalion consisted of white officers and black troops. They arrived in Waterways—having taken the train directly from Camp Claiborne, Louisiana—lacking mosquito netting and repellent, proper clothing, proper training, and the knowledge of where they were and why they had been sent there. The troops of the 388th were to live and eat separately from whites, get the most menial jobs, be last in line for winter housing, be stationed farthest north, and generally suffer the most. Only three of the twelve hundred men of the 388th died in the little more than one year they worked on Canol, and there were "comparatively few cases of serious illness or frostbite," according to the official battalion history that was written by whites.

The plight of these black troops was unusual at that time only in that they were stationed a few miles below the Arctic Circle. There were more than eighty thousand blacks or "colored," as they were then called, in the army. Secretary Stimson, who came from an abolitionist background, confided in his diary in early 1942, "We are suffering from the persistent legacy of the original crime of slavery." Roosevelt left the nagging problem of how to deal with blacks in the armed forces to Stimson. According to historian James MacGregor Burns, the president looked on race relations during the war "more as a problem of efficient industrial mobilization than as a fundamental moral problem." Stimson, while recognizing the injustice of servitude, could not bring himself to break down the barriers of segregation. Historian Burns commented, "If Stimson seemed weak on Negro rights, within the military circle he was virtually a reformer." A memo from the Adjutant General's Office, referring to black civil-rights leaders who were attempting to improve conditions in southern army camps, stated, "It is well known that the Negro population has been a focal point of subversive action."

A contemporary study noted, "The traditional mores of the South govern Army policy on the Negro soldier." Somervell was a southerner, as was the commanding officer of the 388th, Kentucky-born Major Thomas A. Adcock. Referring to engineer units, the study undertaken by an aide to Stimson stated, "The intention was to confine Negroes to small service detachments performing nonmilitary duties of unskilled and menial character that should be performed by civilian employes not available for military service." The aide, William H. Hastie, advocated integration; but this concept was shot down by the army chief of staff, who noted the service should not "adopt a policy contrary to the dictates of a majority of people." General Marshall elaborated in a memo to Stimson: "Experiments within the Army in the solution of social problems are fraught with danger to efficiency, discipline, and morale." Integration was to come only after World War II.

The whites looked on the performance of the 388th as a sort of sub-Arctic minstrel show. In interviews and written accounts, frequent references were made to the blacks dancing, singing, or shooting craps. The 388th was put to work cutting wood for fuel on the paddle-wheeled steamboats carrying men and equipment downstream to Norman Wells. They also became skilled at loading and unloading the vast stockpile of four-inch pipe— "stevedoring" work, as observers described it. At one time the soldiers cut two thousand cords of wood by hand, only to have some of it consumed by a forest fire. A lot of time was spent just slapping at the swarms of mosquitoes and flies. The task force history noted, "It was a strange Northland setting as the Negro soldiers, first of their race whom most of the natives had seen, labored through the long hours of daylight against a background of dark, cold, and dangerous waters (the rapids and whirlpools are just a few hundred yards north) on one side and the stunted spruce, jack pine, and aspen poplars on the other."

The troops were depicted chanting:

Crackers in the morning, crackers at night, here comes the
    Athabaska [a steamboat] with more damn pipe.
The night is light, mosquitoes sho' do bite, look up de river
    and see mo' damn pipe.

In July the rumor spread that the troops would return to the United States before winter. In late August, when the ice was already forming in washpans, the troops learned they were to spend the winter in the North. There was not much time to prepare. At Norman Wells about four hundred blacks were put to work cutting lumber that was used for housing for the white troops and civilians. The blacks erected log structures with moss chinking for themselves. The sawmill detail lived in pyramid tents all winter. Temperatures dropped to minus fifty degrees. By the end of October the soldiers were going to bed fully clothed to keep warm. A wood-cutting detail got marooned on an island in the Slave River and managed to survive night temperatures of minus twenty degrees for three weeks.

With the arrival of the first movies in late December, morale picked up a bit. When food was short, caribou were shot or rabbits snared. For weeks at a time no cigarettes were available. Matters improved in the spring. A band was formed, and there was a PX. By September 1943, Task Force 2600 had departed, leaving the job for the civilians. There were eight deaths in the task force. No limbs were lost to frostbite, and the venereal disease rate was very low.

For civilians, conditions were little better. Eventually a total of 52,900 persons worked on Canol, and this is the warning they read at hiring halls in the United States and Canada:

> THIS IS NO PICNIC. Working and living conditions on this job are as difficult as those encountered on any construction job ever done in the United States or foreign territory. Men hired for this job will be required to work and live under the most extreme conditions imaginable. Temperatures will range from 90 degrees above zero to 70 degrees below zero. Men will have to fight swamps, rivers, ice, and cold. Mosquitoes, flies, and gnats will not only be annoying but will cause bodily harm. If you are not prepared to work under these and similar conditions, DO NOT APPLY.

Despite the stern warning, there was a high turnover. Slightly more than one-half of the civilians did not finish their nine-month contracts. As one Imperial Oil employe recalled, "It seemed there were 2,000 coming, 2,000 there, and 2,000 going to Canol Camp." This camp, on the west bank, was across the Mackenzie River from Norman Wells. At the peak of activity, there were ten thousand persons working on the project at one time. About twenty percent were Canadian citizens.

Canol, as the project evolved in August 1942, became not only the one crude oil pipeline between Norman Wells and Whitehorse, but also three distribution lines, roads, and a string of airports. The distribution lines ran from Whitehorse east on the Alaska Highway to Watson Lake, to Skagway at tidewater, and to Fairbanks. The distribution lines to Fairbanks and Skagway operated after the war. The line to Watson Lake, the refinery, and the main crude oil pipeline closed down one year after operations began. The refinery, which cost $24 million to ship from Texas, was sold to Imperial Oil after the war for $1 million. It was moved to Edmonton.

But as the massive amount of supplies started pouring down the eleven-hundred-mile water highway to Norman Wells, nobody thought of Canol in terms of failure. There was a sense of participating in history. The contractors's book claimed that besides laying sixteen hundred miles of pipe, the Canol workers built more miles of road and airports than were involved in the better-known Alaska Highway project.

Although several loads of pipe, a half-dozen tractors, and some graders ended up resting on the bottom of the Slave River and Great Slave Lake, the tricks of navigation were soon mastered; and 5,450 tons of equipment were shipped the first month. Eventually between 60,000 and 70,000 tons went down the Mackenzie River. The total project, whose price was officially put at $134 million but is estimated to have cost as much as $300 million in World War II dollars, consumed more than a quarter-million tons of equipment. Much of this was left on the spot in 1945 when Canol was abruptly abandoned. War is wasteful, but Canol's waste was far above average.

On June 10, 1942, the first airplane flight was made over the proposed pipeline route from Norman Wells to Whitehorse in a twin-engine Barclay Grow. Two Indians from Fort Norman were taken along on the flight, but they were unable to point out the trail over the Mackenzie Mountains because the speed of the plane and fog confused them. Most of the mountain portion of the route had never been systematically explored. The Canadian surveyor, Guy H. Blanchet, abandoned other suggested routes and settled on investigating the Indian trail by dog team. Blanchet and his Indian guide, using the sketch of an old hunter, set out in October.

Blanchet wrote, "The Indian road is a remarkable one, picked out by people who knew every mountain and valley and pass. The trail cuts into the escarpment of the mountains by the deep box canyon of Sheep's Nest River, a tributary of the Carcajou. The walls rise vertically for hundreds of feet, and in the eight miles of the canyon the scenery is wild and romantic . . . . The aerial view of the Mackenzie Mountains in winter is of a sea of white ranges with few outstanding peaks. Narrow dark streaks cross these, the courses of the streams marked by the timber and willow along them. The headwaters of the rivers where timber is absent merge into the general whiteness."

Work started on the pipeline road in January 1943, but it was not until the following summer that the surveyors, using pack dogs and horses, finished their job. As the crude oil pipeline would simply be laid on top of the ground, the route was determined by the grades needed for the accompanying road. The crude oil, because of a wax base, would flow at extremely low temperatures. A feasible route had been found and enough oil discovered to meet the capacity of the pipeline. Somervell's luck was holding, but not for long.

Canol was still far from completed when the Japanese were being driven from the Aleutian Islands in the summer of 1943, and the oil tanker shortage eased. Some factions of the army were having second thoughts, but Somervell squelched the doubters. On July 20, he addressed a memo to the assistant chief of staff of the Operations and Plans Division. It stated, "The project will be completed in December or January. It is utterly foolhardy to talk of discontinuing the project at this stage of the game. It is likewise impractical to review the project as suggested with some representative of Mr. Ickes. We know the oil is there. We know that the refinery will be turning out oil by the time any intelligent further investigation could be made and a report rendered thereon. I recommend that the Secretary of War take a firm stand on this matter. . . . and back up the judgment of the War Department agencies who have examined it."

On September 6, 1943, Senator Harry S. Truman announced that the Special Committee to Investigate the National Defense Program—commonly called the Truman Committee—would take a look at Canol. There were enough opponents of Canol and enemies of Somervell around Washington to draw the committee's attention to the project. Besides Ickes, the Bureau of Budget, the War Production Board, and navy secretary Frank Knox opposed Canol. A subcommittee held hearings in Whitehorse; the full committee scheduled hearings for November in the nation's capital. On October 6, Julius H. Amberg, special assistant to Stimson, wrote his boss a memo stating, "Present indications are that the [committee] report will be critical."

The cover-up phase of Canol began. The vast bulk of documents available on Canol, some classified "secret" until a few years ago, pertain to the attempt by the military, including the Joint Chiefs of Staff, and the War Department to justify Canol or evade giving the committee essential documents. It is interesting to watch how Canol, originally thought of only as a source of fuel for airplanes and trucks along the Alaska Highway, grew in the minds of those seeking to justify it to become a keystone in the over-all strategy to defeat the Japanese. The growth in concept was in direct proportion to the committee's aggressiveness. Finally the Joint Chiefs of Staff cloaked the whole project in the false guise of "national security."

Through the dust of years on the documents and the scribblings in the margins by these giants of the past, one sees the blind lunges of the committee and the evasive tactics of the military. The real waste of Canol was not the abandoned equipment but all the time and manpower spent investigating and defending what was a very insignificant project, considering the total scope of the war.

One unexpected outcome of Canol was the eventual elevation of a haberdasher from Missouri to the presidency. Canol was the Truman Committee's most dramatic find. Roosevelt, impressed with Truman's impartial handling of the committee's activities, made the senator his running mate in 1944. Truman took over when Roosevelt died in 1945.

The Joint Chiefs of Staff "officially" learned about Canol on October 2, 1943. Undoubtedly, the top advisors to the president on military matters knew about it unofficially before that date. The JCS held secret hearings, and on October 26, they upheld Somervell's decision. One of those testifying was James Graham, author of the one-page memo specifying a five-month completion date that Somervell had acted on. Said Graham, "In talking to General Somervell this past summer, I said, 'I don't see how the project could cost so much.' It was always a simple operation from my point of view, except for the adverse weather conditions and difficulties of transportation."

The military heard the special committee was focusing part of its attention on Imperial Oil's lucrative contract. On October 25, the JCS recommended renegotiation of the contract with Imperial, stating, "Imperial should not profit unduly from exploitation done at our expense outside the field of its original discovery and development." Standard Oil Company of New Jersey, the parent firm, rushed a pamphlet into print emphasizing, among other points, the global importance of Canol. Amberg saw a draft copy of the pamphlet and refused to clear it because of inaccuracies. Nevertheless, Standard sent it out to stockholders and the press. Standard officials told the military, "Implication had been made that Standard of New Jersey was deep in the $134 million, and we want to clarify this."

The motives of private industry involved in the Canol project were something less than purely patriotic. A War Department memo reveals the contractors, Bechtel-Price-Callahan, were investigated by at least one grand jury and the Comptroller General's Office. One of Somervell's aides, Brigadier General Walter B. Pyron, a former Gulf Oil vice-president, recalled a conversation with Harry D. Collier, president of Standard Oil Company of California. "Mr. Collier stated that they deliberately entered into the contract to protect their marketing position in northwest Canada and Alaska." Standard of California operated the pipelines and refinery after construction.

At about the same time that Standard Oil of New Jersey started putting together its pamphlet, the military launched its public-relations campaign. Somervell, departing on a trip, instructed his staff: "During my absence the Truman Committee may let off a blast on the subject of the Canol project. You should be ready with our public relations outfit to put our best foot forward so that we can be helped. It seems to me that our best line is that if we had the thing to do over again, we would double the size of the installation."

The general approved an aide's suggestion that a "selected" group of newsmen be sent to Canol because, in the aide's words, "with proper guides they could do us tremendous good even at this late date." Stories and photographs, prepared by army press offices in Washington and Edmonton, began appearing virtually intact in various newspapers and magazines in the United States and Canada. Richard S. Finnie, borrowed by the army from Bechtel, traveled widely to document the project in words, still photographs, and movies. A color movie Finnie shot for the army, and edited with the blessing of Somervell, was never publicly released because at the time of its completion the army no longer wanted to draw attention to what had become an acute embarrassment. Finnie wrote the book published in 1945 by the contractors.

At the time of the initial Truman Committee probes, the first transcripts of pertinent telephone conversations recorded by the military appear in document collections. The transcripts were sent to Somervell for perusal. Here is one example:

> *Hugh Fulton, chief counsel for the Truman Committee:* "The real background of that is that definitely they ought to have in mind conservation of resources in time of war rather than the protection of the name of one man . . . . Undoubtedly there will be a complete investigation of that directive, particularly at the waste of millions of dollars on the project in order to protect the name of a certain lieutenant general. At a later time it will perhaps be one that they will rather regret having taken because every figure I

have seen indicates more the asininity of the project and the continuance of it."

Colonel : "Well, of course, that is your feeling on it."

The Truman Committee staff made a determined effort to obtain the Canol files of the Joint Chiefs of Staff. A blizzard of memos flew back and forth. The staff recommendation for denial that the JCS acted on stated, "It would enable the committee to produce additional evidence and attack the military decision of the Joint Chiefs of Staff made in the furtherance of a projected military operation on the grounds that the decision was made without the Joint Chiefs of Staff being in possession of all data pertaining to the project."

Opposite the name of Admiral Ernest J. King on the memo is penciled, "No examination of JCS files by anyone!" On December 16, Admiral King wrote Truman that the committee could not have access to the files as Canol was a "logistical plan in support of projected military operations, the secrecy of which must be preserved otherwise the national security might be endangered." Truman telephoned King and objected.

Two days before Thanksgiving 1943, Interior Secretary Ickes, representatives of the War Production Board, and Budget Director Harold D. Smith testified against Canol before the Truman Committee. On following days, Somervell and Undersecretary Patterson testified in favor of it. The hearings got wide coverage in the press. The battle lines were clearly drawn in public—the civilian faction of the Roosevelt administration versus the military. It was part of the continuing feud over control of the economy. Deep within the bowels of government, Ickes the infighter was jousting with the military for control over oil production in the North.

Initially, Somervell's appearance before the committee was impressive. He was described as "confident, trim" by the *Washington Post*. The general, with a staff of fourteen officers to back him, began his testimony, "It is a reckless man indeed who questions the strategy that has pulled us up and is going to lead us to victory. We had just as well get off Tarawa after killing off all but one squad of Japs as to get out of [Canol] now." Somervell said the additional drilling for oil at Norman Wells resulted in striking a bonanza of between fifty-eight million and one hundred million barrels. He characterized this amount of oil as the biggest find on the North American continent in the last fifteen years.

Senator Edward H. Moore, a Republican oilman from Oklahoma, was prepared for Somervell's claim. To the embarrassment of the general and his staff, Moore cited twenty oil discoveries in the United States between 1930 and 1936 that were larger than Norman Wells. What Somervell or anyone from the War Department never made clear is that most of the oil in the Norman Wells field lies under the broad Mackenzie River and is not recoverable. To this date, Imperial Oil has been unable to extract that oil.

The day following Somervell's testimony, President Roosevelt was asked this question at a press conference: "Mr. President, General Somervell testified yesterday that in June, 1942, you approved the Canol project in Alaska [again, the wrong location]. Did you know at that time how much it was going to cost?"

The president's answer was, "I couldn't tell you, Pete. I think I did, but I would have to check it up. It was one of those projects to furnish oil, especially at that time, since there was a likelihood of a great deal of action in Alaska and the Aleutian Islands. I approved anything to get a new source of oil up there. It was a war measure distinctly."

The Truman Committee's initial report was issued on January 8, 1944, accompanied by a flurry of press releases, both pro and con. Said Senator Homer S. Ferguson, a Michigan Republican, "It is unfortunate that General Somervell ever ordered the project to be undertaken. The stubborn persistence in completing it is inexcusable." Undersecretary of War Patterson defended Somervell. "General Somervell acted with his customary decision to remedy what might well have been a serious situation. The result of that decision is now being criticized in the light of our subsequent good fortune. Wars are not won in retrospect."

Needless to say, the committee's first report was critical of Canol. It concluded, "The committee is definitely of the opinion that the Canol project should not have been undertaken, and that it should have been abandoned when the difficulties were called to the attention of the War Department." The report cited the great benefits Canada and Imperial Oil obtained from the contracts drawn up by the War Department. The United States paid for the exploration and development of the oilfield but retained no rights to the oil after the war.

The construction of Canol continued. While the Truman Committee was readying its report, the road from Norman Wells to Whitehorse was completed in the winter of 1943. The pipelayers and welders followed the road builders. They worked out of wooden huts, mounted on runners and drawn by tractors. A song of the day, titled "Cat Train to Canol," celebrated the mode of transportation. The project was also romanticized in a 1946 novel.

Of course, the realities were somewhat less than romantic. A worker on the pipeline recalled bailing out of the back of trucks when they slipped off the road. After eating a meal he did not like, one truck driver went outside and drove his vehicle through the mess hall. Three pairs of socks, moccasins, and overshoes failed to keep one man's feet warm. Diesel oil was in the wrong containers and wound up being poured into gasoline tanks. Diesel fuel froze at temperatures of minus fifty degrees, and the fuel tanks had to be warmed by blowtorches. The eight-by-twelve-foot cabooses were confining. And with only three months completed out of a nine-month contract, there was a turnover of six in one fourteen-man crew.

Through blinding, wind-driven snow that whipped across the barren landscape, the two pipelaying crews, working from opposite ends of the route, groped toward each other. On February 16, 1944, they met for the golden weld ceremony. Finnie recorded it thusly: "[Bob] Shivel grinned as he bent to his task. He tacked the pipe, ran the filler bead, and made the cover pass. That was all there was to it. No speeches were made. No dignitaries were present." Two months later, after passing through ten pump stations, the first oil reached the Whitehorse refinery. It was an incredible achievement at the time, but one doomed to failure. Canol was already obsolete.

Not long after the start-up of the pipeline, the War Department put the machinery in motion to close it down. Stimson wrote Budget Director Smith on October 10, 1944, "For some time past the War Department has been of the opinion that action toward an orderly liquidation of this project should be undertaken with the defeat of Germany or as soon as the present critical shortage of petroleum products and tankers may be alleviated." A JCS staff report urging abandonment of Canol because the cost of operating it exceeded the purchase price of oil from other sources was deflected by Somervell from the eyes of the chiefs.

On November 22, he scribbled in the margin, "I approve of this but do not believe it should be submitted to the [Joint Chiefs of Staff] until the war is somewhat further along."

During the early months of 1945, the special committee put pressure on the War Department to end Canol. A closed hearing was held at which committee members made the point that refinery and pipeline workers were needed elsewhere with more urgency. The committee staff threatened another public hearing. Amberg, special assistant to Stimson, wrote a memo to Somervell's top aide urging abandonment. "We feel that otherwise we shall again be attacked publicly by the committee when our budget is being considered, if not before, and very probably an appropriation [to operate Canol] would not be granted."

That same day, February 14, a high-level group met in Amberg's office and decided to visit Somervell the next day and press for an end to Canol. The recommendation was to be kept "highly secret." On March 8, in a four-page press release, the War Department announced the end of Canol by June 30. Operation of the pipeline ceased five days after the announcement. Within one month the workers were gone, leaving table settings intact and beds made.

In May the *Nation* magazine characterized Canol as "the sorriest chapter of the American war effort on the home front." Canol was that. It took too long to build Canol and get it operating. The wartime purpose for which it was legitimately conceived had vanished halfway through the project. When Canol did operate, it did not work properly. Additionally, Canol was a short-term economic and environmental disaster.

From April 16, 1944 to March 13, 1945, the Whitehorse refinery processed 983,844 barrels of crude oil from Norman Wells. Of that amount, a whopping twenty-three percent was refined into fuel oil to operate the refinery. The most desperately needed type of refined product was aviation gasoline. Because of mechanical difficulties peculiar to the North, that portion of the refinery operated for only three months at less than maximum output, and 20,399 barrels of aviation fuel dribbled out.

The special committee estimated that a standard-sized tanker, plying between Los Angeles and Skagway during the three years it took to plan and execute Canol, could have delivered twelve times as much petroleum as produced by Canol. The committee released its final report on September 1, 1946. It was scathing. "The detriment to the war effort from the resulting waste in manpower and materials was greater than any act of sabotage by the enemy which has been disclosed," stated the report.

Canol was also an environmental abomination at the time it was built and operated. No energy project in the North before or after was built with less regard for environmental concerns. The idea was simply to get the job done as quickly as possible. Because of careless handling of the poor-quality pipeline, it began breaking repeatedly after start-up. In the first nine months, forty-six thousand barrels of crude oil were spilled from the pipeline. An eighty-thousand-barrel storage tank on the banks of the Mackenzie River burst while two-thirds full, sending most of its contents into the river. Sewage from the camps was dumped in the most convenient spots. The permafrost was ripped apart; and wildfires, caused by cigar butts dropped from airplanes, ravaged the countryside.

But thirty-two years after Canol was abandoned, it is hard to see any lasting environmental damage. Most of the litter has been cleaned up by government crews or salvaged by private parties, and what remains is more a poignant reminder of one man's hubris than an example of environmental rapacity.

The road is mostly overgrown in the forested sections and fairly well intact through the tundra of the Mackenzie Mountains. An occasional party of backpackers uses the road as a trail over the mountains. All the bridges are gone, so fording the rivers and streams is a major problem. At least two parties of snowmobilers have traveled the route in winter. Some attempted it on trailbikes, but bogged down. One Canadian government official who made frequent flights over the route in recent years said wildlife use the road as a trail. No one could cite any lasting effects from oil pollution, and the islands off Norman Wells are still heavily used by migratory waterfowl and shorebirds.

Imperial Oil, fulfilling the terms of a lease with the territorial government, has burned or buried most of Camp Canol. Scavengers and souvenir hunters, plopping down in helicopters and airplanes, picked over the remains of the "epic of the North." The camp's last inhabitants were trapper Emil Debrock, his Indian wife, and three daughters. They lived in what had once been a well-insulated meat locker.

Audubon, November 1977.

Valdez Foretold

The flight from Anchorage was flawless. The plane rose in the late winter sunrise, ascended over Turnagain Arm, crossed the Kenai Peninsula, and flew east over Prince William Sound, and then that massive corrugated sheet of ice, the Columbia Glacier, came into view. The glacier ended abruptly in Columbia Bay, an arm of Prince William Sound.

Because I had been studying charts and maps of the area for the previous week, I strained to make out additional landmarks. Yes, there was Valdez Narrows hemmed in by snow-covered peaks rising abruptly from the rocky shoreline, a typical glacier-carved fjord. My seat companion, an oil tanker consultant to the state of Alaska, jabbed at the view with his finger, "There, you can see it. A black dot in the middle of the channel." I was tempted to pretend to see what I knew I should be seeing. I tried to imagine seeing it. Then I saw it—the deadly black dot of Middle Rock in the center of Valdez Narrows.

I am not the only one who has had difficulty seeing Middle Rock, nor am I likely to be the last. Seven years after the selection of Valdez as the port from where the trans-Alaska pipeline oil will be shipped, it is just dawning on a lot of government and oil industry experts that there may be serious problems in getting supertankers in and out of Valdez. There is a chance the supertankers will go aground on Middle Rock or, more likely, will wind up on the opposite shoreline while attempting to avoid it. That is, if they can first miss the icebergs from the Columbia Glacier that float in Valdez Arm. Fog or a whiteout from one of the frequent blinding snowstorms (average snowfall is 245 inches a year) do not particularly help matters. Winds gusting up to 120 miles per hour from different points of the compass also can stir things up.

No pilot has yet been trained to bring supertankers into Valdez. Moreover, if such a vessel strayed from the narrow tanker lanes in Prince William Sound, it would find itself in waters last charted in 1860. This interchange took place last year between a federal official and a veteran barge captain:

> *Official*: "On the published chart there is no difference between the 1860 survey of Prince William Sound and what we did in 1973, 1974, and 1975. So if you're outside those traffic lanes, you're on old survey ground."
>
> *Captain*: "We've surveyed a lot of those waters with our keels, you know."

The waters of the sound and, outside, those of the Gulf of Alaska are the stormiest in the Northern Hemisphere. One-hundred-foot-high waves were once recorded on an oil platform in the gulf. This is what the environmental impact statement records: "Adverse navigational factors are thick fogs, sudden wind and rain squalls and snowstorms, as well as the uncommon occurrence of floating glacial ice, 'bergy bits,' and extreme waves . . . . During the winter months the Gulf has the highest frequency of extratropical cyclones in the Northern Hemisphere."

Those are the dry statements contained in a tedious document. Here is what one barge captain said of the winds in and around Valdez: "There's actually no way of getting any idea of how or why or where that wind is going to come from. And it funnels there at the Narrows. You'll get 60- or 70-knot winds right outside the Narrows, and inside Valdez Harbor you'll get 20 or 30 knots."

Add to all this the fact that the supertankers are going to be considerably less safe than what the Nixon administration promised at the time of the passage of the trans-Alaska pipeline act, and the possibility of oil spills along the southern coast of Alaska, already rated high, is guaranteed to increase.

The real dimensions of the problems are not known since no vessel larger than 28,000 deadweight tons (DWT) has ever entered the port of Valdez. The ships that will haul the oil vary in size from 70,000 DWT to 225,000 DWT. "The difference is like piloting a Cessna 150 and a 747," said one tanker expert. The oil industry did not think trial runs were needed, and it sees its recent acquiescence to demands by the state and Coast Guard to one month of trials with a 120,000 DWT tanker as a public relations gesture.

In fact, no one has taken anything near what might be considered a comprehensive look at the problems involved in getting the vessels in and out of Valdez and to other West Coast ports. Already there are six thousand vessel movements a year through the Santa Barbara Channel in southern California. With the additional tanker traffic, new offshore drilling in the channel where the massive 1969 spill took place, and the possibility of explosive-prone liquefied natural gas tankers using a nearby port, the congestion will become acute. The Coast Guard plans no vessel traffic system for the area and has kept the designated traffic lanes within the channel although oil companies have said they prefer the safer outside route for one lane of traffic. Vessels do stray from designated lanes. A collision was narrowly averted recently in the Santa Barbara Channel when two large vessels found themselves traveling straight at each other in the same lane on a clear day.

The environmental impact statement for the trans-Alaska pipeline glosses over the sea-leg portion of the oil transportation system, and since its issuance in 1972, all energies have been focused on building the pipeline and terminal in Valdez. For the oil industry, this omission has been due to overconfidence. The industry's maritime experts cite similar narrow harbor entrances elsewhere but neglect to add all the factors together. The federal regulatory agency—the Coast Guard—has lacked aggressiveness and has been extremely cozy with the industry it is supposed to regulate. The record of the Nixon and Ford administrations is one of broken promises. The only entity that is due credit is the state of Alaska, which has issued a host of warnings that have largely been ignored.

Granted the issues of the sea transportation of Alaska oil are immense, as they have been for the entire $10 billion pipeline project. At no time have domestic shipping and oil firms been called upon to furnish such a large fleet for the transportation of oil from an area about which so little is known. Nor has the Coast Guard ever regulated the movement of such large vessels in such a hostile environment. However, the tremendously rich waters of southern Alaska, through which a variety of whales and millions of birds pass, are a poor place to experiment on such a large scale.

But I am getting ahead of myself. The destination of the flight out of Anchorage was unknown. Nominally, it was headed for Juneau, but for the second day the airport at Alaska's capital city was closed. It took us three days to make it into Juneau, and while I was flying around at thirty thousand feet above Washington, Alaska, and British Columbia, I learned something about the nature of a regulator and those regulated, since Coast Guard brass, Alaska bureaucrats, and oil company executives were all on the same Seattle, Ketchikan, Yakutat, Cordova, Anchorage, Ketchikan, Seattle, Ketchikan, Juneau merry-go-round. We felt like yo-yos on a thirty-thousand-foot cord and shared a sense of camaraderie.

There was, for example, the five-hour wait, starting at 4 A.M., for the departure of the flight from Anchorage. (The next day a Japan Air Lines cargo jet was to crash at this airport, forcing its closure. It was not a good week for commercial flying in Alaska.) The wait was at a time when the Senate Commerce Committee was holding hearings in Washington, D.C., on oil tanker safety and the Coast Guard was taking its lumps on the East Coast. A Coast Guard officer came back from a rack holding a newspaper whose front page headline proclaimed, "STATE RAPS COAST GUARD." It was silently passed around the ranks of gold-braided, dark-blue uniforms until one officer remarked with some vehemence, "We have got to establish that we have the same goal."

Another high-ranking officer, a former master of a commercial vessel, commented, "What problem? You have to establish there is a problem. Why I was down in Texas, and they have these bumper stickers, 'Let the bastards freeze in the dark.' "

Not all the Coast Guard brass fit the same mold. There was a younger officer who sat mostly by himself. He had taken his chances and widely circulated a controversial proposal that pilots be certified according to vessel size, instead of the present blanket certification for all tankers over 20,000 DWT. He was later to take his lumps from industry representatives.

It struck me that there was little difference in outlook between Coast Guard officers and oil company shipping experts, most of whom have been ships' masters at one time. Both groups are essentially conservative. They are not trained to take chances. They revere authority and have developed elaborate systems within the ranks and on board to perpetuate it. Along with airline pilots, ship's captains and the military are the most self-assured professional groups I have met. All these factors add up to a commonality of style, which can form the strongest of bonds. At the Juneau meeting on pipeline tanker traffic, to which we were all headed, the Coast Guard officers addressed the oil men as "captain," and the civilians replied with the appropriate rank of the given officer. As a former enlisted man, I felt like saluting all the time.

Against these bonds and the combined expertise of the two groups, it has been impossible for other federal agencies, coastal states, and environmental groups to assert themselves with any effect in the highly technical field of oil tanker safety. But if ever a change was needed it is now in the wake of all the groundings, explosions, and sinkings of oil tankers in recent months.

Indeed, the Coast Guard's record of decision making on tanker regulations raises the question of whether a military organization should oversee such a civilian activity. Inherent in such an organization are specific tours of duty, then reassignment just when knowledge is acquired. An officer who has developed expertise working on vessel traffic systems the last few years remarked, "I will spend three or four years on this and become an authority. Then I will go back to sea duty. Someone will come into this position with no knowledge and have to learn it over again. That is the gap. We just do not have within our ranks the people with expertise in supertankers, so we have to go outside for it."

A former Coast Guard officer who worked in Washington headquarters and retains close ties with his former comrades took this longer view: "The Coast Guard has always had the job to protect men and ships from the sea. The ocean has always been the enemy. Now the Ports and Waterways Safety Act comes along and they have to protect the sea from dumb crews and antiquated vessels. In the first instance you have the industry and unions on your side. In the second it is the state governments and environmentalists versus the others."

The Ports and Waterways Safety Act of 1972 was signed by President Nixon with this statement: "Under this act the Coast Guard gains much needed new authority to protect against oil spills by controlling vessel traffic in our inland waters and territorial seas . . . and by setting standards for design, construction, maintenance, and operation of tank vessels . . . . The legislation provides a firm basis for the safeguards we will need to handle increased tanker traffic with minimum environmental risk." Thus the Coast Guard, whose primary mission had been search and rescue, found itself squarely in the business of setting standards for design and operation of oil tankers for the first time.

The next ringing promise came from Interior Secretary Rogers C. B. Morton who testified at a hearing of the Joint Economic Committee in 1972, "I am convinced that we must seize this opportunity to set new and exacting standards to govern the marine transport of American oil. This goal is worth accomplishing by itself; but, if our standards can set an example for solving the broader problems of international oil movements, we will have accomplished a task of long range significance for mankind."

Referring specifically to the transportation of Alaskan oil, Morton said, "Newly constructed American flag vessels carrying oil from Port Valdez to United States ports will be required to have segregated ballast systems, incorporating double bottoms." Morton repeated these assurances during the debate in Congress on the trans-Alaska pipeline act during the summer of 1973. Few noticed that the Coast Guard, the agency actually charged with making the decision, was saying very little.

In January 1973, the Coast Guard published in the *Federal Register* an advance notice of rule making and requested public comments on proposed regulations for segregated ballast and double bottoms on supertankers. The notice stated that final action would be delayed until after the Inter-governmental Maritime Consultative Organization (IMCO) conference in London later that year. The position the U.S. delegation took to the IMCO conference was formulated by the Coast Guard. It called for segregated ballast in vessels over 20,000 DWT and for double bottoms.

Segregated ballast consists of separate tanks for ballast water only. This eliminates the chance of discharge of oily ballast waters into the seas. Double bottoms are two separate watertight shells, along the bottom of a ship, that protect against grounding accidents. A double hull is the same type of construction, only carried on up the sides of a vessel. Such construction on the sides helps prevent a spill if a tanker collides with another vessel or rams an above-the-waterline object. To complete the definitions, a gas inerting system is a method of filling empty spaces in oil cargo tanks with an inert gas. Such a chemically inactive gas eliminates the potential for an explosion created by petroleum fumes mixing with air. The oil tanker *Sansinena,* which recently blew up in Los Angeles Harbor, killing eight and injuring scores of others, had no such system.

At the London conference, the U.S. position was overwhelmingly defeated. One participant said, "We were defeated on just plain economics. Nobody wanted to go for double bottoms except the United States." Another member of the U.S. delegation had a different interpretation. An Exxon executive told him the oil firm had lobbied twenty-two countries before the vote. One U.S. delegate felt the Coast Guard did not advance its position forcefully enough. He said, "The speed with which they retreated indicates there may have been some lack of resolve in the first place that easily could have been communicated to their colleagues in other delegations."

Be that as it may, the Coast Guard position was to weaken considerably from this point on. What has maddened critics both inside and outside government is the Coast Guard's insistence that it cannot impose tanker requirements for segregated ballasts and double hulls stricter than those agreed to at the IMCO conference, nor can tougher regulations be applied to domestic vessels than foreign tankers. (The Jones Act requires that only vessels constructed in the United States be used in the domestic trade. If it is decided to ship Alaska oil to a foreign country, namely Japan, foreign vessels could be used.)

The position agreed to at London is binding on no one, since neither the U.S. Senate nor the IMCO member nations have ratified the treaty. It calls for segregated ballast on tankers of 70,000 DWT, but it is not retroactive for vessels whose construction was contracted for prior to January 1, 1976. That requirement was adopted with a similar nonretroactive clause by the Coast Guard in late 1975. It will have little effect on the tankers to be used in the Alaskan trade, since construction of most of these vessels was contracted before the effective date of the regulations; and with the current glut of oil tankers, it is unlikely that many new tankers will be contracted for in the near future.

Because the oil may be hauled farther than originally thought—through the Panama Canal to Gulf of Mexico ports or to Japan—a second fleet of older tankers is taking shape. They include the *Manhattan,* built sixteen years ago and later converted to test the feasibility of an Arctic Ocean route eastward for Alaskan oil and last leased to haul grain to India and Bangladesh. In 1975 the Coast Guard adopted requirements for gas inerting systems, but they were not made retroactive and only apply to vessels larger than 100,000 DWT. These regulations also will have little effect on the Alaskan trade. No regulations have yet been adopted for double bottoms.

Of the thirty-one vessels now scheduled to haul Alaskan oil, thirteen will not have segregated ballast, seventeen will have no gas inerting system, and twenty will not have double bottoms or double hulls. The reason so many were fitted out with safety devices that were not required was because at the time they were ordered in the early 1970s it was thought the tougher regulations would be adopted. Additionally, what makes a mockery out of the Coast Guard's timidity is that chemical tankers and liquefied flammable gas carriers are required by IMCO codes and Coast Guard regulations to have double bottoms. Double bottoms are found on passenger liners, navy ships, Coast Guard vessels, container ships, and dry bulk carriers. The supervisor of salvage for the navy has stated, "I view the probability of a major salvage or pollution incident growing out of the grounding of a large, single-bottom tanker on an order of magnitude greater than for a double-bottom tanker."

Not everyone within the administration was happy with the Coast Guard's position. In August 1974, Interior Secretary Morton wrote the Coast Guard, "The proposed regulations do not, however, require new tank carriers to be constructed with double bottoms, regardless of whether or not the vessels are constructed for, or employed in, the Alaska oil trade. . . . The Department of Interior must strongly take issue with this position as it relates to oil transported from Alaska." The Environmental Protection Agency wrote, "We feel, however, that no valid case was made for not including double bottoms in the regulations." But the opposing view was not pushed hard because, as one official said, "The bureaucratic tendency is to accept the views of your sister agency, particularly when they have some kind of expertise."

Environmentalists went along with double bottoms but preferred double hulls. They did not like the proposed regulations, and eight conservation organizations fired off a letter to the Coast Guard pointing out that the regulations had been put together with the help of a "study group" organized by the American Petroleum Institute. It consisted of six representatives from major oil companies, one from a shipping industry trade association, one an independent tanker operator, and three government officials. The group, formed without public notice, met behind closed doors after the public comment period on the regulations had ended. The chairman was a vocal opponent of double bottoms.

Senator Warren G. Magnuson, chairman of the Senate Commerce Committee, which has jurisdiction over oil tanker safety, wrote Transportation Secretary William Coleman, "I am also concerned that the rules were developed in a manner that relied too heavily on the input of special interests . . . . Heavy reliance on special interest input in a public rule making process can only erode public confidence in our government."

In the letter the senator from the state of Washington, off whose coast these tankers will ply, added, "Instead, the Coast

Guard has accepted—on a political rather than a technical basis—the provisions of the 1973 IMCO conference as the basis of
its regulatory actions. The Coast Guard strained to stay within
the letter of a treaty which had not been sent to the Senate for
advice and consent, which is not intended to be exclusive, and
which does not cover completely the problem of accidental pollution from ships."

Despite these protests, the regulations were finalized.

While most of the debate has focused on construction of vessels, little has been said or done about training and licensing.
Over fifty percent of collision and grounding incidents are attrib-
utable to human error. The Congressional Office of Technology
Assessment pointed out the differences in training and licensing
of airline pilots and ship's officers in a 1975 report. Candidates
for commercial pilot jobs average four years of college and fifteen
hundred hours of flying time. Upon this base the airlines pile on
their own training schools. After graduation, there are annual
retraining sessions. Maritime academies graduate ship's officers,
and from there it is mostly on-the-job training. "Relatively few
shipowners have any formalized in-house training programs," the
report goes on to state. "The contrast with aviation in the area of
licensing is striking. Marine licenses, in themselves, do not as-
sure competency. Licenses of airline flight crewmen come much
closer to doing so in light of the extensive formal training and
proficiency testing required, coupled with the tough hiring practices of the airlines."

The genesis of the Juneau meeting was a study conducted by the
state's Office of the Pipeline Coordinator on a supertanker simulator at the Netherlands Ship Model Basin. The 160 runs on the
simulator did not result in any firm conclusions, but they were

the first excercises to point in some interesting directions. Although some runs were made under extreme conditions when shipping would normally be closed, certain predictable difficulties were excluded. For example, reduced visibility was not factored into the simulated runs, and it was assumed that all the captains and pilots had previous experience on large tankers. No tugs with barges or fishing boats were placed in the channel, as might be the case under real conditions. Using a mock 165,000 DWT tanker, the vessel was run in and out of Valdez Narrows under a variety of conditions. The variables were wind, placement and availability of tugs, ballast or loaded condition, and power and rudder failure. Few of the simulated runs followed the specified track down the center of the channel. Most wobbled from side to side, and some wound up on the rocks. One tentative conclusion was that Middle Rock was more a psychological barrier than a physical hazard, because in trying to avoid the rock, and in trying to veer on a dog-leg turn at the northern end of the track, most captains overcompensated the ungainly supertankers and wound up on the east side of the channel or on the rocks.

The next set of runs on the simulator probably will be with the rock taken out, the dog-leg straightened, and under conditions of poor visibility. The official Coast Guard position is that the rock has not yet been proven to be a hazard to navigation. The Corps of Engineers has estimated it will cost between $12 million and $18 million to remove the rock with conventional explosives. The lower figure is to remove it to a sixty-foot depth, the higher to seventy-five feet. The job would take about two years. With the rock out, the channel would be widened from nine hundred to twelve hundred yards.

When the state of Alaska released the report on the simulator tests, the results shook up a few people. The Coast Guard called a first meeting for December 14 in Juneau, and the Alyeska Marine Advisory Committee told those attending that they did not plan to bring a tanker to Valdez for trials prior to the start-up of the pipeline. Alyeska Pipeline Service Company is the consortium of oil companies building the pipeline; but, despite the existence of the marine advisory committee, when asked to comment, spokesmen for the company say its jurisdiction ends when a tanker casts off its moorings at the Valdez terminal. From that point on, Alyeska officials say, it is a matter for the individual oil companies.

The Coast Guard minutes of the December meeting note, "With regard to maneuverability and other operational data on the TAPS tankers operating specifically in Valdez, industry expressed their intention to rely on existing data from other vessels in other port areas, contending that such data was sufficient and adaptable to the Valdez area."

The minutes don't mention it, but tempers began to boil at this point. Charles A. Champion, the hulking state pipeline coordinator, recalled, "In the hall afterward I frankly threatened to punch a few oil people out. I had one by the tie and six backed up in a corner. I was using basic oilfield language. I went back with the admiral [John B. Hayes, commander of the Coast Guard in Alaska] to the hotel room of Exxon. The result of that meeting was that they came out basically to pacify me and decided to bring up a 120,000 DWT tanker for the trials."

The Coast Guard minutes end with a note, "The meeting adjourned at 3:30 P.M." Then there is this addendum, in capital letters: "AT AN INFORMAL MEETING LATER IN THE DAY, THE ALYESKA MARINE COMMITTEE ADVISED THE COAST GUARD AND STATE THAT, AFTER RECONSIDERATION, ACTUAL TANKER TRIALS

AND FURTHER SIMULATION STUDIES WOULD BE CONDUCTED."

The program for the tanker trials was worked out at the meetings held on January 13 and 14. In addition to assessing the danger of Middle Rock for the first time with a real, live supertanker, the *ARCO Fairbanks* will be used to determine wake damage, train pilots and masters, test the Coast Guard's new vessel traffic system, docking, anchorages, maneuvering in port, and positioning of tugs. Maximum publicity will be sought for the trials. And all this for only twenty thousand dollars a day in operating costs.

≺ ≻

While a start has been made in dealing with the problem of Middle Rock, little has been done about the icebergs disgorged by the Columbia Glacier. A report by the U.S. Geological Survey (USGS) in 1974 noted that although the glacier was presently in a stable condition, it showed signs of being on the verge of a massive retreat. Under stable conditions, the report stated, "Icebergs occasionally drift into the shipping lanes in northern Prince William Sound and the approaches to Valdez. Drastic retreat of the glacier would vastly increase iceberg hazards to shipping, especially to large, unwieldy vessels such as oil tankers." One estimate is that the amount of floating ice would increase tenfold; another cites up to fifty cubic miles of ice over the next thirty to fifty years.

A Coast Guard officer read an account of the report in a West Coast newspaper, and a meeting was called in Washington, D.C. There was talk, but nothing happened. The problem is bureaucratic. Nobody can figure where the jurisdiction of the USGS ends and Coast Guard begins in the case of a tidewater glacier.

Subsequent funding requests for studies to confirm whether the glacier is about to retreat have been turned down within the USGS. The Coast Guard has done nothing but consider air and ship iceberg patrols and a wild scheme to stretch a three-mile cable between Glacier Island and the mainland to keep icebergs out of the shipping lanes. This has never been tried before. There are doubts about whether the cable could withstand the massive pressures of wind-driven icebergs.

Records kept by a Valdez cruise boat and the state ferry show the number of icebergs have increased in the last two years. USGS scientists, after two days on the glacier last summer, felt they had found additional evidence to support the theory that the glacier is on the verge of drastic retreat. Of twenty-seven tide-water glaciers in Alaska, twenty-six have gone through such periods of retreat in historic times. Columbia Glacier is the only one not to do so. "Glaciers just sit and look pretty most of the time. It is hard for people to envision periods of rapid change," said one scientist.

The heads of the maritime divisions of the oil companies tend to publicly downplay the danger of icebergs, but recorded testimony reveals that they have closely questioned Coast Guard officers about the availability of iceberg patrols. What worries ship operators are not the massive, obvious icebergs but the smaller pieces, nicknamed "bergy bits" and "growlers." Along with those larger icebergs, which have a high rock content, bergy bits and growlers float low in the water and are difficult to spot. With moderate to high waves in storm-tossed waters, radar can be rendered useless as an aid to iceberg detection.

Even disregarding icebergs as a danger, by some calculations the number of ship accidents and the volume of oil spilled could be two to three times higher for Valdez than for the Los Angeles area. Moreover, the consequences of a spill at Valdez would be more severe. The draft environmental impact statement for the proposed pipeline project to take Alaskan oil from the port of Long Beach, California, and ship it east states, "It should be reemphasized that Port Valdez supports very rich and diverse intertidal and subtidal communities . . . . Port Valdez waters have not been severely degraded biologically as have Long Beach port waters. The low temperatures result in much longer oil degradation times than for Long Beach. The probability of a major spill in Port Valdez Harbor is considerably greater than Long Beach. One may reasonably assume that the biological impacts at Port Valdez would be significant, but these are beyond the scope of this statement." The same could be applied to the waters of Prince William Sound, which a University of Alaska publication has termed "a resource of unique dimension . . . as yet unassailed by unmanaged human use."

Under adverse weather conditions the Coast Guard says it has the authority to shut down Port Valdez. But the questions arise: How long can it remain shut down and under what adverse weather conditions would the Coast Guard act? There is a maximum of eight days of tank storage capacity at the Valdez terminal. A slowdown or stoppage in the flow of oil through the eight-hundred-mile-long pipeline from the North Slope could congeal the hot crude oil. At one time the Coast Guard estimated the port could be closed for two weeks. An officer who has studied the problem said, "Any conditions we lay on them could have an adverse economic impact. We cannot have unnecessary delays. The government could affect the private economy. We are going to make sure the operation is safe enough, but not too safe."

Outside the port, the vessels are on their own. One report states, "Prolonged periods of fog . . . play havoc with the economics and logistics of the entire tanker transport system for Alaskan crude. There may be strong motivation for a ship's master to proceed through the fog: such pressures might well work to increase the risk of collision or grounding."

As Champion predicted on the flight into Juneau, the day and a half meeting was conducted in an atmosphere of "sweetness and light." In the wood-paneled courtroom on the ninth floor of the Federal Building, Admiral Hayes summed up the results: "Out of each workshop we have gotten specific areas of agreement. We have gotten further than I thought we would. I am just delighted with the input of industry." Champion, representing the state, commended the Coast Guard and the oil industry but cautioned it was only "a temporary commendation." The chairman of the Alyeska Marine Advisory Committee declined to comment at the open session.

And the flight out of Juneau was made on the first attempt.

Audubon, March 1977.

Southeast

It was not the first time the Tlingit Indians of Angoon had faced a crisis, nor was it likely to be the last. There was the time in 1882 when a U.S. naval vessel bombarded the village and destroyed numerous homes and canoes. The ninety thousand dollars that the Indians won in an out-of-court settlement for damages from the federal government in 1973 is now being spent to restore some of the older tribal homes. But it seems that more matters of dire importance than ever before are descending upon the remote village on the western side of Admiralty Island. The same could be said of all southeastern Alaska.

In Angoon there was, first of all, the matter of the liquor license. This issue posed the gravest threat to the continued vitality of the ancient village of 485 inhabitants—ninety-seven percent of whom are Tlingit Indians. A white lodge owner had applied for such a license, and his attorney had not yet found any legal documents establishing Angoon as a dry village. (A joke told locally is that Angoon is the wettest dry village in "Southeast," as Alaskans refer to this extremely humid portion of their state.)

The city council was told the records had been lost because the village business had been conducted out of various private homes before being moved into the city hall in 1973. One council member said of the lodge owner, "He is an outsider and doesn't know our problems. He does not raise children here." Another council member said that should a license to sell liquor be granted, the city should get it. This prompted Mayor Peter Jack, a hunting guide and fishing boat operator, to declare vehemently, "I don't care how much money comes in. As long as I am on the city council, I am not going to be in favor of it. I don't want it on my conscience. In Hoonah when hunting season comes around, they have nothing to support themselves with. They have sold their rods and rifles for drink." Hoonah is a Tlingit village to the north that has a liquor store.

In Angoon, hunting and fishing is more than a sport or wage-paying job. It is a means of obtaining between ten and fifty percent of a family's yearly supply of food. Many refer to Angoon as the last true Indian village in Southeast because of its high Indian population and adherence to the traditional subsistence economy. Other villages either have become inundated by whites or have adopted a wage economy. This is not to say Angoon uses ancient means to attain its ends. Wood canoes have given way to fast, outboard-powered fiberglass hulls used to pursue salmon and take hunters into deer country. The older homes on the waterfront have been mostly deserted for the suburban-modern houses on the hill. But the Angoon Indians have accomplished this transition with a sense of self and roots that is lacking in other similar places.

Angoon is blessed by being in an area having less rainfall than the rest of Southeast and a plentiful supply of wildlife and fish. But it is cursed, at least this year, because it is on Admiralty Island, which has become the focal point in a land-use struggle symbolic of all Southeast. Despite millions of acres of untouched, primeval forests and mountains, there is not enough land to go around to satisfy all legitimate claims.

But back to the city council meeting in the rear room of the Angoon city hall, which also functions as the village library. Even though Angoon is administered as a dry town, there was a certain amount of bootlegging going on; and along with liquor, the council members were wondering where the young folks were getting ammunition for the pistols and rifles being fired indiscriminately near the village. The mayor suggested that perhaps a shooting range should be built where the weapons could be discharged safely. Then he turned to the three white men in the room and asked their business.

Marc Malik, a planner, got to his feet and explained that he headed a National Park Service study team sent to Admiralty to judge whether the island should become part of the National Park System. Robert Leedy, a biologist with the U.S. Fish and Wildlife Service, explained that although he was with the study team, he came from a different branch of the Department of Interior. The Indians tended to confuse Leedy's agency with the Alaska Department of Fish and Game. It was no wonder, since Angoon had been subjected to a lot of different jurisdictions lately. Leedy wound up his presentation with a brief description of the merits of being included in a national wildlife refuge. He said he would pass out some literature on the subject. I stated that my purpose for being in Angoon was to collect material for an article.

Angoon has been discovered in a big way, and the decision makers and opinion molders have started beating a path to its door. Actually, Angoon is accessible only by seaplane or the state ferry, which began service to the island last summer. Representative John Seiberling, chairman of the House Subcommittee on General Oversight and Alaska Lands, and his entourage had spent a day in the village, and the Ohioan had been made an honorary member of the tribe. (One older Indian said, "They put one foot in Angoon and then left.") The National Park Service study team was presently in town, and the next week Assistant Agriculture Secretary M. Rupert Cutler, in charge of the U.S. Forest Service, was due to arrive and would be followed by a Forest Service team that would conduct a public hearing on wilderness proposals for Admiralty and Southeast. As one white worker in the local native corporation observed, "These people can only take so much impact." No one had yet suggested an environmental impact statement be done on the effect that those studying Admiralty Island were having on the human population.

What the Indians were thinking was stated eloquently this overcast afternoon at the city council meeting. The meeting, like the referendum election the council set on the liquor-license issue, was being held on an off-fishing day.

Council member Albert Frank stood up and formally addressed the strangers. "Logging has been mentioned. It is the feeling of our people that they would not like to see what happened to Sitka. These loggers clearcut. They drag logs across streams. Those streams are dead now. We want Angoon the way it is. There are no fish in those streams. A long time ago there used to be. So this clearcut logging, we don't agree to that. We fully support this wilderness area. I think the general feeling is we want it the way it is."

Then Mayor Jack commented, "A lot of loggers come in from the Lower 48. Not many local people work in those logging camps. There is so much debate on that word 'subsistence.' To me subsistence is living off the land. That is the reason why Angoon is here, because of the abundance of hunting and fishing. I think logging affects the land more than anything. I point out many times how our people respect the land. The old people, when they go out to cut firewood, put moss over the stump. If you are good to the land, it will take care of you. We have always tried to protect the land and the resources. And we always stand up for our people's rights. We get more support from outside than from our own people."

But the Indians are not purists. The Angoon natives want no logging on Admiralty Island, which makes them the friends of outside conservationists. But in exchange for not logging the lands around their village that they would obtain under the Alaska Native Claims Settlement Act of 1971, Angoon residents want to be able to log elsewhere in Southeast. Said the mayor, "More than likely it would be an area the Forest Service was going to allow to be cut anyway."

The native village corporations in Sitka and Juneau want to log the lush timber on the west side of Admiralty Island. Angoon has bitterly opposed this. The Juneau native corporation, Gold-belt, has signed an agreement with the Angoon natives that it will look for lands of equal value off Admiralty, but if no such timberlands are available, it will stick to its Admiralty Island selection. The regional native corporation, Sealaska, supports native logging operations on Admiralty. The native corporations set up by the act are designed to be profit-making ventures. The village corporations get to choose 23,040 acres apiece, and Sea-laska gets 279,000 acres. The total amount to be removed from the Tongass National Forest for native claims is 525,000 acres. The commercial timberlands are the lands that are most eagerly sought by the Indians.

It suits the Juneau and Sitka native corporations to log the commercially valuable timber on Admiralty Island. It suits An-goon to log elsewhere. But native land selections are only one factor in the complex brew of Southeast. There are also state land selections, various wilderness area proposals, mining claims, two fifty-year logging contracts plus other timber sales the Forest Ser-vice is obligated to fulfill, commercial fishing, recreation and tourism, and the pending move of the state capital from Juneau.

For instance, if the capital is moved, the economy of the Ju-neau area will collapse. A new pulp mill would partially rectify this, but tourists and hunters and fishermen do not come to Alaska to gaze at clearcuts. The towns need lands to expand, and some would like private lands for timber operations. Yet the fish-ermen from these same towns feel logging destroys the salmon fishing. The long-term logging contracts have to be fulfilled, and the timber companies have been rocked in the last few years by the threatened lack of stability in land use. Yet in this gorgeous region there is not one acre of designated Forest Service wilder-ness. And somewhere in the above equation there is a lot of wild-life to consider, such as the nation's greatest concentration of bald eagles and grizzly bears.

It is said that there are millions of national forest acres scat-tered throughout the Alexander Archipelago and the mainland of southeast Alaska—an amount of land for all with some left over. Not true. It is the narrow coastal strip and a few miles up streams and rivers that are being competed for. This is where the accessible timber is, where towns are located, where Indians live, where fish run, eagles nest, and bears feed. Wilderness use is centered along the water in Southeast. One does not disappear with a backpack into the interior. There are few trails, and the rain forest is virtually impenetrable.

Acreage figures tell part of the story. Southeast extends from Yakutat to the most southerly point of the panhandle, an area of approximately 18.5 million acres, of which only 50,000 acres are privately owned. The population also numbers fifty thousand, and of those employed, about twenty-seven percent are directly or indirectly dependent on the timber industry. Glacier Bay National Monument, near the north end of the region, contains 2.5 million acres, and Tongass National Forest, the largest national forest in the nation, has 16 million acres. Thus, most of Southeast is Tongass National Forest.

With Alaska lands to be apportioned by Congress in 1978, most of the attention has focused on interior and Arctic Alaska. The lush panhandle has been treated as a bastard child. The story of Southeast, at least up to the early 1970s, was the story of Tongass National Forest and the policies of one man—B. Frank Heintzleman.

In 1794, long before Heintzleman arrived on the scene, the explorer George Vancouver wrote a description of Admiralty Island that could apply to much of Southeast: "The island seems to be composed of a rocky substance covered with little soil, and that chiefly consisting of vegetables in an imperfect state of dissolution, yet it produces timber superior to any I have noticed on this side of America." The tone was thus set for the extraction of resources that was to be the distinguishing mark of the panhandle's history.

The Tlingits did not take kindly to the arrival of Vancouver or the Russians who followed; but superior firepower, diseases, and liquor had the same effect on the Tlingits as on other tribes in North America. Because of overhunting, the Russian fur trade declined in the mid-1800s; and Alaska was sold to the United States in 1867. Next came the fishermen who, after depleting southwestern Alaska, centered their efforts on the panhandle. Gold miners on their way to the Klondike in western Canada poured into the state in 1897 and later fanned out in search of gold and other metals. The gold-and-fish boom lasted until after World War I, when few salmon were left and most of the precious metals had been taken out of the ground.

Armed with a master's degree in forestry from Yale University, Frank Heintzleman arrived in Alaska in 1918. He became assistant regional forester in 1922 and regional forester in 1937. As such, Heintzleman represented not only the Forest Service but all of the Agriculture Department's activities in the state. He was also the local representative of the Federal Power Commission and granted licenses for private power development. Heintzleman made Alaska, and particularly Southeast, his lifework. A 1939 report on him by the chief forester said, "My impression is that love of Alaska and determination to help solve its problems are perhaps his strongest motivating forces." Another superior wrote, "Frank's love for Alaska and his intense interest in its welfare lead him to get out of focus on Alaska's importance and its problems."

At the senate committee hearing in 1953 on Heintzleman's nomination for territorial governor, the forester testified, "My principal interest and principal activity in the last twenty years has been working for the development of the resources of Alaska which would help support a big population and bring in a permanent population."

He went on to describe how homesites, towns, and industries

were established in Southeast. "Our forest supervisors would even take [a potential resident] out along the road and show him what lands were open. He could start building his home there the next morning if he wanted to do so, and many of them did . . . . After about a year he would have a nice home. We threw it out of the forest so he could get title to it after three years. The same thing with all industrial plants. We threw land out of the national forests for salmon canneries, sawmills and so forth. We laid out townsites. We divided them into streets and blocks, and as soon as they had 50 or 60 or 100 residents, we eliminated the tract from the national forest so the title could be obtained under the Townsite Act. I think if we can do more of that work in the territory as a whole, it would be very beneficial."

Nebraska senator Hugh Butler, then chairman of the Senate Interior and Insular Affairs Committee, summed up the federal government's policy toward Alaska. "So we are all agreed on that, and I think the substance of the testimony by Mr. Heintzleman this morning is that he believes in the development of all available resources in Alaska not only for the purpose of making somebody prosperous who develops that by private capital, but for the purpose of getting a tax income and a tax base in Alaska that will support state government, if, as, and when it is voted by Congress." Heintzleman's confirmation was unanimous.

Under Heintzleman as regional forester, the Forest Service was successful in confining the National Park Service's area of jurisdiction to Glacier Bay National Monument. The Park Service eyed Admiralty Island as a potential national park, but the trade-off finally worked out by Heintzleman and Interior Secretary Harold Ickes was the enlargement of Glacier Bay National Monument with Forest Service lands. Admiralty Island was left in Tongass National Forest. Said Heintzleman, referring to national parks, "The time is coming when we must limit our one-use reserves." Subsequent Park Service proposals for Admiralty were submerged, and while I was in Angoon, the word the National Park Service study team got from Washington, D.C., was that the Forest Service was nervous because of the team's presence on Admiralty. So a low profile was maintained by keeping the size of the team small. A Forest Service liaison (spy?) was due to join the Park Service team the day I left the island.

Interagency turf struggles are one of the lesser-known aspects of carving up Alaskan lands. Nathaniel P. Reed, former assistant secretary of the Interior Department, testified that the department's first proposal for dividing Alaska was "flawed" by the large expansion of national forests designed to satisfy then Secretary of Agriculture Earl Butz and the Republican members of the Alaska delegation.

Federal agencies were attempting to enlarge their domains and serve their most powerful constituents. Reed said outside mining experts had to be used because Bureau of Mines personnel provided information "often inaccurate and slanted toward a pertinent industry." The Bureau of Land Management, Reed said, would claim that the Federal Land Policy Act of 1976 gave it authority to manage an area like a wildlife refuge or national park. "Frankly," he added, "it will take many years to uplift BLM's standards."

Heintzleman's main achievement while regional forester was to locate pulp mills in southeastern Alaska. He said his instructions from the chief forester at the time were: "Do anything you want to get the pulp mills." Heintzleman started contacting attorneys, bankers, and timber companies in the 1920s. Because of the high costs of operating in Alaska and the availability of timber in Oregon and Washington, the pot had to be sweetened. Despite resistance within the Forest Service, Heintzleman worked out the concept of the fifty-year contract that gave the timber companies a guaranteed source of timber.

Another obstacle was Indian land claims that Interior Secretary Ickes wanted settled. Heintzleman saw native claims not only as a cloud on title to land and a deterrent to any timber operations but also as a threat to the Forest Service. He wrote, "The thought is often expressed by private citizens that the move to set up vast Indian reservations in southeastern Alaska is based, in part, on a desire to eliminate the national forests in Alaska." The claims had to be circumvented if there were to be any pulp mills in Southeast. The Tongass Timber Sales Bill, designed to achieve that purpose, was passed in 1947 with Heintzleman and representatives from both the Ketchikan and Juneau chambers of commerce lobbying for its passage.

The Ketchikan Pulp Company signed a fifty-year contract in 1951 for 8.25 billion board feet of timber, and a mill was built near Ketchikan in 1954. In 1952—at the height of the Cold War—a Japanese delegation came to the United States seeking a source of timber and pulp to replace their previous supply, which had been taken over by the Russians. Heintzleman later recalled, "The State Department said fix these fellows up somehow because they might go back to the Soviets for timber." That fit Heintzleman's policy of economic growth for Southeast. The labor would be American along with some capital. The market would be Japan. A second fifty-year contract, calling for the cutting of 5.25 billion board feet, was signed in 1956 with a Japanese-controlled firm, Alaska Lumber and Pulp Company, and a mill went into operation late in 1959. A State Department document noted the Sitka mill would provide employment and increase the civilian population that was "looked upon by the Department of Defense as necessary to strengthen the defense of Alaska." The

Interior Department gave its "full support" to the development of such industries.

A third fifty-year sale was awarded to Georgia Pacific Corporation in 1955, but the firm later backed out. In 1965 the Forest Service announced the second offering of the third fifty-year sale and attempted to sweeten it with a five-page "Memorandum to Conservation Leaders." By now the timber sales had begun to attract criticism. The third sale was particularly sensitive because it included tracts of land on the west side of Admiralty Island. In a series of spirited articles, *Field & Stream* magazine aggressively took on the logging practices of the Forest Service in Alaska. The articles stung the agency enough for it to put out a rebuttal. Here is an example:

> *Field & Stream:* "The cut-and-get-out policy of the nineteenth-century timber barons is being duplicated here with the official approval of the U.S. Forest Service."
> *Forest Service:* "Mr. Young's [Ralph Young, an Alaskan guide] article contains untruths, half-truths, and irresponsible generalizations which convey an alarming and false impression of land and wildlife management on Admiralty Island."

In December 1965, the Forest Service announced the St. Regis Paper Company was the successful bidder on the long-term timber sale. The press release stated, "This is the largest sale of timber ever made by the U.S. Forest Service. It marks the final phase of plans conceived many years ago by the late B. Frank Heintzleman to establish a pulp industry in southeastern Alaska." Heintzleman had died earlier that year. He served as territorial governor until 1957, and then spent his last years promoting the economic growth of Southeast.

St. Regis subsequently backed out of the sale, and U.S. Plywood-Champion Papers Company took it over in 1968. The Sierra Club, Sitka Conservation Society, and guide Karl Lane filed suit in 1970 challenging the sale. Southeast was thrown into turmoil, particularly when local fishermen filed a suit aimed at halting clearcuts on existing operations. The Sierra Club suit dragged on until the Forest Service and the timber company both agreed in 1976 to cancel the sale. The two previous fifty-year sales were validated by the National Forest Management Act of 1976. Between fifty and seventy percent of Southeast's wood products derived from the Sitka spruce and western hemlock trees are shipped to Japan.

The Forest Service in Alaska, which some said operated like an independent fiefdom, was jolted by the court suits and the environmental fervor of the early 1970s. Shortly after taking office, Governor Jay S. Hammond wrote Regional Forester C. A. Yates, "Serious differences concerning forest management and fish and game management have arisen between the Forest Service and the state." The Alaska Department of Fish and Game had asked the Forest Service since 1961 not to log along thirty streams it considered critical to fisheries; despite this request some of the areas were logged. The state came close to filing suit against the Forest Service in 1975. Yates replied to Hammond, "I am sure you realize the sudden impact on land management by the environmental movement of the last ten years. It has required some drastic changes on the part of both industry and government, both state and federal."

A 1975 background paper prepared by the Hammond administration noted, "The nature of the Forest Service as an agency, characterized by its reluctance and inability to change, requires that this be viewed as a long-term contest of attrition." The state document added, "In many respects, the plans adopted by the

Forest Service for the Tongass National Forest will dictate the future evolution of all southeastern Alaska. Therefore, it is critical that the state government and various interest groups be involved in the planning process to the fullest extent possible." Referring to the so-called cooperative review of planned timber operations, the paper noted, "Proposals enter a tunnel period where, in effect, the Forest Service makes its decisions and ignores the recommendations" of the state and others.

Guy R. Martin, then commissioner of the Alaska Department of Natural Resources and chairman of the Governor's Task Force on Southeastern Alaska, told a senate subcommittee, "The lack of any recognizable fair and agreed process for allocating land for purposes other than logging has created an atmosphere of mistrust and an inevitable litigation-filled future for southeastern Alaska." Martin has since become an assistant secretary of the Interior Department.

As a result of these pressures, the Forest Service attitude began to change, and with the arrival of the current regional forester, John Sandor, the land-use planning process was turned around so that state, industry, conservationists, fishermen, and others got the opportunity to make substantial contributions. The Forest Service issued a "Southeast Alaska Area Guide" in 1977 that upgraded logging practices and gave some indication of how the land would be used. Robert E. LeResche, who took Martin's place, testified last summer, "Southeast Alaska is one area that is finally. . . . being competently planned and considered on a comprehensive land-use planning basis."

Along with developing a land-use plan, the Forest Service started to take a new look at designating wilderness areas in Southeast, where none exists to date. Whether the new direction will continue when the Forest Service gets past the phase of outlining alternatives and starts making some hard decisions remains to be seen.

< >

Any discussion of the panhandle inevitably comes back to Admiralty Island. Like so many environmental issues, the island is not necessarily the most relevant one, but it generates the emotional force needed to become a rallying point. Other parts of Southeast are equally if not more scenically attractive, but they are too difficult to reach and too amorphous to constitute a good issue.

Before departing for Washington, Martin caught the significance of Admiralty in a memo to Governor Hammond. Citing its "lasting symbolic importance for southeastern Alaska and the [Hammond] administration," Martin said the island should be set aside as a national recreation area where no logging, land sales, or road construction would be allowed. He said the governor would win "substantially more credit than condemnation" by such action. Martin's opinions were backed up by Alaska attorney general Avrum M. Gross, who contended in another memo to Hammond: "I have always thought that the timber industry has missed a real opportunity here since there is timber available from other sources to fulfill economic needs, and if they were willing to join with conservation groups in setting aside Admiralty, I am reasonably sure some accommodation could be worked out to insure that other timber." It seemed last summer that southeast Alaska's future was headed toward such a compromise solution.

What is Admiralty? The island has a middle-range type of grandeur. The mountains, reaching close to five thousand feet, are snow-capped, and the irregular coastline, backed by thick, dark forests, forms undulating bays and coves. It has a feeling of wetness and, like well-aged meat, a soggy gentleness. It is where the sky comes down to the land, and the drifting tendrils of clouds filter through the treetops. It is solemn. Admiralty has little humor or lightness, but it does have lots of grizzly bears and bald eagles.

Admiralty consists of 1,064,960 acres, of which about 2,400 hundred acres, mostly in the Angoon area, are privately owned. The remaining acreage is within Tongass National Forest. A little more than one-half of the island is classified as commercial forest land, and the Forest Service estimates this area contains 14.8 billion board feet of timber. The native corporations of Angoon, Sitka, and Juneau have identified 65,000 thousand acres on the west side of the island they would like to control. Angoon's selection of 23,040 acres includes the village and its historical hunting and fishing grounds in Mitchell Bay to the east. Sitka and Juneau are seeking the timber-rich lands formerly held by U.S. Plywood-Champion and its unsuccessful predecessors. At one time or another, about 12,000 acres of Admiralty were logged in scattered parcels.

Admiralty is not wilderness in the strict sense of the word. About five hundred persons live on the island, most of whom are located in Angoon. The Indians are attempting to purchase the lands and businesses owned by the whites in Angoon with funds from the native corporation, Kootznoowoo. The Forest Service maintains some cabins for public use on lakes and inlets and a cross-island canoe trail. There is a private lodge at Thayer Lake.

The history of mining activity on Admiralty has been one of a lot of searching but little production. Prospectors have combed Admiralty since 1855. The Noranda Exploration Company is currently looking for copper, lead, zinc, and nickel on the north end of the island, and WGM Consulting Company is search-

A Summer with Alex

Every once in a while I have this imaginary conversation with a friend, or a friend of friends, who has come to California from the East to sample our golden life. The friend asks me where he should go, what he should see. I tell him to drive south on Highway 1 along the magnificent Big Sur Coast, then cut inland and cross the fertile San Joaquin Valley to the ranching and oil city of Bakersfield. From there the ideal tour progresses north on U.S. 395, where the eastern flank of the Sierra Nevada plunges from near fifteen-thousand-foot heights to the floor of the high desert. Lake Tahoe would be a good place to turn west. The trip should end at one of the better restaurants of San Francisco.

Those are the places. The imaginary friend has only to go to one location to see the people, and that is a busy Pacific Southwest Airlines (PSA) terminal on a Friday evening. Through those sterile airport lounges—be it in Los Angeles, San Diego, San Francisco, Sacramento, or a half dozen other cities—pass the people of California in their myriad, freedom-loving, sun-blessed disguises. PSA is a true commuter airline and an integral part of California life. The passengers are herded like cattle through the gates with only receipts for tickets, and the intrastate flights are never long enough to establish any type of permanence in this state of transients.

If the friend were particularly discerning on a Friday evening, he or she would observe a weekly ritual. As the 6:50 P.M. flight arrives at Los Angeles International Airport from San Francisco, anxious men can be seen craning their necks to glimpse the passengers as they are disgorged. They have to stand a little higher because what they seek is a little lower. The children are brought into the terminal by stewardesses clad in hot-pink miniskirts. Another one of those achingly short weekends is about to begin for divorced fathers and their offspring.

I know whereof I speak, because for a number of years I waited once or twice every month on Friday evenings at Los Angeles International Airport for my son. Now I wait at the Greyhound Bus Terminal in Sacramento. But it is the same. The weekend is short, intense, unfulfilling; and quickly are the children gone, with the emptiness returning to be dealt with in other ways until the next short visit.

Alex, who at ten is an experienced traveler, and I have taken a number of trips together. We have backpacked in the Sierra Nevada, kayaked on western rivers, skied in Colorado and New Mexico, and camped in Baja California and on the Navajo Reservation in Arizona. He has also traveled the world with his mother, Dana, who works for an airline.

Never had we spent more than three weeks together. When he was two I left for South Vietnam to be a newspaper correspondent. When I returned, Dana and I separated and then divorced. I have consoled myself since then with the thought that when Alex and I are now together there are not the disruptions that occur in a normal family relationship. But the day-to-day intimacy is lost.

I am not sure when the idea first came to me—a summer to be spent with my son exploring the wilderness areas of Alaska. But it clicked in my mind as something that was inherently right and that it should be done before it was too late. The first opportunity presented itself when I knew that I wanted to leave the *Los Angeles Times.* But I was offered a job in the administration of Governor Edmund G. Brown, Jr., and that summer had to be passed by. A year in government was enough. So when I was offered the job as western editor of *Audubon,* I accepted with the stipulation that I would begin work after the summer ended.

Alex and I headed north from Sacramento on June 15. Both of us had trepidations about whether the summer would work. He asked his mother whether he could return by plane if he wanted, and after she passed that request on to me, I assented. I left with almost impossible expectations about seeing a magnificent wilderness and establishing a close relationship with my son over a long period of time. But, somehow, the summer did work. We returned feeling like an old married couple who had discovered each other's weaknesses and strengths. We learned how to accept and deal with these idiosyncrasies in gentle, understanding ways. And on our journey we saw some fine,

and not so fine, places. We know that despite other airline
and bus terminals, at least we had that summer together in
Alaska.

As a writer, I had to decide whether to take notes on the trip
for a future book or magazine article. After much thought, I
decided not to since this would be an intrusion into the undisturbed time I wanted with Alex. Also, I wanted to experience
Alaska without a notebook coming between me and the wilderness. But the memories are still vivid. Here are some snapshots
of the trip, as we both recalled them later.

We collected a lot of things that summer—like hot springs,
cherry pie, Peanuts' books, Richie Rich comics, bears and bald
eagles, accouterments for G.I. Joe (a male doll), miscellaneous
shells and stones, new friends of various sizes, dust and mud on
the Alaska Highway, and a cracked windshield and two flat tires,
not to mention a monstrous gas bill that went a long way toward
subsidizing the oil companies that were constructing the trans-
Alaska pipeline that bicentennial summer.

A few words follow about hot springs, cherry pie, tents, and
bears. We quickly discovered that the mineral baths scattered at
haphazard intervals through western Canada and Alaska were the
most pleasant way to get clean. Alex's favorite was Radium Hot
Springs in Banff National Park, British Columbia. It has two
large pools, one hot and one cool. One of the pools had a small
concrete island in the middle. I preferred Liard Hot Springs, near
the border of the Yukon Territory. It was a natural pool set
among trees a short distance off the Alaska Highway. A wooden
boardwalk carried bathers across a marsh, where moose were
grazing, to the sylvan setting. I found that frequently Alex's and

my opinions of places would split on aesthetic versus practical considerations.

Our fetish for cherry pies saved us from changing a flat in a dangerous situation on the Alaska Highway. On days when there was a long drive, we would make it a practice to stop at a cafe around midmorning for a piece of cherry pie. We developed a rating system for the excellence of pies, or the lack thereof. One morning we stopped at a remote outpost in the Yukon Territory for gas, then went into the attached cafe for pie. When we came out, the right rear tire was flat. We fervently thanked the cherry pie, because the prospect of changing a tire on that narrow road was not pleasant. Aside from the drenching downpour, huge trucks pounding north with materials for the pipeline had been slipping off the road all day.

Usually we could tell what kind of day we had and how well we were in sync when we put up our tent at night. Taking a bright orange tent was the one logistical mistake I made on the trip. With close to twenty-four hours of sunlight, sleeping inside the tent was like trying to sleep under a sunlamp.

We developed a routine for putting up the tent that worked better on some days than others. I would mark the location. Alex would hand me the pegs to hammer into the ground. With each working on opposite sides of the tent, we would insert the poles and pull it erect. Each would cinch the tie lines on his side. Lastly, we tossed the rain fly over and tied it down. Some nights we were all thumbs, particularly when clouds of voracious mosquitoes added an element of desperation. One day in the cold rain near the end of a kayak trip through Glacier Bay National Monument, we were all coordinated, fluid motion. The functioning together felt good.

Our best day for spotting wildlife was when we drove out of

Mount McKinley National Park (now known as Denali National Park) after a week's camping. We saw caribou, Arctic ground squirrels, grizzly bears, moose, and Dall sheep. We camped in a small state park on the road to Anchorage that night.

It started out inauspiciously, then took a turn toward the unusual. The earth shook with a mild earthquake; it felt like quivering jelly through our sleeping pads and bags. Later, something woke me up—probably the bright orange glow—and twenty feet from our tent I saw a black bear sniffing around our picnic table and station wagon. The bear tried to raise itself onto the luggage rack but evidently decided the thin rain gutter that circled the car roof was not sufficiently firm to use as a clawhold.

I was petrified. With only the thin fabric of the tent separating Alex and me from the claws of the bear, I felt like I was lying nude under the threat of razor blades. I did not awaken Alex, thinking the bear might frighten him into a sleepless night, as it had me.

The beast returned in the morning and went through its same act. Alex was lying awake in his sleeping bag this time. "I felt all excited. Wow! I wanted to go out and hug him, he looked so friendly. I wasn't scared. I was more excited than scared," he recalled. So much for the protective ability of fearless fathers.

From Fairbanks, shortly after our arrival in Alaska, we took off by plane for the remote Eskimo village of Point Hope on the Chukchi Sea. We both could not wait to get out of Fairbanks. It seemed crowded and sordid from all the oil pipeline activity. Alex put it succinctly, "Yuk. It was an ugly city. So many factories and that kind of stuff, and it was always raining." I don't remember any factories.

What I do remember was walking down the main street on the way to see Mel Brooks's *Blazing Saddles,* one of Alex's all-time favorite movies. Alex's hand was in mine. While we waited for the traffic light to change, a prostitute made me an offer I could easily refuse. How do you explain that to a ten year old, I wondered?

"What did she want, Dad?"

"She was only being friendly, Alex."

I also remember spending a lot of time worrying that an expensive, collapsible kayak might be stolen from the top of our unattended car, and listening to the owner of a gas station complain that it was so crowded in Fairbanks that he could no longer tell people about his favorite fishing spots for fear they would be desecrated.

But Point Hope was different, although its share of trash was strewn along the shoreline. This prompted Alex to comment, "Why does all this pollution happen? I don't think the Eskimos deserve to live here unless they treat the land properly or get rid of all the trash." My only comment was that perhaps there was a reason for the trash being there. Perhaps it could not be buried because of the permafrost; and in any case, it would soon be covered by winter snows.

In Point Hope, Alex learned what it was like to be in the minority. He was the only small, white face with freckles at the July 4 bicentennial celebration in swirling snow. "It started when this kid said 'warts' or something, and then said, 'No, they are freckles.' And then he goes and announces it to everyone. The Eskimo kids were running around me saying 'Chinese freckles, Chinese freckles.' I felt mad. I wanted to slug them, each of them in the face. There were so many. That's a little difficult. They came up and pushed me when I had my back turned and then, when I turned around, they would split off around the building. I didn't want to cry, but I did. I didn't cry until we got back to our room."

How do you advise your son in that situation? To ignore the children because the taunts were not directed at him as a person, but rather as a stranger? To put his back against a wall so they could not push him from behind? I tried both suggestions and felt they were inadequate. His sobs devastated me. Later Alex made friends with some of the children, and one came to play with him in our room. The situation resolved itself.

Our stay in Mount McKinley National Park was the turning point in the trip. We both, separately, felt depressed. Unbeknownst to me, Alex was homesick. It rained. There were the ever present mosquitoes. Our hikes bogged down in the soggy tundra. The awesomeness of interior Alaska depressed me, and I began to yearn for a more gentle, recognizable land.

We talked about it recently while camped at Point Reyes National Seashore, north of San Francisco.

Father: I felt a few times that things were not going too well on the trip.

Son: Like what?

Father: Like at Mount McKinley, I wanted to get out and hike for a long distance, and you didn't want to. Then I got to thinking. If I sent you home, the trip wouldn't be much fun anymore. It would be an empty time, and there would be no one there to talk to in the morning.

Son: That's what I thought. That's one of the reasons why I didn't want to go home.

Father: So I thought I would change what I was doing. I wouldn't push you to take hikes. We could do that another time. This time I thought I would just enjoy your company.

Son: Yeah.

Father: So from that point on, I felt better about the trip.

Son: I sort of felt better at that point. I thought I would have enjoyed the trip if it wasn't so long, like just one month. I missed Mom, and Missing [Alex's mispronunciation of his grandmother's nickname, Missy], and my room, and Blue [his cat], my friends, and all that stuff.

Father: The thing about that trip is that it really did work out. We got along well. We really were good friends at the end, and if we never take another trip like it, at least we had one such trip.

Son: Yeah.

Father: Because I'm not with you all the time, although I would like to be. We were with each other for three months.

Son: Almost three months.

Father: It's kind of hard not being around your son all the time and watching him grow up, you know.

Son: Yeah.

Father: How do you feel about it?

Son: What do you mean?

Father: Not being around all the time, just on weekends.

Son: I don't feel that great about it, and the other thing is I don't really like to answer these kinds of questions. It sort of gets me embarrassed. I don't know what to say.

The highlight of the trip for Alex, he admits reluctantly but honestly, was the go-carts in Anchorage. He also liked the three-day return ferry ride to Seattle, checking out toystores and bookstores, making up games in campgrounds, pizza, movies, and the occasional motel rooms we treated ourselves to.

"I sort of like being around people on camping trips," he said.

I would have preferred it if he could have cited some wild,

natural scenes. But I realize this would not be normal for a ten year old. I think he senses my preference, which is why he was a bit reluctant to mention the go-carts.

For me, the highlight was our eight-day kayak trip through Glacier Bay National Monument. We started at the head of Muir Inlet and ended at monument headquarters at Bartlett Cove. It was as close to a valid wilderness experience as we got, if you don't count the daily tour boat and the occasional cruise ships that ply the inlet.

We celebrated Alex's tenth birthday camped on the shores of Adams Inlet with porpoises, seals, and rafts of seabirds for company. I cooked our favorite camping dinner, Japanese noodles mixed with fried salami. Dessert was chocolate pudding with a match stuck in the middle of it for a candle. I wrote descriptions of the presents waiting in the parked car at the Juneau airport on slips of paper that surrounded Alex when he awakened the next morning.

Alex recalled, "Oh, no, I won't forget that birthday for a while. It was different from all the others."

Of Glacier Bay, Alex remembered the pods of whales that surfaced around us and paddling among the icebergs shortly after they had calved off the glaciers. "When you got right up to them, that really frightened me. The big ones, with this tiny kayak paddling by, that really freaked me out a little bit. I was thinking the icebergs would come over us and crush us. I guess it is the way they melt. They take off weight on top and turn over."

That's okay. I owed him a little fright from the bear episode.

We talked about wilderness and wildlife.

Son: Well, I don't think man should be able to walk in wilderness if he can't treat it right. All this shooting, killing grizzly bears for money and killing moose.

‹ II ›

The West

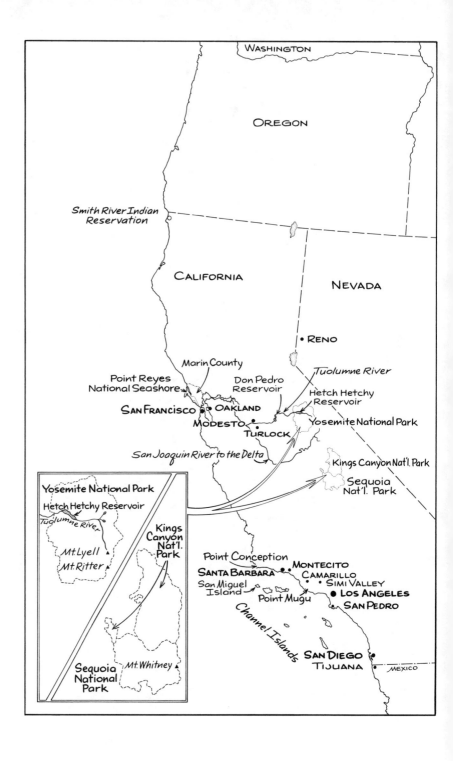

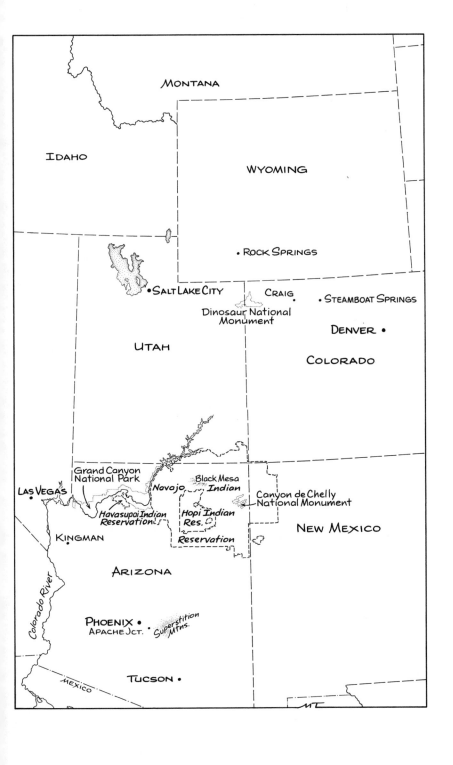

The Fall from Grace

The Indian of old believed he was born of the Earth Mother and the Sun Father and that life's main purpose was to live in harmony with nature. He did not wish to master nature, but to live alongside it. The land was left intact, an admirable concept in this time of environmental awareness, but one from which many a southwest Indian has strayed, if it was ever true that the original concept was practiced on as wide a scale as it was preached.

Today's Indian is alienated from the land. The evidence is found in the abuse that the Indian has wrought upon his own lands, an abuse that goes beyond the white man's strip mining coal, building power plants, and extracting other resources from Indian lands with the permission of the Indians.

The Indian has fallen from grace with a forceful push by the white man in the form of monetary inducements and legal trickery. The white man has encouraged industrialization of Indian lands in the name of progress and material benefits, while at the same time restricting the Indian to a limited land base. But the Indian is also responsible for the poor condition of his lands. The Indians are querulous among themselves and seem unsure of how to proceed with others. Should we allow the land to be exploited further, or leave it intact? This question is being faced by many tribes in the western states.

In northern Arizona, the heartland of Indian Country, the reservations are overpopulated and the land is badly overgrazed and turning to dust in this year of drought. Use of the land is at the center of extremely bitter tribal disputes. These are some of the most remote lands in the nation. The long fingerlike mesas are dotted with juniper and piñon, the translucent green leaves of cottonwoods flutter against massive red sandstone cliffs, and a birthday-cake fringe of snow lies along the ledges of the Grand Canyon, whose exposed rocks predate known life on earth.

Humans have lived longer in this region than anywhere else in the nation. The sense of having endured for so long gives the land and its people a sense of timelessness. To them, the white man is a short-term interloper. Search far enough and a sense of harmony with the land can still be found. More commonly though, the opposite is true.

The men and one woman sit quietly in pickup trucks with heaters turned up. A few talk briefly to each other. The red, Cyclopean eyes of burning cigarettes flicked out car windows describe an occasional arc to mark their passage and the only visible movement. Two red-tailed hawks are tethered above the chief's stone and adobe home. A dog barks in the Hopi village of Shungopavi. It is freezing cold.

First one then more of the dozen or so people sitting in their vehicles, as if at some unspoken signal or a sign that I cannot decipher, enter a small house and take their seats on benches or chairs arranged along the walls. I follow.

Nothing is said. The men sit, seem to doze, cough, spit, and smoke their pipes and cigarettes. The stillness brings repose and a gathering of thoughts.

The water boils over on the propane stove. The hiss of gas lanterns seems to grow louder. Two men sitting by the pot-bellied stove exchange pipes without a word. The tobacco is pungent. The room becomes stifling.

After what might be a half hour or forty-five minutes, a few scattered words are uttered. There is a general murmur of "ai," and the meeting to discuss the mining of coal on Black Mesa begins. The coal will be shipped to two power plants, where it will be converted to electrical energy to feed the homes, businesses, and industries of Southern California. When the plants are completed, a homeowner, such as myself, will flick on a switch and the effects will be felt all the way back to the remote Indian village of Shungopavi, one of the oldest continuously inhabited communities in the nation.

In the search for or extraction of ever-increasing amounts of water, coal, oil, natural gas, and other raw materials, Southern California's insatiable maw is draining the western and northern halves of the continent and, in the process, changing the way life is lived in such remote places of greater antiquity.

These are the voices I heard recently on the Havasupai, Hopi, and Navajo reservations:

• One hundred years ago Uncle Sam came along and said, "Stay at home and be good Indians and we will feed you." Welfare is a terrible thing to do to an Indian.

• I remember the old people saying, "Don't take anything from the white man. There will always be strings." It is true.

• An Indian environmental activist: "We go into the chapter houses and try to tell these people about what is happening to their land and they kick us out and call us Indian hippies."

• An older Hopi: "The white man is trying to grab the resources of the land. They are trying to divide us from the Navajo with this land dispute. It is the same old divide and conquer all these years."

• A white woman fresh from the Harvard Graduate School of Education: "I had to toss everything I learned out the window and structure these classes rigidly. These children get no discipline at home."

• An Indian teacher, a middle-aged woman, holding her Head Start Class rapt by reading *The Coyote Tales* and explaining what a feast is by asking what the children do before a Kachina dance: The almost unanimous reply is "eat." One small pig-tailed girl added, "We went down into the kiva and there was dancing down there."

• A Public Health Service doctor: "There is a lot of diabetes and there is some tuberculosis, but you don't see many Indians getting heart attacks. There is the problem with alcoholism, though."

• A Havasupai woman holding one of her grandchildren on her lap: "There are pretty bad people out in the towns. I just got back with my girlfriend from San Diego. They were robbing stores and everything. Here we can raise our own vegetables and live on that. It is too expensive in the towns."

• A Navajo on prices at the nearest trading post: "They used to be pretty high when the white men ran it, but now it is better since it became Navajo-owned."

• A white trader confided at another post: "We lent them the money to go to Washington to testify in the land dispute against the Hopis."

• An elderly Hopi after being interviewed for about two hours: "Why don't you tell me about your way of life?"

"Of course, what questions do you have?"

He pondered for a moment. "I guess I really don't have any."

These are the places:

No community is more remote than the Havasupai Indian Reservation, eight miles by trail down the Grand Canyon. It has the last post office in the nation where the mail is delivered by mule. The reservation has been described as a Shangri-La. For the most part, it is that. A year-round stream gives the canyon valley a lush carpet of green in an otherwise desert environment. Waterfalls below the village form pools the equal of any Polynesian setting. Transportation is by foot and horse, and peace reigns without the automobile.

But all is not well in a paradise that threatens to be lost. In 1901 President Theodore Roosevelt visited the Grand Canyon, and the outcome of his visit was recorded in the unpublished memoirs of Mark Hanna, a Havasupai Indian:

> Teddy Roosevelt said there was going to be a park placed at Grand Canyon and there was going to be people there that run it. I asked (Chief) Manakadja if we were going to get run off this land. Some other fellows asked him if the Supais would get money for the land for the park. That is Supai land and we owned that place and they took it away. Manakadja told us to wait and see what they do. He said, "I don't think they'll kick us off that land." Captain Navajo [another chief] told us to wait, too. We waited, but we got kicked off the land and we didn't get money for it. We just got kicked off.

The Havasupai, spurred on by the example of the Taos Indians of New Mexico who regained their sacred Blue Lake from the Forest Service last August, are now seeking to reclaim a portion of their former lands that were placed in Grand Canyon National Park. The reservation will strangle on itself unless the Indians get land on the mesa top in order to supplement their crowded canyon holdings. Two Prescott College professors concluded in a recently published book, "The Havasupai live perched on the brink of environmental and population disaster at the beginning of the 1970s."

The plight of the Supai has been described by Lee Marshall, a former chairman of the Tribal Council, thusly: "Unless something is done, the canyon reservation will become a jungle of government housing piled high with undisposible tin cans and inhabited by senior citizens of the tribe on welfare. The stream and the falls will reek of pollution from the sewage, and the young will be dispersed and no longer identify with the tribe."

From a population of little more than one hundred at the turn of the century, the tribe increased to more than four hundred, most of whom are crowded into the small valley with an equal number of horses and mules. The Bureau of Indian Affairs is supplying the Indians with fifty new prefabricated houses, which are being built in the middle of the fields and thus taking more land out of production. The design of the houses relates more to a white suburb than to a remote canyon in Indian Country.

Building these homes is temporarily boosting the Indians's income, since construction jobs pay about seven dollars an hour. Government jobs, derived from various antipoverty programs, along with tourism account for the main source of income. Between seven thousand and ten thousand tourists a year visit the remote canyon, either on foot or horseback. At Easter, the peak of the tourist season, about two thousand persons were jammed into the reservation and a Park Service campground below it. Administrators at Grand Canyon National Park have now placed a one-hundred-person limit on the campground, and tribal officials fear that their $75,000 yearly income from tourism will be cut by three-fourths because of decreased use.

To supplement their tribal income and cut the costs of supplies, among the highest in the nation because of packer's fees, the Indians have discussed building a tramway that would haul tourists and foodstuffs into and out of the canyon. They have also considered selling their water to white business interests. The water now runs into the Colorado River. A third alternative, if the Indians were granted mesa-top land, would be to pipe the water up to this land and go into the cattle-raising business, as other tribes have done. Some of the tribe sees this last alternative as the best way to preserve their traditional ways, gain needed income, and resist domination by white tourists and water users.

The Hopi reservation is a small island surrounded by a vast sea of Navajos. A total of 130,000 Navajos, the largest Indian tribe in the nation, surround some 6,000 Hopi. The Hopi reservation is a 650,000-acre enclave within the 16-million acres of the Navajo reservation that sprawls over four states. About half of the Hopi reservation is moderately to severely overgrazed, but it still looks good in comparison to adjacent Navajo lands. Overgrazing leads to soil erosion, and this loss of topsoil decreases the productivity of the land and changes it into a wasteland—a more widespread alteration of vegetation than any strip mining could ever achieve.

For more than one hundred years the Navajos, a seminomadic tribe with a birth rate far above the national average, have been encroaching on the Hopi, a village-dwelling people. In recent months the conflict has erupted into a border war, with the Navajos erecting fences and the Hopi tearing them down and impounding Navajo cattle that strayed onto the Hopi reservation. A few shots have been traded back and forth and some butchered cattle have been found in isolated ravines. Because of the devastation to their own lands by overgrazing and increased population pressures, the Navajos have pushed the Hopi off 1.8 million acres designated as joint use, arguing that possession is nine-tenths of the law.

Along with battling the Navajos, the Hopis have been internally split into two factions—the progressives headed by the government-commissioned and recognized tribal council and the traditionalists composed of the old religious chiefs. The traditionalists express a philosophical closeness to the land, and their sympathies lie with the Navajos in the present struggle. They hope that the Hopi Tribal Council will lose face and be defeated in its efforts to partition the joint-use land.

Two conversations illustrate the polarization. A progressive said, "We will not have peace in our land until we come to terms with each other. The young people are going to prevail and the traditionalists are dying. They do not have the zeal any more. But if we do not restrain the younger generation, we will be just as bad off because we will lose what we have, what has kept us together for centuries—a sense of tradition."

A traditionalist replied, "If the young people continue to fool with the land, they will ruin it. The land does not belong to the government to split up. We should hold onto the land and be self-supporting. But the young people just hang around looking for government jobs. They farm less and they have neglected the fields and the orchards are drying up."

≺ ≻

Canyon de Chelly is the heartland of the Navajo Nation. It contains two of the Navajos's most sacred shrines, White House Ruin and Spider Rock. Following a scorched earth policy by troops led by Kit Carson, the Navajo stronghold in the canyon was broken and the tribe subjugated in 1864. The present Navajo reservation grew from 3.5 million acres surrounding the canyon in 1868 to its present size. The trees have grown back in the canyon bottom since Carson and the U.S. calvary passed through with torches, and life here among the rock paintings and Anasazi ruins that date back nearly two thousand years hasn't changed greatly.

There is a closeness to the earth that sustains the families who live among the cottonwoods and towering sandstone cliffs. There are no paved roads or electricity. A few pickup trucks drive the sandy bottom of the river bed, but a more reliable form of transport is the horsedrawn cart. The Navajos farm the canyon bottom in the late spring and summer months and then move their herds up to the mesa tops for the winter. They live in traditional hogans, log- and-mud-chinked structures with bright blue roofs that reflect the color of the clear sky above. Dogs lie about, and sheep skins and harnesses are draped on poles.

On one such plot of land lives Chauncey Neboyia and his wife, Dorothy. They have four daughters, one son, and twenty-six grandchildren, some of whom live in the four hogans. The farm, just under four acres, is called Zuni Trail for the Indian slave who escaped up the near-vertical cliffs many years ago. These cliffs have sheltered the canyon's occupants from raids by other tribes and encroaching civilization.

From the trading post in Chinle, Neboyia and his wife buy flour, coffee, sugar, salt, and lard. Their flock of about one hundred sheep and goats and a few cattle supply them with meat and cheese. Neboyia has planted a section of his land with corn, melons, beans, and squash—traditional Indian crops. There are peach and apple trees in the orchard. The sheep, driven out from a corral fenced by branches in the morning and returned at night, are tended by Mrs. Neboyia or one of her daughters and grandchildren.

The elderly couple is fairly affluent by Canyon de Chelly standards. They have the only well in the canyon, and when dressed for a photograph, he in clean jeans and she in a long velveteen dress, both are adorned with a heavy load of Navajo jewelry. Neboyia proudly declares, "We are the only ones between White House and Spider Rock who are not on welfare."

There are problems. The prices for lamb and wool have been low for the last two years. Neboyia had to set fire to the dry leaves under the fruit trees to scare away the porcupines that had destroyed some of the trees. But altogether, it is a good life for the couple. "We live fairly well. The earth is our feeder. What we grow here we eat," said Neboyia, who earns some cash by working summers on Park Service archaeological digs.

A raven circles on the updrafts near the cliffs where the corn cobs of a people long gone lie amongst the ruins. The Anasazi were also guilty of overcrowding and overuse of natural resources, and disappeared around A.D. 1300. The Navajos are their successors. They, too, are interlopers.

Two dogs fight for a bone. A sharply uttered Navajo word separates them. The tinkling bells indicate that the sheep are heading for the corral in the late afternoon, and a flatbed truck pulls into the yard to let off a half dozen joyful grandchildren who romp across the dusty ground.

Los Angeles Times, May 1972

A Coastal Journey

There is no mistaking where the California coastline begins. The traveler on U.S. Highway 101—two lanes here but a freeway by the time it reaches the Mexican border more than one thousand miles distant—leaves Oregon behind just after the Winchuck River. On the right is an agricultural inspection station. These stations are placed at every major road entry into the state to filter out dangers to livestock and crops, and to warn travelers that they are entering a different land.

Land is the most important commodity in the nation's most populous state. Nowhere is land more sought after than along the coastline, where agriculture is in decline but recreation, commerce, tourism, industry, and the pursuit of the good life are booming. This is land to be bought, sold, traded, and held for speculation. It is land to be drilled, graded, paved, furrowed, and trod upon by millions of people who want to work and play where the continent ends in unparalleled splendor.

And it all begins a few feet over the border. A sign on the ocean side of the highway declares, "Development opportunities. 112 acres. Motel sites. Commercial sites. Home sites. Private airstrip." A little further away a companion sign reads, "No trespassing. Violators will be prosecuted." Both themes—inclusion if you have the money to live here, exclusion if you don't—will be repeated with little variation and increasing tempo on the journey south.

On this day, ignoring the signs, I turn off the paved highway and drive to the edge of the Pacific Ocean. It is one of those vivid early-fall days. A thin sliver of fog hangs over the horizon. Each form is sharply edged. It is a world of fresh greens, of intense blues, of dazzling white surf, and the comfortable gray of weathered driftwood. Further south the tones become more muted. They shade off into the more representative California hues of the olive-green vegetation, the dull yellow grasses, and the soft brown soils. But here, on this day, the light and colors have an aching intensity.

The north coast, ranging from the Oregon border to San Francisco, is bucolic California. The low coastal hills are lush with second-growth timber, the old growth having been extensively logged. Here, in a near rainforest environment, there can be up to one hundred inches of rainfall a year. Small ranches unroll along gentle slopes, while offshore the guano-splattered rocks indicate where powerful ocean swells have separated these outposts from nearby headlands.

The winter storms flush out the coastal hillsides, and the rivers disgorge tree limbs, logs, and miscellaneous debris, much of it plastic, onto the ocean beaches. Pelican Beach is littered with driftwood. A child's imagination runs wild, and an adult can see art in the many variations of forms and textures. Then with the next high tide and storm, the beach is rearranged.

It is a tranquil, warm day. A hawk and a few gulls circle slowly—the perennial hunt. The swordlike dune grass sways softly. Above, on a bluff, is the Smith River Indian Reservation, a few dilapidated shacks, and the How-On-Quet Cemetery overlooking the beach. Plastic flowers add splashes of unreal color to the carefully tended graves, and a weathered picket fence keeps out encroaching sand dunes. The grandest tombstone belongs to Mattie Richards, "Beloved wife and mother."

A few miles to the south, a fisherman clad in hipboots sits on a bench overlooking the Smith River and laments, "Not much luck here now. We need a rain to raise the level of the river so the salmon can go up and spawn."

The man is older, retired. He wears a yachtsman's cap and on the sleeve of his brown windbreaker there is a National Rifle Association patch. Definitely a sportsman, as they call themselves. He likes to come here, he tells me, because there are trees and grass and shrubs and he can walk upon the ground. He lives far to the south, in the direction of my journey.

If you had to balance the coast of California, the fulcrum would probably fall at Point Conception, which lies a little more than two-thirds of the way down the coastline. To the north, with a few exceptions, are areas of great natural beauty. To the south are the people and the works they have created. The California coastline is both of these, mostly in conflict, a few times in harmony.

The point is a physical barrier. The one time I passed it at sea in a small sailboat it was an utterly calm, moonlit night. There was no wind, so the boat's small diesel engine put-putted away. A few lights from ranch buildings twinkled benevolently on shore, and the boat's wake spewed up phosphorescent organisms. The night had a languid, tropical feeling. At other times the weather off the point can be fearsome.

Here is the mixing bowl of the coastline, where the cold California current sweeps down from Alaska to meet the warm Davidson current from the south. The result, most of the time, is wind and fogs and the dividing line of the two Californias—north and south. When they speak about splitting the state, this is where the Mason-Dixon Line would fall.

The moderating effect of the ocean currents cancel out any great seasonal changes. The sluggish California current, about four hundred miles wide, moves a large body of cold water south. During the spring and summer, when the sun would be expected to be warming inshore waters, the prevailing northwest winds push them steadily south and they are displaced by colder subsurface waters. This phenomenon, called upwelling, brings deep, nutrient-rich waters to the surface near shore, thus providing a rich marine environment. Warm Pacific air masses blow over the cold inshore waters, and presto—summer fog, the bane of tourists but natural air conditioning for the natives. In the fall and early winter the upwelling ceases and the warmer Davidson current takes over. These are the golden months.

In the balmy months near Point Conception it is not difficult to guess that a major population center lies nearby. To keep out the weekend crowds, the neighboring ranch owner has strung concertina-type barbed wire around his property and employs guards riding in radio-equipped, four-wheel-drive vehicles with German shepherds sitting beside them to keep the people out. Surfers circumvent the land-bound guards by arriving in sleek speedboats from as far away as Santa Barbara, forty miles to the east, and anchor offshore. The chase scenes are sometimes worthy of a James Bond thriller.

The intrepid Spanish explorer, Juan Rodríguez Cabrillo, was the first European to sail up the coast of California fifty years after Columbus discovered America. Cabrillo was seeking a passage to India and treasure but instead met with death on a barren, windswept island. The Spanish were never very lucky in California.

Cabrillo broke his arm on the Isla de Posesión, later renamed San Miguel Island, but continued his voyage up the stormy coast against the prevailing winds. The journal of the voyage provides the earliest recorded description of the coastline. Cabrillo may have been in the vicinity of the Big Sur coastline when he wrote, "There are mountains which seem to reach the heavens and the sea beats on them. Sailing along close to land it appears as though they would fall on the ships." The two small boats were forced back and again landed on San Miguel Island where, on January 3, 1543, Cabrillo died of complications from his arm injury.

San Miguel and the other Channel Islands off the crowded coast of southern California have changed little in the past four hundred years. They are long steps back into time. Man's mark is upon them, but not yet with any degree of permanence. To walk across San Miguel, the northernmost of the group of islands, is to feel an unknown presence. It could be Cabrillo or any one of a number of odd, mysterious twists that life has taken on this island. The presences, in fact, do not begin with Cabrillo. They date back at least five thousand and perhaps as far as thirty thousand years when, it is estimated, Indians first ranged over the Channel Islands.

Jutting out into the cold arctic waters of the California current, Point Bennett, on the northwestern tip of the island, is alive with squirming, prehistoric masses. Up to ten thousand seals and sea lions can be resting on the white sands of the crescent-shaped beach at one time. The tawny masses, dark and sleek when they emerge from the water, are coated with sand after lying on the beach. The grunting shapes are sprawled over and under each other, and are sometimes intertwined in tight clusters. Flippers are draped over fat guts. Necks arch upward, and the dark holes that house unblinking eyes stare at the intruder.

The path across the island leads up over a gentle slope to an overgrown rutted road used long ago by ranchers and the military. The dry, brown headland rises here from the iridescent blue of the ocean water. Spume trails from the many rocks offshore. Up from the grass, permanently bent from the force of the winds, jumps a tiny fox like toast from a toaster. The San Miguel fox is a strange adaptation of a mainland variety; it is smaller because of the harsher environment. The fox pauses, then darts off as I approach. Soon others start popping up along the way.

The animal and plant life has gone awry out here. There are white-nosed burros grazing in the distance. Brought here long ago, they have now grown wild like the pigs, dogs, cats, rabbits, goats, and sheep on some of the other Channel Islands. Of the thirty-four types of mammals found on the islands, fourteen are native to the area and the rest, including a herd of buffalo left on Santa Catalina Island by a movie company, were introduced. In addition, there are eighty plants that are not found elsewhere or are a different type from the mainland variety.

The gently rising track dips over a series of rolling hills. The island is treeless, except for a forest of the past. The pygmy copse has been calcified by the salt spray. The contorted limbs are wrapped in white shrouds. Top another hill and there are the remains of a wooden antenna forest once used by the military. Rusting cables and other debris lie nearby.

More ruins are at the foot of the hill. An iron bedstead stands upright amidst the rubble of past lives. A few gleaming porcelain bathroom fixtures stand in contrast to the dark rot. The story is told of an eastern socialite who found peace by ranching with his family on this desolate island but had to be evacuated at the start of World War II. The thought of leaving was too much, and he committed suicide. Down the steep canyon from the ruins there is a long, white sandy beach. The water around these offshore islands is a deep indigo color and marvelously clear. In Cuyler Harbor the starkly edged ribs of a wooden vessel lie in the shifting sands.

For the last fifty years there have been proposals to make the five northernmost Channel Islands into a national park. Of the five, three are already owned by the federal government. San Miguel is not accessible, but the smaller islands of Anacapa and Santa Barbara are administered by the Park Service as the Channel Islands National Monument. The much larger islands of Santa Cruz and Santa Rosa, which have greater recreation potential, are privately owned. To the south San Nicholas and San Clemente islands—the latter once the site of an atomic weapon's test—are controlled by the Navy.

A coastline does not exist alone. It is not a detached landform but is dependent upon what happens behind it, as well as upon the more visible human and natural forces that sculpt its facade.

It is more than thirty miles to the ocean. There is no water to be seen at this time of year in the crackling, dry brushland at the summit of Santa Susana Pass, the dividing line between Los Angeles County and its neighbor to the north, Ventura County. But what begins as a ditch beside the Simi Valley Freeway at the summit of the pass and wends its way through a typical cross section of southern California suburbs and farmland ultimately has a very definite effect on a shallow body of water teeming with marine and bird life—a coastal lagoon.

The hillsides here in this early fall month could be aflame in a second, with fire leaping through the explosive chaparral to create one of those periodic infernos for which the area is known. From the ditch, the dry creek bed tumbles westward down the canyon walls, while the carefully engineered freeway takes a more circuitous route. The creek skirts a knoll where the Pass Club is perched: "Legal poker and pan. Open to the public seven nights a week. Ladies Welcome." On this weekday San Fernando housewives with beehive hairdos and tapered slacks are seated about the card tables.

The creek levels out in the Simi Valley where it is held within bounds by rock-lined walls. Here, as it passes cheek-by-jowl tract houses that are the urban spillover from Los Angeles, the creek is technically known as a flood-control channel. Down again goes the arroyo through Moorpark and past the new college, whose freshly watered, green lawns belie the desert environment. Below the college is a dusty community where Mexican movies play on Saturday nights for the farm workers and cowboy tunes issue forth from the café jukebox.

"For sale" signs are displayed on neglected ranch buildings or tacked to trees on vacant lots. Agriculture in this inland valley is about to give way to more suburbs. But the land is still pastoral, a reminder what Los Angeles County was thirty years ago. There are well-tended rows of orange and lemon trees. It is a smogless (although getting less so) Garden of Eden.

Near Camarillo the creek passes under Highway 101, now a four-lane freeway. There is a trickle of water from the treated wastes of a sewer plant and from the runoff of the agricultural fields. When it rains, a torrent rushes past. From Camarillo to the Pacific Coast Highway the creek bisects the rich, dark, soil of the Oxnard plain. Flowing under the highway, its bonds are loosened. The rock walls give way and the creek bed widens into Point Mugu Lagoon and then the Pacific Ocean.

The lagoon is the last remaining landform of its type that has not been significantly altered in southern California. Along the whole coastline, but particularly on the south coast, such easily filled areas near the ever-desirable water have been the first to yield to housing developments, marinas, and shopping centers. There are now 125,000 acres of wetlands remaining along the coastline, down sixty-seven percent, or 256,000 acres, from what existed at the turn of the century. These wetlands are essential to the more than one million birds, representing about thirty-five species, that use these marshes as stopovers when migrating along the Pacific Flyway.

The teeming life that exists above and under the waters of Point Mugu lagoon is as rich and varied as that found in a tropical rainforest. It is still mostly dependent on historic, natural cycles. There are problems, though. Pesticides from agriculture, silt from new construction, and sewage find their way into the lagoon from the creek. Most of this alien material is flushed out by winter rains or the twice daily influx of high tides.

The lagoon's complex web of life becomes visible as the waters recede. A white egret stalks slowly through the shallows. A great blue heron rises in alarm, flapping furiously in takeoff but quickly streamlining its form in flight. Brown pelicans rest on the sand spit at the inlet's mouth, while a harbor seal pokes his nose above water a short distance away. Swimming about are top smelt, staghorn sculpin, barred surfperch, and the shovelnose guitarfish. Most of the teeming life is out of sight, burrowed under the sand. The mollusks, crabs, echinoderms, and annelids, if not devoured by the birds, will eventually rot and form the rich organic material that later generations of lagoon dwellers will depend upon for sustenance.

Into this natural setting, the U.S. Army Corps of Engineers would come with a lined flood-control channel. In terms of the current environmental movement, these are the bad guys and this would be a bad idea. But here they may be the good guys, since a small part of the lagoon may have to be destroyed in order the save the remainder.

Allowing nature, albeit altered, to follow her course would mean that the lagoon would stifle within a short period of time on the materials brought downstream by the creek. Then the last good example of this rich form of life would be lost in southern California. So, the thinking goes, divert the silt, pesticides, and sewage through a flood-control channel to the ocean (where there may be further difficulties) in order to let the lagoon live—frozen in time. It is a Hobson's choice.

I live on a bluff overlooking Los Angeles harbor and the ocean. From my window on a clear winter day I can see the snowcapped peak of Mount Baldy where I could be skiing. Below me is the line of breakers on the ocean side of Cabrillo Beach, populated by a few surfers, one or two hardy swimmers, and a few wanderers soaking in the aloneness of a winter beach. Whether to hike, ski, sail, or surf today; it is one of those California decisions that can tear a person apart.

Although I have lived in the Point Fermin area of San Pedro for only three years, I feel very possessive about it. In a region where so much is homogenized, San Pedro has its own peculiarities and a strong sense of separateness. Part of this comes from being a port town with varied ethnic mixes.

There are waterfront dives—or there were a lot more before

the sterile redevelopment project replaced them—Yugoslavian restaurants, Italian and Scandinavian bakeries, corner grocery stores, and a few other personalized amenities that are nonexistent in mile-long shopping centers. San Pedro is still a real place, not a backdrop for tourists as are so many other shoreline communities. The scale is close and understandable.

Then there is the beach. Cabrillo Beach is quite unlike any other in the state. In the summer and early fall months it comes alive. It is used. Down from the southcentral and eastern portions of the city come the blacks and the browns. There is the rich smell of roasting barbecue sauces. Mexican women go wading in their dresses, while small, lithe brown bodies dart about their legs. There is the mock scream of a young girl being carried into the water by young boys who are feeling their machismo. The activity is constant—running in and out of the water, throwing and catching, jumping over rocks, climbing the bluff. Amplified rock music adds an insistent beat.

On most other south coast beaches, the action is languid. Supple young women, inevitably bikini-clad with long blond hair and bronzed bodies, are the norm, along with their moustached Robert Redford lookalikes. Like feedlot cattle, they seem captives of an exclusive diet consisting of sun, honey, milk, and gin. They are the seeming epitome of good health and vapid minds. It is a scene duplicated few other places in the world, and it has been celebrated many times in the media.

Believe me, it is not make-believe. The overall impression on these sun-warmed sands is one of passive surrender of the body. It is an almost compulsive sacrifice of the body, not the inner release that the others bring to the edge of the ocean.

Back at Cabrillo, the blacks are on the concrete fishing pier, collecting the ingredients for gumbo—fishing not being a sport here but a serious search for the next meal. The Orientals are out

on the boulder-strewn breakwater, gathering up those small crea-
tures and plants, bypassed by others, that comprise their ingen-
ious feasts from the sea.

There is a funky museum tucked away in the palm trees on the
beach, with shells and stuffed fish downstairs and ship models
and nautical displays upstairs. The amateur collections that make
up most of the displays were donated by local inhabitants, adding
a personal touch. The polar bears, as the lusty old men who sun
and swim year round call themselves, face their thick nude bodies
toward the sun in the sheltered lee of the men's shower room and
talk about their grandchildren and the Old Country. Their
younger counterparts lift weights next door.

A minor miracle, considering that the beach is within the Los
Angeles city limits, takes place each spring and summer on Cabrillo Beach. This is the running of the grunion that occurs at
night when the high tides drive water far up the sand. These
small fish, resembling sardines, flop onto the sand in silvery lay-
ers just at the moment the tide begins to recede. The female,
with a side to side motion, digs her way into the sand. The male,
excited by this motion, curls himself around her slippery body.

The female lays from one thousand to three thousand pink
spherical-shaped eggs, and the male emits milt that seeps down
into the sand and fertilizes the eggs. Freeing herself from the
sand, the female flops back into the water. The whole process
takes about thirty seconds. If the eggs escape predators, such as
long-beaked shore birds and small children building sand castles,
then the next high tide, in about two weeks's time, will agitate
the embryos and out pop the baby grunion, which then swim
away. I have watched this happening on the beach below where I
live, against a backdrop of ships gliding in and out of the harbor.

Those who arrived first in California did not have many good
words to say about San Pedro. To the explorer Cabrillo, the most

striking thing about the area in 1542 was the large amount of smoke in the sky. The smoke came from the fires set by Indians to flush the game. He named it Bahia de los Fumos in honor of the smog. Richard Henry Dana, the seaman-lawyer-author who wrote *Two Years Before the Mast,* thought that San Pedro was the worst spot he saw along the coast during his 1835 sojourn in California. Two of his shipmates were flogged there, and it was a difficult place to load hides.

One hundred and thirty-seven years later, I treasure this place.

For better or worse, but with true overall magnificence, it all comes to an end at a pyramid-shaped monument marking the extreme southwest corner of the nation. Agile Mexican boys wiggle through a rusty barbed-wire fence to sell chewing gum to the traveler. On the other side of the fence is the Tijuana bull ring. There are no trees on the low bluff rising above the gray sand beach that sweeps south in a broad crescent from San Diego. The 1,072 miles of the California coastline, whose equivalent length on the East Coast would run from Boston to Charleston, begins in a rainforest environment and ends in the desert.

Along the way the sand and rocks and mountains and river plains have bisected three climactic subprovinces and encompassed nine geological types of shoreline formations, not to mention an uncounted number of human impediments. There have been sixteen distinct biotic communities and, by coincidence, an equal number of rare and endangered species, ranging from the gray whale to the Santa Cruz long-toed salamander.

In large part the coastline is California, since eighty-five per cent of the state's population is huddled within thirty miles of the ocean. The water's edge, whether fresh or salt, exerts a magnetic attraction. By their large numbers, people threaten to destroy the very unspoiled wonders they covet so avidly. However, there are still places of natural grandeur and piercing stillness to discover; but they are not marked on a roadmap.

There is one small place along the coastline (I won't say where it is) where a visitor can sit on a rock, close his eyes, and feel surrounded by good, silent things. I don't mean that there is no sound, because there are sounds. But the sounds fit, one within the other and all within the context. No sound intrudes by itself, although it may seem separate for a short time. There is the rhythmic sound of surf, the scurrying of windblown sand, the rattle of bushes, grasses swaying softly, and the rush of wind about the ear. This is silence.

Along with the sounds are the smells that rise from the pungent warmth of the chaparral, the new green growth, the fertile decay of seaweed, the moist salt air. The smells are heavy, but they too meld together.

Now, if the visitor sits long enough with his eyes closed in this one small place, the inner rhythms begin to match what is happening quietly outside. They never completely mesh, because random thoughts intrude (the mind, at least my mind, is impossible to control); but they are close enough to leave me with a sense of tranquility.

As long as there are such places, people will keep coming to the edge of the continent searching for something I prefer not to ever completely know; because, if I did, the essential mystery of something very satisfying would be lost. By comparison, the works of humans seem insignificant.

From *California, the Golden Coast,* Viking Press 1973

The Dimming of the Range of Light

O n April 28, 1971, the Nixon administration used the full resources of the White House to publicize its proposals for the establishment of new wilderness areas. The president issued a brave statement, and Interior Secretary Rogers C. B. Morton briefed reporters on the administration's proposal to set aside portions of fourteen wildlife refuges, national monuments, and national parks (all jurisdictions that already had a high degree of protection) in nine states as official wilderness areas. The hoopla made front page news. Preservation of wilderness, in one stroke, was raised to the level of presidential concern one year after Earth Day.

The largest such area proposed for wilderness status was

721,970 acres in Sequoia and Kings Canyon National Parks in the Sierra Nevada. A close look at the condition of the wilderness values in those two national parks, however, indicates that something less than true wilderness, as defined in the Wilderness Act of 1964, exists in the back country. The act states, "A wilderness, in contrast to those areas where man and his own works dominate the landscape, is hereby recognized as an area where the earth and its community of life are untrammeled by man, where man himself is a visitor who does not remain."

Consider what I found this year in my travels through four wilderness areas: Hikers into the remote back country are warned to boil their drinking water for ten minutes or use purification tablets because the otherwise crystal-clear mountain water might be contaminated by human bacteria. Some glacier-fed lakes at the ten-thousand-foot level of the High Sierra have been closed to camping because of human pollution. Because of overcrowding others have a one-night limit, a buffer area between tent and water, and numbered campsites similar to vehicle campgrounds at lower elevations. A boot stirs up dust where grass once provided a soft carpet for a tent and sleeping bag. The campfire is almost a tradition of the past, because firewood has been stripped from around most campsites. In their search for wood, campers are chopping down green trees and leaving ugly stumps that provide no shade. It is not safe to leave a fishing rod, camera, backpack, or sleeping bag unattended along the trail, where they often are stolen. Cars are broken into at trailheads. Wildlife is disappearing and trees are dying because of smog in the mountains that are called "The Range of Light."

The problems caused by overcrowding are not only confined to Sequoia-Kings Canyon. They can be seen up and down the Sierra Nevada in other national forests and parks. Although such overuse is most evident in California, where the largest population and the greatest number of wilderness areas are located, other western states are beginning to encounter the California experience. Hikers were turned back from the descent into the bottom of the Grand Canyon in Arizona over the Easter weekend if they did not have advance reservations for camping sites. A limit of ten thousand river runners—the number that shot the rapids of the Colorado River last year in commercial raft trips—has now been imposed by the Park Service, which administers Grand Canyon National Park.

Although permits are required for the first time this year in wilderness areas administered by the Forest Service in California, they have been mandatory for a number of years in the Boundary Waters Canoe Area in northern Minnesota. In that wilderness area, which competes with the John Muir and Minarets wilderness areas in California for the dubious distinction of being the most crowded in the nation, cans and bottles have been banned in an attempt to deal with the litter problem.

Wilderness, and the freedom the word implies, is part of the American ethos. The implications of gross overuse of wilderness areas are daunting. If there is overcrowding in the mountains, where most wilderness areas are located, then where else is there to go to escape the bondage of everyday life? The concept of wilderness has been synonymous with America. Has America, and particularly California, lost its last vestiges of wilderness?

Those were my thoughts as I set off up the John Muir Trail. A woman, a few hundred yards from the parking lot, asked me, "Aren't you afraid to go up there alone?"

No, I replied. What was there to be afraid of? There were no freeways, no television. Should I be afraid of myself? Of solitude?

The track that had been beaten into the forest duff was covered with dustlike pumice from an ancient lava flow in the Minarets Wilderness Area. The trail climbed through a forest of red fir, silver pine, lodgepole pine and mountain hemlock. The first steep grade was a catharsis. The tensions of city living flowed out of me in the still heat. The first drink of mountain water was biting and sweet. The trees smelled like Christmas.

While the heavy use of wilderness tends to be concentrated along a few well-known routes, such as the John Muir Trail through the Minarets, more people every year are getting further out only to be still confronted by the vestiges of civilization. The sonic boom is ever present as are the below-grade trails incised in the meadows by countless feet pounding over them for years and the charred remains of old campfires. Traffic along the trails is constant during the height of the season, from mid-July through August; and it is, indeed, a rare lake or stream that does not have at least one camping party along its shores. In California, water is a magnet.

Many more people are going into the mountains because there has been a revolution in backpacking. Space age technology has joined the back-to-nature movement to spawn a technical and cost revolution in camping food and equipment. Freeze-dried foods that are easy to carry and prepare make it possible to dine sumptuously in the mountains. Pack frames are lighter, as are down sleeping bags and jackets that weigh as little as two pounds, yet are warm at below-freezing temperatures.

Wilderness used to be for the elite, meaning that entrants were either the few who were able to make a living there or those who were advocates of unspoiled nature and had the means and time to make the long trip into the mountains. The hardy rancher or Sierra Clubber traveling in the mountains is now the exception, not the rule. A wilderness trip is within the reach of anyone who does not have a physical disability, thanks to the ubiquitous automobile, proliferating backroads, the availability of good food, and lightweight equipment.

Where I camped that night, there was just enough wood around the granite-ribbed shores of Minaret Lake to keep the campfire going for a couple of hours. Some people dropped by. The talk was of society's ills, how to make government more responsive, the good life, poor marriages, and letting things hang out. The middle-aged pediatrician offered marijuana to his campfire mates. Dope seemed like a sacrilege in that setting.

For the next day's portion of the trip, I referred to a hiking guide, *High Sierra Hiking in the Devils Postpile Area,* that stated, "Fair campsites may be found around Shadow Lake, but there is no wood, and we would discourage camping here to lessen human impact around the lake." As if to prove the power of the written word, there were relatively few campers around Shadow Lake where a Claremont College student was conducting a pollution study. About seventy campers were clustered around Lake Ediza, a few miles further up the trail. That lake had been featured in a recent issue of *The National Geographic.*

There are figures to document the huge leap in back-country use. The Desolation Wilderness Area near Lake Tahoe has experienced an average twenty-three percent increase a year in wilderness use, and in Sequoia-Kings Canyon there has been a one hundred percent jump over the last five years, compared to only a ten percent increase in total park visitors. This tidal wave of humanity has resulted in confusion. The public agencies that administer wilderness areas work at cross-purposes to each other, share no common goals, and lack consistency within their separate jurisdictions.

Consider these examples: The State Department of Fish and

Game objects to the Inyo County Board of Supervisors pushing a road into the Horseshoe Meadows area where the proposed Trail Peak ski area would be built with Forest Service approval. Fish and game officials state that the rare golden trout will be wiped out by the large number of visitors that the road will bring to the area. Yet the Forest Service objects to the department's planting of trout in lakes that are overused, a practice that encourages more use.

The Forest Service, lodged within the Department of Agriculture, first made wilderness areas more convenient and liveable by installing various facilities, despite the "untrammeled" wording of the law. Now it has reversed itself. Toilets, picnic tables, and fireplaces are on their way out of the Inyo National Forest wilderness areas on the east side of the Sierra Nevada. Yet at neighboring Sequoia and Kings Canyon National Parks, administered by an Interior Department agency, the wilderness proposal endorsed by the Nixon administration calls for five enclaves of semicivilization in the back country. Into these one- to two-hundred-acre enclaves toilets, tables, and fireplaces will be installed.

Yet another federal agency, the Department of Transportation within the Department of Commerce, wants to push a trans-Sierra highway across Minaret Summit near the Mammoth Lakes area. Although authorization for the road exists, funds for its construction were deleted from this year's federal budget. The highway would bisect the John Muir and Minarets Wilderness areas. It has been vigorously opposed by Norman B. Livermore, Jr., head of the State Resources Agency. Livermore, the chief voice for the environment in the administration of Governor Ronald Reagan, operated a pack station in the area for a number of years.

Parallel to, and perhaps because of, the recent large-scale impact of humans on wilderness areas, the federal agencies responsible for their administration have shifted toward managing those areas for their legally declared values rather than letting them evolve into trash pits. A Park Service official in Yosemite National Park said, "I can sum up our thinking in three words—managing for naturalness." The Park Service is using prescribed burns ("We write prescriptions"), chain saws, and axes to return valley meadows, the back country, and the Mariposa Grove of Giant Sequoia trees to what photographs depicted the vegetation as looking like in the 1890s.

In Yosemite and Sequoia-Kings Canyon, where the practice for years had been instant suppression of fires, the present policy is to let lightning fires burn themselves out unless widespread damage is likely. Without wildfires, which existed in the park before man began to extinguish them, small trees and shrubbery have infringed on meadows and the giant trees. So fires have been set to cut back on the undergrowth that has choked the meadows, and axes and chain saws have been used on white fir in the Mariposa Grove to restore those areas to a pre-1890 look.

But all of this beaverlike activity brings up an interesting question: Who is to say the 1890s look is the "natural" look, since homesteaders and visitors had previously been in the park and the Indians had certainly preceded them. Criticism of the management-for-naturalness programs comes from those who fear additional air pollution from the burning or cite the colossal conceit it takes to presume to manage nature.

Then there is the effect of the hordes of backpackers on wildlife. Managers are proposing zoological zones in the High Sierra where the shy Sierra bighorn sheep can remain undisturbed by hikers. Game biologists believe that populations are down in two of the five herds at the higher elevations of the Sierra Nevada because of human intrusion. The count of rare animal, bird, and fish species has dropped from a maximum of 390 in 1948 to 215 at the present. The fishing limit for the rare golden trout has been halved and a zero limit is being considered.

A game warden, who has spent eighteen years patrolling the High Sierra, said, "In the past twelve years I have seen the Mount Whitney trail go from a wilderness to a crap pile. They used to have pine martin, blue grouse, and deer along the trails. Now, not any longer."

Two battleship gray outhouses were recently airlifted by helicopter to the 14,495-foot summit of Mount Whitney where five hundred hikers have rested at one time. A count of two thousand hikers was made one weekend along the summit trail and over three hundred backpackers were camped at one time beside tiny Mirror Lake, the major stopping place for a weekend climb of the highest peak in the contiguous United States.

Some wildlife remains. I saw a brief flash out of the corner of my eye. Then the tawny smudge halted, and each of us regarded the other with surprise—the marmot and the man who had paused beside Garnet Lake. The small furry creature did not give ground. Showing no fear, the marmot advanced slowly from a distance of fifteen feet. Rabies? A wave of fear swept me followed by a wave of foolishness. The marmot veered away. I was the alien in that environment where animals should have the right of way.

There are 53 million acres of federal lands that qualify as potential wilderness areas under provisions of the 1964 act. So far, only 10.1 million acres have been so designated. Areas that have already been declared wilderness comprise about one percent of the land area of California and one-half of one percent of the national land base. It took seven years to get the wilderness bill through Congress, and in the process a number of compromises had to be made.

Both individuals and public agencies have taken advantage of the loopholes in the law. Grazing and mining are permitted in Forest Service wilderness areas. Where I was hiking that weekend, a minister had a mining claim and used the site and old buildings at Minaret Mine as a summer camp for his church. Another church group was seeking road access across the wilderness area to a mining claim in the Nydiver Lakes area. A Southern California college used an old cabin at another mining claim for recreational purposes.

The ranking minority member of the House Interior Committee, Representative John P. Saylor, a Republican from Pennsylvania who is a staunch advocate of wilderness areas, has introduced a bill that would designate twelve areas on Forest Service lands as wilderness. In proposing the legislation, Saylor noted that the Forest Service, perhaps purposely, could render these areas useless as wilderness by allowing logging and other development proposals to mar these lands.

The next day I planned to climb Mount Ritter. The best way to read an account of John Muir's ascent of Mount Ritter one hundred years previously was to dine on oxtail soup, beef stroganoff, chocolate pudding, cookies and a shot of brandy. Then I curled up in a warm sleeping bag snuggled between two rocks at the west end of Thousand Island Lake. At the ninety-eight–hundred-foot level of the lake the glow of the setting sun lingered on the crenellated peak, which was thought to be unclimbable until Muir made his solitary ascent.

Muir wrote, "After gaining a point about halfway to the top, I was brought to a dead stop, with arms outspread, clinging close to the face of the rock, unable to move hand or foot either up or down. My doom appeared fixed. I must fall."

After mastering this temporary impasse, Muir, who knew how to turn a dramatic phrase or two, scrambled to the top and discovered that day was done. With only a crust of bread to eat all day, he still had many miles of hiking in the night to make it back to his camp in a pine thicket, where he slept without blankets in the biting cold.

John Muir would be greatly saddened, perhaps more than when he lost the canyon of Hetch Hetchy to a reservoir site, if he were to return and tramp along the crest of the Sierra Nevada today.

First, there is the matter of health. Signs along the Muir trail declare: "RECOMENDED THAT ALL DRINKING WATER BE TREATED WITH PURIFICATION TABLETS OR BE BOILED BEFORE USE. BOIL 10 MINUTES." Bacteria counts of human wastes in lakes and streams exceed U.S. Public Health Service standards in Sequoia-Kings Canyon. In the Inyo National Forest, the Forest Service has hired a hydrologist for the first time to test High Sierra water for pollution this summer in the wilderness area named after the famed conservationist.

In Muir's beloved Yosemite, the park superintendent said, "Because of the human wastes emptying in from the back country, we don't feel confident of the water source. The only way we could feel confident is to chlorinate the streams." A longtime Yosemite climber said, "It gets so bad that if you turn over a rock to hide your garbage, you are liable to find another camper has been there before you."

Then there is the matter of crime. At Yosemite a park official said, "If you put a $60 Kelty pack or a $150 sleeping bag down you just might lose them. It is sad but true." At the Arch Rock entrance station, where visitors are most likely to have come from San Francisco, park rangers keep a "hippy sheet," a listing of the license numbers of cars that contain hippy types. These vehicles and their occupants are then monitored in the park. Rangers mounted on horses recently charged the flower children who were illegally camped in a valley meadow. Drug use is rampant. Rangers are now trained in law enforcement and carry guns. The city has come to the wilderness.

It wouldn't make sense to John Muir, but it did to me as my long weekend drew to a close. The trail on the last day rose and fell along the east bank of the middle fork of the San Joaquin River. It passed through lush growths of larkspur, shooting star, and other vividly colored mountain wildflowers that contrasted sharply with the basic gray-green landscape. Across the canyon that was gouged out by Ice Age glaciers and up the tributary hanging valleys, the black spine of the incisorlike Minarets stood out in stark relief against the clear blue sky. It was a grand summation of a four-day hike over the fourth of July weekend.

That woman should have known there was nothing to fear in the wilderness—nothing to fear, that is, except people and their wastes.

Los Angeles Times, August 1971

Living with Fire

On a drive or walk through the area of Sycamore Canyon two months after the Santa Barbara fire, these were some of the sensations: There was the *pffft, pffft, pffft* of rotating sprinklers spewing out the water desperately needed to get newly seeded grasses and plants growing before the first heavy rains of winter and the almost inevitable mudslides that would follow. The grating noise of chain saws echoed across the canyons as dead trees were cut and neatly stacked for firewood. By this time most of the debris from the fire had been cleared. There seemed to be a fetish for neatness in this place—a visible denial of a catastrophe having taken place. The predominant smell of burnt rubble and vegetation was cloying in a slightly sweet sort of way. Some ash was white, indicating great heat, and hillsides were mottled shades of gray. In some places nothing stood. The vegetative cover was completely removed, like burnt hair from a skull. In other places, for no apparent reason, a home was intact surrounded by an island of green shrubbery. Stacks of new lumber, piled neatly on the pads of former homes, signified what was to come. And in the distance was the underlying reason for it all, sailboats setting off from Santa Barbara Harbor for an early evening race in the Pacific Ocean—symbols of the good life viewed from the deadly hills above the city.

It was not always this way, a scene of neatly arranged destruction in the midst of Mediterranean-like beauty. (Indeed, one portion of the fire area is called the Riviera.) Sprawling $100,000 and $200,000 homes on large lots were sheltered by graceful eucalyptus and pine trees. Evergreen brush, growing higher every year, hid the custom-designed homes and provided a sense of privacy. The narrow, winding streets contributed to a rural atmosphere, and the steep slopes, some forty-five degrees, insured that many had a view of either the ocean or mountains or both. Tranquillity begat security.

Winds sweeping down in hot dry gusts from the three-thousand- to four-thousand-foot heights of the Santa Ynez Mountains behind Santa Barbara were good for kite-flying in the early evening hours of July 26. They were also good for fanning flames. Because of the winds, heat, and extremely low humidity, fire-fighting units in the area were on a red-flag alert. They were out patrolling neighborhoods and warning residents of the high fire danger. The kite being flown by a twenty-three−year-old man near Coyote Road and Mountain Drive hit a powerline. It arced, and the sparks fell to the ground. The man and others nearby tried to put out the small blaze. At 7:38 P.M. the first call was made to the Montecito fire district. Montecito, an area of even greater wealth, adjoins Santa Barbara on the east. Two minutes later a fire truck and three firemen were at the scene. They hooked up to a hydrant, but the water pressure was not sufficient to work the deck gun atop the engine. The firemen got out a one and one-half–inch hose attached to the truck's tank, but the small hose could not reach the head of the fire, whose thirty-foot-high flames were now burning along 150 feet of Mountain Drive and spreading 175 feet downslope. Twelve minutes later, when the first helicopter arrived, the flames were fifty feet high. Modern fire-fighting technology swung into high gear at 8 P.M. when an air tanker dropped two thousand gallons of fire retardant. At 8:10 P.M. the first home burned on Banana Road, and the holocaust began.

Given the conditions—ninety-five–degree temperature, thirteen percent humidity, winds gusting up to fifty miles per hour, and thick chaparral—there was no chance of halting the fire, although 116 trucks and eleven hundred firemen responded from all over southern California. The firemen and their equipment have been termed the best in the nation for fighting wildfires. They have to be. The combination of a large population and potential for wildfires is unmatched anywhere else in the world.

By midnight, almost four and one-half hours after the fire had first been reported, most of the damage had been done. It was not until 8 A.M. the next morning, however, that the fire was under control. Two hundred and sixteen homes were destroyed, and another sixty-four were damaged. The preliminary damage estimate, due to rise, was $33.5 million. Nearly eight hundred acres burned, a minute amount compared with that of other blazes. No one was killed "by the grace of God," said one fire chief.

In a way, the very affluence of the area set it up for destruction. The large homesites meant lots of vegetation. The sense of privacy and the natural feeling achieved by letting the brush grow tall became the downfall of many a structure. The crowns of eucalyptus and pine trees exploded in fireballs when their oil and resin heated up, showering flaming debris on a much wider area. In southern California, one pays more to live near such trees. The charm of narrow, winding streets became the terror of trying to escape, or the hopelessness of a fire crew trying to reach the flames through the congestion. The steep canyonsides, great for views and homes that seem to thrust out into space, are where flames travel fastest. With more persons seeking this type of life-style, the water system became overtaxed and failed, just when it was needed most. But the Santa Barbara fire was not unique. The only surprise was that anyone was surprised.

Fire has been an integral part of the natural scene of California for the last two million years. Growth of vegetation and richness of the soil depend upon it. Lightning and volcanoes were chief causes of fire before man first appeared on the California scene, perhaps fifteen thousand years ago. Then the incidence of fires began to increase. Indians adapted fire for their own uses—to promote the growth of desired grasses and herbs and chase game from the dense brush. These fires would roar out of control peri-odically, and vast sections of the state, particularly the southern half, would be blackened. Some ethnologists claim fires set by Indians changed the balance of vegetation from grasslands to the more fire-dependent chaparral. Others say there is no evidence that the Indians had any effect on the land by using fire as a harvesting tool.

The Europeans did not see a totally natural landscape when they first arrived in California only a short time after Columbus discovered America. When the first Spanish explorers sailed up the coast from Mexico to California in 1542, fire is the first thing they saw. In early fall, the height of the fire season, Juan Rodriguez Cabrillo saw "great smokes" at what was to become San Diego and Los Angeles.

With the introduction of livestock by the Spanish missionaries in the late 1700s, the spread of fire-dependent brush was hastened. Overgrazing combined with introduction of seeds from the Mediterranean area changed California's perennial grasslands to annual brush. In *The Destruction of California*, Raymond E. Dasmann wrote: "The combined effects of the tamed and wild livestock were to change the nature of the California rangelands, to destroy the old California prairie, and replace the native plants with alien species. This was the first major destruction of the wildlands of California to be charged against the influence of the white man."

In 1793 the Mexican governor proclaimed the first fire-control regulations because of "widespread damage which results to the public from the burning of the fields." Like subsequent regulations and laws, these had little effect on stopping disastrous fires. There is this contemporary account of an 1831 fire by Santa Barbara resident Alfred Robinson:

> About this time we were much alarmed, in consequence of the burning of the woods upon the mountains. For several days the smoke had been seen to rise from the distant hills of St. Buenaventura [modern-day Ventura] and gradually approach the town [Santa Barbara]. At last it had reached the confines of the settlement and endangered the fields of grain and gardens. Soon it spread low upon the hills, and notwithstanding a strong westerly wind was blowing, the flames traveled swiftly to windward, consuming everything in their course. It was late at night when they

reached the rear of the town, and as they furiously wreathed upwards, the sight was magnificent, but terrible. The wind blew
directly upon the town, and the large cinders that fell in every
direction seemed to threaten us with certain destruction. The
inhabitants fled from their homes to the beach, or sought the
house of Senor Noriega, where prayers were offered and the saints
supplicated. The vessels at anchor in the bay were also much
endangered, for their decks were covered with burning cinders,
and their crews incessantly employed in keeping them wet. During the entire night the ravages of the fire continued, and when
daylight broke it had seized upon the vineyard belonging to the
mission. Here the green state of vegetation somewhat checked its
progress, and it passed over to the mountains again, to pursue its
course northward. On the uplands everything was destroyed, and
for months afterwards, the bare and blackened hills marked the
course of the devastating element.

Four years later Richard Henry Dana, Jr. arrived in Santa
Barbara on board the brig *Pilgrim,* and he described the fire-
blackened hills in *Two Years Before the Mast.* At that time the
population of Santa Barbara was nine hundred, and most lived in
adobe homes with tile roofs that were much more fire-resistant
than the wood-frame and wood-shingle houses the Anglos were
to start building in the 1870s.

After the Indians and the first Europeans arrived on the
scene and made their respective alterations in the landscape, the
third major change came with the burgeoning population after
World War II. Southern California's population doubled and then
doubled again, and California became the nation's most populous
state. With the aid of giant earthmoving equipment developed
during the war, the population pushed up into the fire-prone
canyons and foothill areas. Now the fires burned not only the

chaparral and oak woodlands, but also homes and people. They even jumped freeways. The tempo and devastation of wildfires increased greatly, once more because the landscape had been altered.

One factor in this recent equation was the increased fire protection demanded by homeowners and agreed to by public agencies. There were fewer small fires and more large, devastating blazes because the flammable chaparral was not allowed to go through its natural fire cycle. Controlled burns were considered unsightly, could escape, and produced smog. Mature stands were permitted to grow to the point where the dead brush would virtually explode under the right conditions.

Between 1953 and 1964 three major fires in Santa Barbara County burned 210,695 acres, or twelve percent of the county's total area. The Coyote fire of 1964 was the most destructive of the three blazes. It burned 67,000 acres and destroyed or damaged 118 homes and structures. One fire fighter was killed. Both the Sycamore Canyon fire and the Coyote blaze started in the same area, and some of the same ground was burned. In 1964, as in 1977, a Governor Brown (the present governor's father) toured the burnt area. The elder Brown said he was "shocked"; thirteen years later the younger Brown said it looked "bad."

I have a sense of déjà vu about the Sycamore Canyon fire, since my first assignment for the *Los Angeles Times* was to drive up to Santa Barbara and cover the start of the Coyote fire in 1964. A photographer and I arrived in late afternoon. The flames seemingly had been quelled in the first few hours, so we drove the ninety miles back to Los Angeles with pictures of a charred home or two. In the early evening hours the "sundowner" wind rose in force, and the flames ripped through Montecito. That is when Avery Brundage's mansion burned, and he lost part of his Asian art collection. Robert M. Hutchins, president of the Center for the Study of Democratic Institutions, lost his home. Fire is a great equalizer.

The photographer and I drove back to Santa Barbara that night and arrived in time to have a Forest Service fire official tell us that he expected the fire to cut a swath through Santa Barbara to the ocean. That is what I telephoned the rewrite man for the last edition, and that is what the banner headline proclaimed the next morning. But the winds had changed again in the early morning hours, and the fire raced back over the mountains to burn for the next twelve days.

Following that fire, a committee of the county board of supervisors held an inquiry; and Harold Biswell, a professor at the University of California's Santa Barbara campus, warned, "The Coyote fire of 1964 was very bad indeed, but it could have been worse . . . . Under slightly different circumstances probably even more houses would have been burned, or people could have been trapped in large numbers and burned. This is something to keep in mind when speculating about big fires in the future, for probably our most destructive fires are yet to come."

Prophetic words, indeed. Nine months later 78 of the 100 homes destroyed in the Coyote fire were being rebuilt, and the *Santa Barbara News-Press* editorialized, "There is a spirit of rebirth abroad in Santa Barbara's outer areas which is to be admired and commended." In October 1971, the Romero fire struck east of Santa Barbara and above Montecito and Carpinteria. It killed four fire fighters and burned sixteen thousand acres. More destructive fires followed.

Five days after the Sycamore Canyon fire, the *News-Press*, acting as town cheerleader for the fire victims (and, incidentally, preserving its circulation base), stated, "But in rebuilding self and rebuilding home concurrently, these people will rediscover their inner fortitude, and that's what makes America great." Two months after the Sycamore Canyon blaze, fifty-five building permits had been granted to rebuild and 123 homeowners had applied for Small Business Administration loans. The pattern seemed clear.

Although the Sycamore Canyon fire, another called the Marble Cone fire in the mountains above Big Sur, and a third fire at the far north end of the state made it seem like California was ablaze from end to end last summer, it was far from the state's worst year. During a thirteen-day period in the early fall of 1970, more than a half-million acres of brush and timbered wildlands burned from one end of the state to the other. Sixteen people were killed, and 722 homes were destroyed. In Southern California during those thirteen days in 1970, sixty-eight percent of the affected area was burned as a result of fires started by powerlines. The cause of the recent Santa Barbara fire was not a fluke.

Why such fires? The answer: people plus wind plus chaparral. The dense, dwarflike forest is found mostly along the southern half of the coastal area, which happens to be the most populous area in the state. The leaves of such vegetation are small, thick, stiff, hard, and evergreen—designed to withstand periodic drought. Chamiso is the most dominant shrub, but there is also bitterbrush, toyon, mountain mahogany, sumac, coast and live oak, manzanita, deer brush, yerba santa, laurel, and poison oak. The chaparral is dormant during the dry summer and early fall months, husbanding the use of water in its stubby, wax-covered leaves, which are designed for that purpose. While the foliage is deceptively green on the outside, it is quite dry inside.

By August the plant's growth rate may be down ninety-five per-cent from its rainy-season maximum. This is when destructive fires begin.

Driven by strong Santa Ana winds, it is not unusual for a fire to grow at the rate of four to six square miles per hour with numerous spot fires extending as far as four miles out in front. A Forest Service study states that a fire expanding at the rate of four square miles per hour will produce between 400 and 800 billion Btu's of heat per hour—the equivalent of burning between three million and six million gallons of gasoline. A fuel management expert for the Los Padres National Forest figures that one thousand acres of heavy chaparral, if burned in one flash, would gen-erate the heat equivalent of one Hiroshima-type atomic bomb.

There is no stopping such fires, especially when the Santa Ana wind blows. These hot, dry winds descend from the interior de-serts through coastal canyons to the ocean at speeds sometimes exceeding one hundred miles per hour. They parch mouths and jangle nerves. People become more irritable. Tension builds. There is an air of uncertainty. The winds are fickle, blowing in gusts or changing directions by 180 degrees in a few seconds. Fire follows the wind.

These foehn-type winds, replacing the usual cool, moist winds from off the ocean, occur when a high-pressure system builds up over the interior deserts and Great Basin, most frequently in the dry months. Originating as cold, dry air in the troposphere, the winds are warmed by compression as they sweep over the desert rims and into coastal areas. The relative humidity drops to near the vanishing point. The chaparral, with little moisture left in its system after the summer drought, becomes extremely parched. All that is needed to start a major conflagration is a spark.

Chaparral thrives on fire. Fire is a necessity, and whether humans like it or not, it is likely to occur every fifteen to forty years in a given area. As chaparral reaches maturity, growth ends, and the elfin bushes begin to wither. Fire is needed for rejuvenation. When it does come, flame temperatures can exceed 2,000 degrees, while at the surface of the soil it is fourteen hundred. At the same time temperatures a few inches below ground will be range from 130 to 150. This is the secret of survival for some plants and animals.

A short time after fire has destroyed some species of chaparral above ground, numerous shoots drawing on the plant's water reserves will emerge from the root-crown burls. Chamiso, the dominant species, survives in two ways. Although not resistant to fire, it produces large amounts of seed so that some seed is liable to survive. Its root system remains intact after a fire, and it is a vigorous sprouter. Many nonsprouting species have fire-resistant seeds that lie dormant for years and germinate only after a fire, when the blaze has sufficiently weakened the seed coat so water can penetrate it.

Birds and animals have their own strategies for surviving fires. Some species of rodents are seemingly decimated by a wildfire, but the burned area is found to be repopulated by the same species the next summer. Other rodents prefer burned areas after a fire and will migrate from unburned areas. Those that live in burrows can go six inches or farther underground and be safe.

Studies following a 1953 fire in Berkeley suggested that "the effect on birds was indirect, chiefly in terms of available nest sites and food types . . . . Avian grassland species increased, and chaparral species declined following the fire. Predatory birds such as hawks, owls, and ravens increased markedly in the first year following the fire, then slowly declined, though remaining above prefire levels for at least three years," according to a professor of zoology at Pomona College. Deer, which need open range, begin to thrive again when dense, overmature stands of chaparral are cleared out by fire. And in seven to ten years most of the chaparral has regrown and the customary species are back again.

People, as well as plants and animals, return quickly, probably for three reasons: Institutional policy, both public and private, dictates this direction; fire-prone areas are aesthetically and socially attractive for certain people; and one becomes conditioned to natural disaster just by living in California.

Following the most recent Santa Barbara fire, various private institutions went out of their way to offer aid to fire victims. Most of this aid was aimed at eventual rebuilding. Much was just plain good neighborliness. Some was commercially advantageous. The Chamber of Commerce held informational meetings. The Board of Realtors offered help in relocating. Local contractors and architects lectured. Banks were obliging. It was as if these segments of the community were acting in concert to keep their own from leaving. But there was a curious set of values. Offers of local help were regarded as altruistic. Similar offers made from such areas as Los Angeles were regarded as threatened invasions by "suede-shoe operators."

Public agencies were equally obliging. If the same home was to be rebuilt, the building permit fee and plan check were waived. Planning officials, rather than concentrating efforts on restrictive zoning for such fire-hazard areas, narrowed their efforts to making sure homeowners did not put illegal structures on their lots. The city, like the county, now required fire-retardant roofs and siding. Such requirements gave a false sense of security, since homes with such construction burned in the fire. The tax assessor said he would waive payment for the first twenty-five days of the new tax year. Flood-control officials handed out grass seed to homeowners and planned to reseed the area by helicopter and take other actions to lessen the chance of mudslides. Governor Edmund G. Brown, Jr. was in town shortly after the fire promoting a bill recently passed by the state legislature giving tax breaks to those who build with solar-energy devices. At the federal level the Small Business Administration set up an office to grant low-interest loans. In the Los Padres National Forest above the city, the Forest Service continued to build firebreaks and spray them with Vietnam-era herbicides to keep down the new growth of chaparral.

Seemingly, no one was aware that the State Board of Forestry in May had passed a resolution urging local governments to discourage construction of homes in high fire-hazard areas. As a Santa Barbara County planning official said, "You can't legislate a life-style."

The public and private sectors have made rebuilding the most attractive economic alternative for many fire victims. Because of the skyrocketing prices for homes in recent years, most of the fire victims were underinsured. Consider this example: The market value of a charred lot is $65,000. The house and lot cost the owner $55,000 some years ago. It was insured for $50,000. To replace the home now would cost $90,000. With the $50,000 insurance money and a low-interest loan for $40,000 the owner could construct a new home which, if sold, would bring $155,000 today and much more tomorrow. Consider other pressures and factors, such as tax breaks for rebuilding. Would you sell the lot for $65,000? The choice was further narrowed when one considered the location and the fact that new vegetation will hide the scars of the fire in a few years.

The gleaming wood-frame skeleton of Brian Fagan's new home was rising on the ashes of his old house, built just eighteen months previously. Fagan, a professor of anthropology at the

University of California, was sailing in Yugoslavia at the time of the fire. He lost all his books and research notes. The chance to rebuild allowed him to correct some of the mistakes he made in the previous structure. Solar energy will be used to heat the water for the new hot tub, among other things. Gesturing about the neighborhood enthusiastically, Fagan said, "This guy is rebuilding, so is that guy and that. This is going to be a beehive of activity." He thought for a moment and then answered the question of why rebuild: "It is a very distinctive type of living. There is quiet and one of the best views in California. What I miss most is the spiritualness of it, just enjoying the views."

Of course, natural disasters are nothing new in California. San Francisco was rebuilt atop the San Andreas Fault after being shaken to pieces in 1906. Predictions of another major earthquake in the near future are made frequently. There is the argument that the West has its fires and earthquakes, and the East, its snowstorms and hurricanes. Other sections of the country have tornadoes. Floods and droughts are less restrictive in a geographical sense.

But Southern California does seem to have more than the usual share of disasters. Some say such an unstable area should never have been allowed to become so highly populated. There is little that can be done now with the fait accompli, except to learn to live with it as Roger Horton has done. Horton, president of the Sycamore Creek Property Owners Association, was a lifelong resident of the area. He kept a box handy with critical papers, candles, food, and water, and grabbed it and ran before his home was burned to the ground.

He said, "I lived here so long, the possibility of a natural disaster became pretty deeply ingrained with me. In a short period of time we had an oil spill, an earthquake, floods, and three major fires. I knew by living here disaster was a possibility. I never had the sense that fate dealt me an evil blow. I knew it could happen. We talked about it."

Like the plants and animals, humans have adapted to fire in California.

I write these words in my home atop a pine-clotted ridge that badly needs to be cleaned out by fire. I have a magnificent view of a bay, underneath which runs the San Andreas Fault. The chaparral has grown up around the wooden structure to give me a sense of privacy and closeness to nature. I have experienced fires, floods, and earthquakes in this state, yet I would live nowhere else. But perhaps I should call my insurance agent next week to increase my coverage a bit. Someday I hope to get around to trimming the chaparral.

Audubon, January 1978

Living with Drought

Above all else, California is one big, complex plumbing system. That is the reason for its existence—not the movie industry, aerospace firms, the stupendous coastline, Disneyland, or the pleasures of its cities. The same could be said of the rest of the West. The power and the glory, not to mention the money, center around water and the means to convey it. Woe to any president or governor or legislature that attempts to thwart this system. It consists of ditches, flumes, penstocks, dams, canals, laterals, pipelines, and more ditches, all laid across nobody knows how many miles, that bisect mountains, deserts, farmlands, and cities. It represents billions of dollars of irrigation projects in California alone and less but appreciable amounts elsewhere, making possible more billions of dollars's worth of farm products sent to millions of hungry mouths around the world. If California stood alone, it would rank sixth among the nations of the world in value of farm products.

These basic facts tend to become lost in normal years. But this is not a normal year in the West. It is the year of the Great Drought. Records are being broken, but records are deceiving. They have been kept for less than one hundred years. Undoubtedly, the West has suffered greater droughts and survived, and may survive again. The Anasazi, an ancient Indian culture that predated any of the existing tribes, disappeared from the Southwest around A.D. 1300. Experts say that their disappearance was due to drought.

Earlier this year, I felt the land would wither and the people would have to move. Once again I sensed the tenuousness of existence where floods, droughts, fires, and earthquakes periodically scour the land. I am not an alarmist, but a few times I privately said thanks for the fact that my salary was being paid by an organization based on the East Coast. This would allow me to stay and record the end of a civilization.

Land that should have been green with winter rains was crackling and desiccated. A whole wet season, winter, had just not occurred. My biological time clock was off. I was troubled. The common expectation is of an earthquake causing California to slip into the ocean. This year it seemed the state would simply atrophy. And then just enough rain came to green up the land. It was a deception. The land was beautifully green again, but the snow was not in the mountains to provide water during the hot summer months.

Besides setting records, this year in California was different for a number of reasons.

They talked seriously of water conservation for the first time.

Environmentalists were dinged for opposing water projects, but these criticisms were just scattered potshots. The problem, and people's perception of it, seemed to go deeper. For the first time—and the parallel with the energy shortage was striking—there was an appreciable cutback in the use of water, which, if maintained, would obviate the need for many more dams and water projects. Nobody was laying any bets that the decreased use, both mandatory and voluntary, would be maintained over the long haul; but at least it had occurred this one time.

Conservation was the theme of the Governor's Drought Conference held in Los Angeles. The implication of the proceedings was that there were more drought conferences to come in succeeding years, an ominous prospect. While the various speakers and panelists droned on in the main meeting rooms, the most interesting action was taking place in two smaller rooms at the Los Angeles Convention Center. The center of attraction was the common household flush toilet in all its unadorned glory. Salesmen and models pressed their wares on the passing crowd. There were brochures and pamphlets to carry home and study later. Portable exhibits, with working parts revealed through clear plastic, vividly demonstrated the workings of a number of water-saving devices.

Most assuredly, at no previous time has so much attention been paid to this common convenience, which for so many years has been taken for granted. In the main sessions of the conference, attended by nearly one thousand persons who constituted the state's water establishment, there was open discussion by adults about what to do with human wastes. Frequently recited was the phrase so in vogue in certain water-short communities: "If it's yellow, let it mellow. If it's brown, flush it down." It is not uncommon to go to one of the finer homes in Marin County, the affluent suburban area north of San Francisco, and find toilet paper and urine mixed in the bowl, add one's own contribution, and then reappear among the guests feeling virtuous. Clearly, things have changed.

But it is not with the flush toilet that things will change radically in California. That is only a symbol of waste and people's growing willingness, even when it transcends propriety, to deal with the problem when they are clearly confronted by the lack of water. Down on the farm is where conservation counts, because in California eighty-five percent of water use is for agricultural purposes. This is where traditionally the greatest waste has occurred, and this is where the message of conservation has to be comprehended. There was mixed comprehension and certain conflict as California headed toward the mid-point of the driest year (1977) on record and the second of two dry years in a row.

Take the case of the Tuolumne River. It demonstrates, on a scale applicable to other rivers in the West, the great and varied demands being placed on a limited supply, the frictions between uses that are beginning to emerge, and what steps are being taken to deal with water shortages.

The Tuolumne is neither the greatest nor the least of California rivers. But the use of its water, particularly in this year of drought, is emblematic of the remainder of California and the West. Like most rivers in the West, its waters are overcommitted. Like other rivers, such as the Colorado River, the people who regulate and use it think of the river—not their plans—as being deficient.

The Tuolumne starts its flow from two small glaciers on the northern face of 13,114-foot Mount Lyell, the highest point in Yosemite National Park. The trickle that becomes a torrent in a normal year becomes a trickle again 158 miles downstream when the river, after numerous uses and reuses, empties into the San Joaquin River on the floor of the great Central Valley. The San Joaquin merges with the Sacramento River, which empties into Suisun Bay. From there the water flows through San Pablo and San Francisco bays to the Pacific Ocean. That is one of three endings.

By a different route, the Tuolumne also terminates in the faucets of San Francisco and the peninsular cities to the south after being diverted just outside Yosemite into a maze of aqueducts, pipelines, and reservoirs. This year, through a precedent-setting manipulation of the plumbing system that extends throughout the West, Tuolumne River water will also be shuttled to parched Marin County. Tuolumne River water also ends up on the land in the Modesto and Turlock irrigation districts, the two oldest such entities in the state. There in the San Joaquin Valley, the richest farmlands in the world bring forth bountiful crops, or at least they have in the past.

In summer there are superb alpine meadows and lake-dotted basins near the base of Mount Lyell. Small rills from the snowmelt trickle down to form larger streams, such as the Maclure Creek tributary of the Lyell Fork. Above Tuolumne Meadows, the National Park Service is rerouting trails around the fragile meadows because of overuse and erosion. There probably will be little erosion danger this year, but with a longer high-country season the use will be greater. Other than the fact that bears have come out of hibernation earlier this year, and there will be more fishermen out after trout, park rangers and State Department of Fish and Game officials see little impact on high-country wildlife. From Tuolumne Meadows—the best spot where automobile-bound tourists can glimpse the park's high country—the river, now beginning to be augmented by many small tributaries, enters the Grand Canyon of the Tuolumne and then the eight-mile-long Hetch Hetchy Reservoir, backed up by the City of San Francisco's O'Shaughnessy Dam.

It is here in the national park that the river gains significance for conservationists because of John Muir's fight against the dam in the early 1900s. The use of the river was in the eye of the beholder. Muir said of San Francisco's plans, "Dam Hetch Hetchy! As well dam for water tanks the people's cathedrals and churches, for no holier temple has ever been consecrated by the heart of man." John R. Freeman, the engineer retained by the city to design the project, remarked, "Plainly it is an absolute impossibility to obtain a softer or better water supply than from the upper Tuolumne, and plainly it is impracticable to secure a cleaner reservoir site, or one that will possess a larger proportion of bare granite walls all the way between the high water and low water limits." The dam was built, and Hetch Hetchy Valley, ranking a close second to scenic Yosemite Valley, was flooded. The scars of that battle exist to this day. The city built a second dam, Eleanor, within the national park and subsequently raised the height of O'Shaughnessy.

Oral L. Moore is general manager of the city's Hetch Hetchy Water and Power Department. Moore, who radiates decisiveness with San Francisco polish, is termed the most difficult man to deal with by officials of the Department of Fish and Game. To some U.S. Fish and Wildlife Service officials, the Hetch Hetchy system is an environmental abomination. "So much is lost with so little mitigation," says Jody Hoffman, who headed a multi-agency flow study of the river. The study concluded that releases from Hetch Hetchy were inadequate to protect the downstream fishery and recreational and aesthetic values. San Francisco has appealed those conclusions and asked for releases in this dry year below the minimums presently in effect. Moore puts it succinctly, "I am sure the stream will survive anything. All I am asking the Secretary of Interior to do is share the mandatory reduction of 25% in San Francisco with the fish in Tuolumne County."

It will be a hard year for the fish and wildlife, but experts are talking in terms of stress on populations, not extinction. Within the eighteen hundred square miles of the Tuolumne River drainage area are blacktail deer, California mule deer, black bear, bobcat, badger, jackrabbit, gray squirrel, coyote, beaver, mink, muskrat, raccoon, striped skunk, California quail, mountain quail, blue grouse, band-tailed pigeon, mourning dove, and dipper. An occasional mountain lion and southern bald eagle are about. The sport fish in the Tuolumne below Hetch Hetchy are brown and rainbow trout. Below New Don Pedro Dam, the last major structure on the river, there once were annual runs of Chinook salmon numbering 100,000. The dams lowered this number to between 1,000 and 2,000, and in this drought year there is a question whether any will survive.

The hardier specimens of wild trout below Hetch Hetchy probably will survive by hanging in deep pools. The city did not help the situation last fall when it flushed Early Intake Reservoir and sent a load of decomposed granite downstream onto spawning beds. Riverbank vegetation accustomed to higher flows will suffer, as will the wildlife communities dependent on this habitat.

Cattle and deer will be in close competition for whatever remaining forage there is. The effect of decreasing amounts of shrubbery on wildlife will show up in future years. It will hurt some and benefit others. There will be good fishing in reservoirs this year, since the fish will be more concentrated; but there will be poorer fishing in future years. Quail and pheasant will have poor nesting success because of the lack of good spring rains. The two dozen or so bald eagles spotted near the foothill community of La Grange will go hungry with few or no salmon on which to feed. On the floor of the San Joaquin Valley, where normally there are seventy-five thousand acres flooded in the fall when waterfowl migrate through the Central Valley, this year there will only be forty thousand. With increased proximity, disease among waterfowl will be greater. And so it goes. The needs of people and wildlife are in greater competition this year than ever before.

There are also conflicts between city people and farm people. At Early Intake, a few miles below Hetch Hetchy, San Francisco draws off its drinking water and sends it west by aqueduct. The water remaining in the natural riverbed is trapped below by New Don Pedro Dam for use by the two irrigation districts. San Francisco's share of the water that is released to New Don Pedro, when the city can't use it, goes into a bank account. The city has built up a large enough bank account—400,000 acre-feet—to cover the total amount of expected runoff from the Tuolumne River drainage this year. So the irrigation districts have to rely on the carry-over storage in New Don Pedro. For Turlock, which improvidently decided last year to use its full allotment, this means very little water. San Francisco's Moore, whose city imposed a mandatory cutback, shows no sign of charity. "That's tough," he said. "I can hold all the water and not release any to the Turlock Irrigation District. Obviously the highest obligation is to drinking water." Leroy Kennedy, irrigation engineer for the Turlock district, says nothing but asks what Moore said.

Normally the city and two irrigation districts have a close working relationship. They built New Don Pedro Dam together and closely coordinate the flow of the river for drinking, irrigation, and power generation. Six dams, several with built-in powerhouses, and two other separate powerhouses serve the three partners who would like to build an additional three dams, enlarge Lake Eleanor and one existing powerhouse, and build two new powerhouses. These plans have been in existence since 1968. They are primarily aimed at increasing power generation, which provides the revenues that underwrite the costs of running San Francisco and cheap water for the two irrigation districts. A small side benefit of the projects would be an increased 11,900 acre-feet of water storage. Everyone now expects the water storage aspect of the proposed projects to be played up.

What these projects would do, besides completely harnessing the river to benefit the partners, is wipe out a magnificent stretch of white water and some wild canyon areas. The river can be run in an eighteen- or twenty-seven–mile segment, and it poses one of the greatest challenges amidst scenic grandeur in the state. With New Melones Dam scheduled to inundate the popular white-water run on the nearby Stanislaus River, the Tuolumne has become the prime target of "save the river" campaigns in the state. This stretch of the river is also the subject of a Forest Service study for possible inclusion in the Wild and Scenic Rivers System. The draft study should be available this summer. It is being prepared in a climate of drought, which has forced the planners to look more carefully at the proposal for dams. This year the Tuolumne is too low to be run by white-water enthusiasts in kayaks and large rubber rafts. But for the first time in history, the wild stretches of the river will be suitable for inner-tubing.

There is one other energy project planned in the area that could tap Tuolumne River water. The Pacific Gas & Electric Company, along with the two irrigation districts, would like to build a nuclear powerplant in the foothill area of Stanislaus County. Although the source of cooling water has not been specifically identified, the districts are studying the Tuolumne River. Kennedy said it would be the cheapest source. "That would be rather difficult to sell this year," he added.

The white-water run terminates at the upper end of New Don Pedro Dam. And here again, at another dam, one of those bitter struggles between conservation interests and dam builders has left memories that persist to this day and influence decisions. From 1961 to 1965 a fight was waged with the California Department of Fish and Game and the Interior Department on one side and the two irrigation districts on the other. The districts opposed releasing adequate water for salmon runs, but in the end they lost. The agreement they reached calls for release of sixty-four thousand acre-feet in a dry year, but as of October 1, 1977 (the beginning of the new water year), the Department of Fish and Game may have to agree to a reduction of about fifty percent in that dry-year figure. The farmers and their irrigation districts want to halt the release of water for fish entirely. Kennedy said, "A lot of farmers feel deeply that if their crops are dying, they would rather see some fish dying." Fish and Game officials believe they are not even receiving the reduced dry-year flows they are entitled to because farmers are pumping and diverting water below the dam.

For the San Joaquin Valley, the value of water cannot be overemphasized. Without water, the valley would revert to sand dunes and grasslands. The motto of Modesto is, "Water, Health, Contentment, Wealth." The Modesto district will have a near normal irrigation year because it conserved its allotment last year, but Turlock is going to hurt badly. The crunch, everyone agrees, will come around July when the temperatures soar to over the one-hundred-degree mark and the farmers call for more water. This year, unless the farmers have sunk wells, there will be no more water. Kennedy explains the district's decision thusly:

"Last year we started the irrigation season early. We decided to go with the full allotment because we had a full allotment available. It seemed ill-advised to shorten the allotment. On the basis of the record, there had never been two such dry years in a row. Had we held back last year and had this been a decent year, we would have been criticized."

And so, the district and its farmers are desperately trying to sink more wells to tap the underground water supply. The underground water table is only a few feet below the surface in much of the district because of the practice of flood irrigation, which results in an excessive use of water. To pump it will take energy, expensive this year because the utility companies—lacking sufficient hydroelectric power—have to purchase power from more costly sources. The Pacific Gas & Electric Company says it will be walking the thin edge of energy supply as it meets demand. There could be shortages if generating equipment breaks down unexpectedly. Kennedy, asked what conservation measures farmers are taking, replied, "I have to chuckle because this year there is conservation because there is no other choice."

A few miles below New Don Pedro Dam, completed in 1971, the La Grange Diversion Dam funnels the water out of the river and into two holding reservoirs, one for the Modesto and one for the Turlock district. Turlock Lake holds that district's share, and from there it is fed into two main canals, the Turlock and Ceres main canals. Laterals run from the two main canals, and the district operates the two main canals and laterals. The farmers take over from there. Water is spread onto 172,000 acres within the district via a plumbing system comprising 2,529 miles of canals, laterals, ditches, and pipelines. The most important crops are alfalfa, corn, peaches, almonds, walnuts, and grapes. California supplies almost one hundred percent of the nation's almonds and walnuts, sixty-five percent of its peaches, and ninety percent of its grapes; so what happens in the Turlock Irrigation District, no matter how seemingly remote, will have some effect on what will go on the nation's tables.

When the water, which originated in the Sierra Nevada, flows down the Turlock Main Canal, it is diverted west into Lateral Number Five and thence into Frank La Chapell's division. La Chapell, a graying fifty-nine, is one of thirty-eight ditch tenders in the irrigation district. Although the occupation has not captured the imagination of the media, which tends to glorify the West, the profession of ditch tender is one of the oldest and most valued in these arid lands. It is the ditch tender who regulates the flow of water onto a farmer's land. A few years ago the district's management wanted to change the job title to something more euphemistic; but the ditch tenders, mindful of their ties to western history, would have none of it.

La Chapell says, "Our job is public relations. We are the communications link between the district and the farmer."

In his orange compact, with his record books beside him, La Chapell tours his division twice a day, waving at farmers or stopping when they have a request for more water. Frank, who has been with the district for sixteen years, relates, "There is a saying about us: 'Old ditch tenders just go down the drain.' " He asks a visitor, "I expect you have heard a lot about the negative aspects of the district this year? They just expected the district to be God and put snow on the mountains. The mayor called a prayer week, and we had one good shower after that. It just emphasizes the seriousness of the situation."

As La Chapell drives around the forty-five hundred acres of his division, he explains what each farmer is doing to deal with the drought. "Pasture operations could be hurt. More than likely some will drop out of the operation for a while. Lots of farmers are going to a single crop instead of double-cropping. Now you see over there, that guy spent a little money and hired a dozer to level his land more carefully. There will be a more efficient flow of water. Most of the land in my division is flood irrigated. But some went to furrows, which saves water. That farmer has graded his land so it tilts toward one end of the field. The water collects there and is pumped back to the top. That's real conservation. This one guy usually raises grain and corn. But they take a lot of water, so he's putting in melons, which take less. Some are putting in beans, which take only two irrigations, but that is a desperation crop because the price is never good."

On this day there is water in the canals and ditches because the district has authorized an emergency release for a few crops. The regular irrigation season, over a month late, has not begun. With the water flowing placidly in the canals and gurgling over the drops, it is hard to imagine a shortage. Nobody is hurting yet. There is only the expectation of shortages at this time, not the reality.

La Chapell points to some sandy soil. "This territory could go back to a desert pretty quick. All the ingredients are there."

Audubon, July 1977.

The Eating of the West

In 1977 Americans ate 25 billion pounds of beef, which averaged out to about 126 pounds per person. While other less fortunate countries have sought their protein in grains and fish, from hamburgers to filets mignons America has historically been a nation of beef eaters. What is little known, though, is the high environmental cost attached to this indulgence, particularly on the public lands of the western states.

Simply put, no other activity covers so much land area in this country as cows eating grass. Nor, with particular reference to the eleven western states where more land is grazed than in any other region, has any single activity or combination of activities contributed more toward altering the shape and texture of the land and the wildlife that is dependent upon it.

Approximately 1.2 billion acres, or sixty-three percent of the total land area in the continental United States, has been or is being grazed. More than one-half this amount—622 million acres—is in the eleven western states. The 622 million grazeable acres represent eighty-three percent of the land areas of Washington, Oregon, California, Idaho, Nevada, Arizona, Utah, Montana, Wyoming, Colorado, and New Mexico. And of the 622 million acres in the West, 504 million were being grazed in 1970, the base year the Department of Agriculture used in a study. Of this amount, about half were private lands and the other half were those public lands containing the vast majority of the nation's national resource lands, national forests, national parks and monuments, national recreation areas, Indian and military reservations, fish and wildlife refuges, and wilderness areas where cattle and sheep have been nibbling away, in some cases, for four hundred years.

Almost no area in the West has been left undisturbed by livestock. The ubiquitous cow can be seen grazing from below sea level to the twelve-thousand-foot heights of mountain peaks. As biologist Carl B. Koford of the Museum of Vertebrate Zoology at Berkeley wrote, "Natural grasslands are so rare that rangemen are forced to search the corners of old cemeteries for pieces of protected ground." The impact of countless hooves and mouths over the years has done more to alter the type of vegetation and landforms of the West than all the water projects, strip mines, power plants, freeways, and subdivision developments combined. The changes, in most cases, are irrevocable.

Overgrazing by livestock and remedial programs like fencing, chaining, plowing, and dumping of herbicides on millions of acres in the name of range "improvements" have had a greater

effect on wildlife in the West than any other factor except the
climate. Speaking at a symposium in 1974, zoologist A. Starker
Leopold said, "I am increasingly convinced that fish and wildlife
habitat in our western forests and rangelands, both public and
private, is undergoing a steady, chronic deterioration under existing patterns of multiple use. Livestock grazing in particular
may be having cumulative ecological ill effects on the productivity of both lands and waters." A 1977 Department of the Interior seminar on wildlife and range management concluded,
"Livestock grazing is the single most important factor limiting
wildlife production in the West. It has been and continues to be
administered without adequate consideration for wildlife, especially on federal lands."

Vegetative cover can be changed by overgrazing in the following manner: Cattle move onto an undisturbed range and first
select those plants that are most accessible and palatable. Such
species, called "dessert" or "ice cream plants," tend to have the
highest nutritional values and are the sweetest. With prolonged
grazing, these prime grasses and weeds—mostly perennials—are
replaced by less desirable annuals. Shrubs, such as sagebrush and
pinon-juniper, now invade and take over the weakened area. Less
nutritious and even such poisonous species as larkspur and loco-
weed (which literally drive cattle crazy) appear. Exotic plant
species—perhaps from Mediterranean Europe or the steppes of
Asia—proliferate and crowd out the native species. The compo-
sition of vegetation is altered, as are the small mammals and
invertebrates and their prey that are dependent upon it.

Where there is heavy use over a number of years in an arid
climate, the grassland yields to a desert in a process called desertification. In a paper for the 1977 United Nations Conference on
Desertification, the Worldwatch Institute warned, "Where land
abuse is severe and prolonged, and especially where extended

drought intensifies its effects, grasslands and fields can be reduced to stony, eroded wastelands—or even to heaps of drifting
sands. More commonly, the quality of rangeland vegetation de-
clines as the more palatable and productive plants are nudged out
by less desirable species. On croplands, yields may gradually fall
as soil nutrients are dissipated and the topsoil is eroded by wind
and water." Overgrazing is the prime cause of desertification, and
much of the West is arid or semiarid.

Consider how the landscape can be altered by overgrazing: Livestock trampling about denudes the vegetation and compacts the
soil. There is greater runoff, and the sediment load of nearby
streams and rivers increases. Downstream water users and public
works erected to dam or divert rivers are inundated by silt. With
the lessening of grass cover and subsequent invasion of woody
bushes, gullies and arroyos start cutting through the bare land.
The water table is lowered. Springs and seeps dry up. This can
be disastrous in a dry land.

The best documented study of what overgrazing can do to a
specific area is contained in *The Changing Mile,* by James Rodney
Hastings of the University of Arizona and Raymond M. Turner
of the U.S. Geological Survey. They selected an area that lies
between Tucson, Arizona, and Sonora, Mexico and traced its
grazing history along with the corresponding alteration in the
landscape and vegetative cover.

Before the white man came, the Indians caused the first landscape alteration by the widespread use of fire to herd game.
Grasslands were thus formed and maintained. Four hundred years
ago the Spanish introduced domestic animals to the area, and
livestock numbers increased to eight million sheep and one million cattle. In the early 1800s large Mexican herds, numbering

between 50,000 and 150,000, roamed the region south of the Gila River and north of the border. Still there were no important alterations, except the first noticeable spread of mesquite. Grass was still plentiful in the northern Sonoran Desert, the landscape was open with none of the infestations of shrubbery that were to come later, and the rivers and streams flowed, more or less perennially, through open, marshy bottomlands. There were no established channels.

By 1890 Arizona Territory had a population of sixty thousand, and there were 315,000 or more cattle south of the Gila River. Then a strange thing happened that summer to the San Pedro, Santa Cruz, Sonoita, San Simon, and Babocomari rivers. Their lazy, unchanneled courses changed to steep-walled arroyos or trenches, and with the increase in gradient, much of the surrounding topsoil washed away. At best, the rivers and streams became intermittent. The mesquite and other shrubs started crowding in, and the saguaro cactus disappeared from some areas. Drought hit in 1891 and 1892, and by late spring of 1893, up to seventy-five percent of the livestock had been lost. It was possible in that huge region to throw a rock from one rotting carcass to another. Of that time and the intervening years down to the present, the authors said, "Taken as a whole, the changes constitute a shift in the regional vegetation of an order so striking that it might better be associated with the oscillations of Pleistocene time than with the 'stable' present."

They attributed the drastic change to the cumulative effects of too many cattle and a warm, drying trend in the climate. "By weakening the grass cover, domestic grazing animals have reinforced the general tendency toward aridity. They have contributed to an imbalance between infiltration and runoff in favor of the latter. This imbalance, in turn, may have been the event that triggered arroyo cutting. Because of the weakened grass cover, the establishment of shrubby species has been facilitated. At the same time livestock have aided in the dissemination of shrubby species, and the increased aridity has favored plants with their rooting habits."

Consider what can happen to wildlife as a result of overgrazing: Starker Leopold traced the decline of mule deer herds in the West to the "widespread deterioration of the deer forage." He stated that "persistent livestock grazing would appear to be a prime suspect in contributing to this effect." And he blamed the decrease in quail on the reduction of seeds from plants grazed by livestock. Leopold and other researchers think overgrazing has ruined many trout and salmon streams in the West. When streambanks weaken because of loss of vegetation, sediment loads increase and channelization projects are undertaken, riparian vegetation disappears, and water temperatures rise. Speaking of other harmful effects on fishlife such as the clear-cutting of timber, road building, and subdivision development, Leopold said, "The combination of uses, with grazing the most insidious, is having cumulative effects on most western watersheds."

In Nevada, a Bureau of Land Management (BLM) report states, "Stream riparian habitat where livestock grazing is occurring has been grazed out of existence or is in a severely deteriorated condition. Within the state, 883 miles of streams were identified as having deteriorated or declining habitat." And Nevada is not a state known for many miles of streams.

Herbicides, among them 2,4-D and 2,4,5-T of Vietnam fame, and such mechanical methods as plowing or hauling a chain between two tractors have altered millions of acres of western rangeland. In Nevada alone, the BLM has plowed or chained four million acres. The Forest Service, which administers less rangeland, has altered about 3.5 million acres nationwide by chemical or mechanical means. The idea is to knock down the shrubs and seed the areas with nutritious grass. The result can be vast monocultures—such as thousands of acres of the exotic crested wheat grass.

Although the use of herbicides has been temporarily halted, throughout the 1950s and 1960s massive amounts were dumped on western rangelands by the Bureau of Land Management, Forest Service, Fish and Wildlife Service, Bureau of Indian Affairs, and the military. Nobody has yet assessed the over-all impact of that indiscriminate use of chemicals on wildlife and humans in the West. The Environmental Protection Agency wondered about the massive dumping of herbicides on western rangelands. It commented, "The use of chemical manipulation by aerial spraying needs to be evaluated in greater detail. The potential hazards seem to far outweigh the benefits."

While such programs attract some public attention, it is the undramatic day-to-day chomping of grass that has had the most widespread effects. Cattle have crowded bighorn sheep out of their traditional ranges in the Southwest and have been the major factor in their becoming a rare sight. "One of the most convincing bits of evidence that livestock grazing is a depressing influence on bighorn sheep in Arizona is the fact that there are no thriving populations in ranges now grazed by cattle," says Steve Gallizioli, head of research for the Arizona Game and Fish Department. A colleague of Gallizioli's, David E. Brown, traced the disappearance of prairie chickens, sharp-tailed grouse, bob-white quail, Montezuma quail, and scaled quail from large areas. Wrote Brown, "Even a conservative utilization of forage in the neighborhood of twenty to forty percent could be highly detrimental to grassland birds during drought periods because it could remove that percentage of the bird cover habitat for the next year. Unless some areas are left free from livestock, grazing would then result in increased mortality and eventually more erratic population levels and the elimination of marginal populations."

With things not going too well out on the western range, the question arises how bad are they as measured in those precise numerical equivalents Americans love to apply to impossible situations? The numbers game on the condition of the range is similar to the body counts in South Vietnam. Figures are arrived at by extrapolation of a few known facts applied to a vast, unknown area and tend to support existing policy. At best they represent trends, at worst wish fulfillments. In 1936 the Department of Agriculture and its member agency, the Forest Service, published "The Western Range," the first comprehensive survey of range conditions. It was a document of doom and gloom and a bid by the Forest Service to take over all the federal government's range programs. At that time the Grazing Service had just been formed within the Interior Department and Interior Secretary Harold Ickes was trying to wrest the Forest Service from the Department of Agriculture. The survey said there was a fifty percent depletion in the carrying capacity of rangelands. Those lands administered by the Forest Service were in great shape; those administered by the Grazing Service, later to become the Bureau of Land Management, were in terrible condition. The fact that the survey was unduly influenced by the drought of the mid-1930s and that Forest Service officials today admit to its bureaucratic expediency does not make one feel particularly secure with current surveys—whether they be by the Forest Service or BLM.

The livestock industry had its story to sell and replied to the

1936 survey with a publication entitled, "If and When It Rains." The arguments are the same as those used today. "The stockman is not a despoiler of the range. He is necessarily a conservator. His livelihood depends upon feed for his livestock. . . . Dust storms come and dust storms go, and bureaucrats build up the need for big appropriations based thereon, while sensational writers harvest a big crop telling about it; but when the rain comes, the grass grows again and all is well on the range."

The rains came last year after two years of drought over most of the West; the grass grew, and the price of beef rose. Ranchers were happy, or at least as happy as chronically pessimistic businessmen can be, and the Utah state office of the BLM warned, "A lot of the 'greenery' this year is composed of annual grasses and forbs, many of which are not eaten by livestock or wildlife and only appear during spring periods of above-normal precipitation. This appearance does not mean the ranges are suddenly restored to abundant forage."

The Public Rangelands Improvement Act, which provides $365 million over a twenty-year period for "on the ground range improvements," was signed by President Carter on October 25, 1978. Its need was documented by a 1975 BLM survey claiming that 135.3 million acres or eighty-three percent of the rangeland administered by that agency was in an unsatisfactory or worse condition.

If most of the range is in an unsatisfactory or worse condition and the effects of overgrazing are so widespread and virulent, then why hasn't this issue received greater attention? First, when compared with a coal strip mine or a dam, a bunch of cows munching on grass lacks a certain amount of drama. Raging dust storms and eroded badlands are atypical symptoms. More characteristic are deeper arroyo cutting, a greater silt load, and less nutritious and altered vegetative cover. These symptoms are a matter of degree, not headline-grabbing absolutes. And a good rain year, like the last one, tends to green up the land deceptively.

In addition, the West prefers to treat its particular needs and problems in an insular manner, even though the solution may be sought in such a national forum as Congress. After all, how many outsiders have mastered the complexities of water projects or rangeland management? The academics at the western land-grant colleges and universities, who have developed an expertise in range matters and could have raised the issue, have first served the needs of the livestock industry. The history of the use of western range lands has been obscured by the popularization of the cowboy culture.

Grazing, the first form of agriculture, got its start in the Middle East more than four thousand years ago. It is an activity that has spread over one-half of the world's surface. The first hints of overgrazing appear in the Old Testament. The prophet Ezekiel warned, "Woe unto thee, shepherds of Israel—seemeth it a small thing unto you to have eaten up the good pasture, but must ye tread down with your feet the residue of your pastures?" Perhaps Ezekiel's was the first range management program.

When Coronado marched up from Mexico into the Southwest in 1540, he brought the first horses, cattle, and sheep into the area. Seventy years later the first livestock were landed at Jamestown on the East Coast. In the frontier days grazing practices were rudimentary. As one study put it, the ranchers "mostly grew up with the pioneer idea that when the feed in a certain region was gone there was more 'over the range' to which they could move their herds and flocks." The precedent of free and abundant range had been set. It haunts public-policy making to this day.

The real ranching history of the West spans only slightly more than one hundred years. After the Civil War the great cattle drives came up from Texas, and the hardy longhorns, mixing with the finer breeds migrating from the East, spread over the western range. It was the first widespread land-use revolution in the West. In comparison, the mining boom was confined to small pockets. Investors from the East and Europe poured capital into western cattle operations. Ranching boomed to the point where cattle instead of grass came to be regarded as the principal resource. One government study of this period noted, "Not an acre of grazing land was left unoccupied, and ranges that for permanent and regular use would have been fully stocked with a cow to each forty acres were loaded until they were carrying one to every ten acres. No one provided any feed for the winter, the owners preferring to risk the losses. Gradually the native grasses disappeared. As fast as a blade of grass showed above the ground, some hungry animal gnawed it off." Drought and intense cold, part of the normal western weather cycle, nearly wiped out the livestock industry in 1886 and 1893. The cattle and sheep came back, but never in as great numbers.

Scattered voices spoke up for government regulation of these lands. John Wesley Powell, the one-armed Civil War major who was the pioneer explorer of the Colorado River and later headed the U.S. Geological Survey, made a passing reference to overgrazing in his 1878 "Report on the Lands of the Arid Region of the United States." Powell's main interest was the use of water, the chief beneficiary of which was livestock; but his attempt to assert the government's control over lands susceptible to irrigation led to his being hounded from office by a Nevada senator. It was not the last time an angry western congressman was to cause the retirement, dismissal, or transfer of a federal government employe who was trying to protect a wider public interest than the needs of the lawmaker's immediate constituents.

With Theodore Roosevelt in the White House and a conservation ethic abroad in the land, the Forest Service took over rangeland management on forest reserves in 1905. Gifford Pinchot, chief of the Forest Service, issued this muted warning: "In new forest reserves where the livestock industry is of special importance, full grazing privileges will be given at first, and if reduction in number is afterward found necessary, stockmen will be given ample opportunity to adjust their business to the new conditions." The Forest Service is still trying to cut back.

But the Forest Service only had jurisdiction over a small portion of the public domain, and the remainder went unregulated. These were the vast tracts of sagebrush desert and rolling, shrubby terrain a traveler sees when crossing the West in an automobile. Most of the choicest parcels, like national parks and forests, were carved out of what is now called the national resource lands. With grazing conditions worsening in the early 1930s, the Taylor Grazing Act was passed in 1934, creating the Grazing Service within the Department of the Interior to regulate rangeland use on these national resource lands. The weak bill gave the livestock industry a captive agency that was supposed to control it. In 1946 the Grazing Service and the General Land Office, created to sell off these lands, were merged into the Bureau of Land Management.

The first BLM director, Marion Clawson, wrote, "The political influence of the range livestock industry differs in no essential respects from the political influence of other economic groups. It is simply more powerful in relation to the number of people involved." Clawson noted that the "oldest and best" families in the West, who had the most political muscle, were associated with ranching; and western congressmen "often dominated legislation regarding federal lands because they were the best-informed and most interested in it."

Congressmen from the western states form the majority of those obscure subcommittees where such legislation is shaped, passed with little debate before the full committee, and frequently enacted by voice vote on the floor of the House or Senate before being passed on as a fait accompli to the president for his signature. As with water projects, this is the pattern of politics developed by a region that has found it has special needs that are likely to be uninteresting to ill-informed, unsympathetic outsiders. It is hard to run over such a cohesive bloc, as President Carter and other presidents have discovered.

The real importance of livestock to the West, at least at its present excessive levels, is debatable. About 150 million acres of BLM land is administered for grazing, and the comparable figure for the Forest Service is 94 million acres. The remainder is taken up in much lesser chunks by the Fish and Wildlife Service, the Bureau of Indian Affairs, and the military. The total 250 million acres of public lands used for grazing in the West represent an area larger than the fourteen Atlantic seaboard states. But the five million head of cattle using public lands represent only eight percent of the total beef cattle in the nation. Ranching does help sustain some small communities, but others in recent years have become more dependent on tourists and energy projects. However, it is a good thing that ranch life still exists in the West, whether it be third generation or wealthy newcomers interested in an investment or hobby. Cattle and sheep fit the land better than power plants and condominiums. But it is hard to justify excessive numbers.

The two federal agencies that have the most to do with regulating grazing, the Forest Service and the Bureau of Land Management, have gone about their tasks in different ways. The BLM has put more reliance on a single grazing management system, called rest-rotation. This system was developed by a former Forest Service employe, Gus Hormay, who spread the gospel with fervor throughout BLM ranks.

The system fits political needs by holding out the promise of improving the condition of the range while at the same time allowing more cattle to graze it. The problem is that rest-rotation is not a proven technique, as the bureau admits in its environmental impact statement on grazing. The document states, "Hormay has largely been a pioneer in advancing and adopting new concepts of management, many of which are not yet tested by research investigations."

Generally the Forest Service is given credit for being more resistant to rancher and political pressures and having lands in somewhat better shape than the BLM. There are reasons for this. The Forest Service got into the business of regulating earlier. Grazing is only one of a number of constituencies it has. (The BLM, up to recent years, has traditionally been a one-constituency agency.) Timber and recreation rank higher in priority. Also, Forest Service lands are at higher elevations; thus they get more rainfall and recover more quickly than the hotter, drier BLM lands.

But the Bureau of Land Management is changing, and this has sent a wave of unease through the ranks of the livestock industry, whose ultimate fear is that its members will be kicked off the public lands. Starting with the energy crisis, the BLM's other role as leasing agent for offshore oil and most of the western coal lands widened its dimensions. Recreation has increased on BLM lands, and there are greater demands for such diverse uses as off-road vehicles and wilderness designation—nearly as great an anathema to ranchers as a reduction of stock. More college-educated technicians and fewer cowboy types are joining its ranks. And the Federal Land Policy and Management Act of 1976 gave it a true multiple-use mandate.

On top of all this, a lawsuit filed by the Natural Resources Defense Council required the BLM to file meaningful environmental impact statements. The result, besides a possible break for wildlife on the range, was to make the agency aware of the clout of other interests. It also brought the ranchers and environmentalists together for the first time, as both thought the bureau was dragging its feet on implementing the court order, and both, for different reasons, wanted to see an improvement on the range.

The BLM also issued new grazing regulations in 1978 and started vigorously drawing up allotment management plans for individual ranchers. All these factors, plus the bill passed by Congress that attempted to solve the nagging problem of grazing fees and set the BLM up with the funding for a massive range improvement program, amounted to an upheaval in the customary way of doing business. The bill, which got environmentalist support, sanctified the policy of more intensive management instead of less cattle. Add the Carter administration's attack on water projects and a few other "sacred cows," and you have the ingredients for the Sagebrush Rebellion, a move by westerners to reassert control over their perceived domain.

Nowhere has the sense of uneasiness that has pervaded the western range for the last couple of years been more noticeable than in Arizona and Nevada, two of the most overgrazed states in the West. Besides getting heavy use, these two states are the most arid and possess large amounts of federal lands—eighty-five percent of Nevada's area being federally owned. Only eighteen percent of Arizona is in private hands. The strong desire for independence from federal controls in these two states verges on lawlessness in some cases, vindictiveness in others. Nevertheless, the West traditionally has been heavily dependent on federal largess.

Arizona and Nevada harbor their own special grazing stories.

Regardless of which way Kingman is approached on U.S. Highway 66 (now Interstate 40), the scenery in this part of northwest Arizona is typical of BLM lands. Hot, dry, scrubby desert is mixed with jagged heaps of desolate mountains running north and south between wide alluvial valleys. This is country where one cow needs one hundred acres of grazing land. Driving west at about this point, one drops off the rim of the Colorado Plateau and begins the gradual descent into the summer furnace of the Colorado River and Needles, California—frequently the hottest spot in the nation. Kingman is between the south rim of the Grand Canyon and Los Angeles, and the only reason for the traveler to stop is to grab a quick meal, gas, and some rest.

The casual passerby probably would not know that Kingman has been getting less rain in the last fifty years and that excessive grazing has caused a dominance of snakeweed, rabbit brush, turpentine bush, and goldenweed. But if that traveler got off the highway and drove north of town to where the new freeway will be routed, he would see all the symptoms of unplanned growth in Mohave County, which billed itself as the fastest-growing county in the nation in the 1960s. With an estimated need for 6,259 new lots during that decade, 127,017 were actually created. The population for the greater Kingman area is 22,800, of which 100 are ranchers and their families. Yet the ranchers are one of the most dominant voices in the community.

In January 1977, Gary McVicker arrived in Kingman to start

work as the new BLM area manager; and John Neal, whose family has been ranching in the area since the 1880s, was on hand to meet him that first day. The two were to become bitter antagonists in a classic struggle with many precedents in the West.

McVicker felt no hint of trouble when he first arrived, although he later believed the ranchers had been out to get him from the start. The first indications that things were not going smoothly came in the spring at a meeting with the ranchers when they complained to McVicker that he was unsympathetic.

McVicker, who represents the new style of BLM employe, had replaced an area manager with a reputation for leniency. A draft environmental impact statement was being drawn up for the area, as were individual allotment management plans. All the other pending changes descending from the outside world heightened the ranchers's fears of a reduced livelihood.

The complaints about McVicker centered on his attitude. He was accused of being curt on the telephone, possessing "total negativism" toward the ranchers's plight, and "lacking sympathy" or being "uncooperative." In other words, he was not one of the "ole boys."

Those who worked under McVicker and the previous area managers said the newcomer lacked a sense of camaraderie and that he questioned ranchers's proposals closely but acted fairly. According to one colleague, he was more of a resource manager than a diplomat, a role to which the ranchers were accustomed.

By June 1977, the situation had deteriorated to the point where the Mohave County Livestock Association had formally requested the BLM state director, Robert O. Buffington, "that Gary McVicker be replaced by someone who will work with the ranchers in the Kingman Resource Area." They asked that the former area manager be returned.

Copies of the request went to the Arizona congressional delegation. The state's freshman senator, Dennis DeConcini, had already visited Kingman and listened to the ranchers's complaints. On July 7 he wrote Interior Secretary Cecil Andrus, asking that McVicker be replaced and someone be appointed "who will better reflect the intent with which our governmental employes are to serve." Assistant Secretary Guy Martin replied, "Until such time as specifics are identified and our investigation shows McVicker is not performing satisfactorily in carrying out his job responsibilities, I most respectfully decline to act on your request." The congressman for the area, Bob Stump, made the same request and received the same reply. Other more powerful and experienced members of the Arizona delegation—Senator Barry Goldwater and Representatives Morris K. Udall and John Rhodes—watched the situation unfold but did not commit themselves.

On receiving the requests for removal, Buffington began to investigate the complaints. This involved a number of meetings and interviews with the ranchers. Things quieted down. John Neal said of this period, "We had romped on him pretty hard, and it looked like he wasn't going to bother us for a while." Meanwhile, the local newspaper, the *Kingman Daily Miner,* had become fairly strident about the issue. The editor, Mike Alan, wrote, "If it turns out the BLM 'gets away' with ignoring the requests of the people of this country which were made through their elected officials, then that which many have suspected for a long time will be proven true. This nation is no longer a democracy."

DeConcini called a late-fall meeting in Washington, D.C. Attending were aides for other members of the Arizona congressional delegation; George Turcott, the BLM's acting national director; Buffington, the state director; and Dan Beard, deputy assistant secretary of the Department of Interior. The

meeting failed to resolve anything, but Beard later told De-
Concini that the feeling within the department was that the
situation was poisonous and it seemed best to transfer McVicker.
DeConcini thought he had a commitment and told the ranchers
the good news.

It would be a few months before the agreement would filter
back to Buffington and McVicker in Arizona. They thought
things were going better in the spring of 1978. Frank Gregg,
who became BLM director in mid-February, later said of the
agreement, "Any efforts to salvage the situation were compro-
mised by this promise and predestined to failure."

On January 5, 1978, Secretary Andrus wrote to Daniel A.
Poole, president of the Wildlife Management Institute, who had
become concerned about the McVicker case, "Pressure on the
employes from one or more special interest groups is not new
or unique. When pressure from a single group becomes pronounced, as is currently the case in the Kingman Resource Area,
we will review the facts and allegations in order to arrive at an
[informed] judgment. Employes acting within the law for the
good of the general public will receive my full support."

At about the same time, Buffington completed his report on
the investigation and forwarded it to Washington. It stated, "It
is my conclusion after this investigation that Gary McVicker has
and is carrying out the policies and programs of the bureau in the
Kingman Resource Area in a fair and equitable manner and that
I can find no reason to recommend that he be transferred at this
time." Buffington pointed out that McVicker had arrived in
Kingman at a difficult time and wondered what the effect on
other BLM employes would be if the area manager "is transferred
due to public and political pressure."

When Gregg took over the bureau, he decided to make his
own decision on whether McVicker should go. He traveled to

Kingman, which had rarely, if ever, seen a national BLM director before; and it was on this trip in early May that McVicker, Buffington, and Gregg jointly decided the ranchers were not going to let up. If the BLM program was going to go anywhere at this critical time, the area manager would have to leave. It was agreed that McVicker would be replaced by another strong person. Said McVicker, "I knew the ranchers couldn't cry wolf twice in a row and be effective about it."

There was an additional aspect to the situation. DeConcini had played a key role in getting the Panama Canal treaty ratified by the Senate in a close vote and had accrued some national publicity and, more importantly, some points at the White House. BLM officials did not want any superiors dictating a decision at DeConcini's request, especially with Beard's promise to transfer McVicker hanging over their heads.

The transfer decision was made public in June by Buffington, and by then most BLM and Forest Service employes had heard about the case and were aware of its ramifications. Gregg said, "It was a sticky case. It is going to raise a signal that we are not going to support our field people. There is going to be some damage."

At the Department of Agriculture, Forest Service chief John McGuire had been watching the McVicker case unfold, and he foresaw the possible effect on his range personnel. "I think it is a mistake to give in to pressures like the ones McVicker encountered," said McGuire. "I urged Interior not to cave in." One of the letters Buffington received criticizing him for his action was from Earl D. Sandvig, who in 1951 had been coerced into transferring by Forest Service superiors who did not like his strong stance on grazing.

For Neal and the other ranchers it was a complete victory they thought could be repeated, if necessary. They had received inquiries from ranchers in other western states who were facing BLM-imposed restrictions on their grazing. These ranchers wanted to learn the successful techniques used in Kingman. All they had to do was consult the grazing history of the West.

Nevada, if anything, is more fiercely independent and disdainful of federal control than Arizona. Outside the glitter capitals of Las Vegas and Reno, Nevada is hard-rock ranching and mining country. It is a closed, cut-off society. Few have taken the time or care to interfere with the use of these Great Basin lands, which are removed from the mainstream of urban civilization in the West. And where attempts have been made to alter existing land-use patterns, they have been rebuffed.

There are these examples: When a Sierra Club chapter was formed in Elko, development-oriented citizens joined to subvert its purposes. In response to restrictions being placed on motorboat use at Ruby Lake National Wildlife Refuge, boaters arrived in large, organized numbers and zoomed around wherever they pleased. BLM employes caught twenty-four horses that were trespassing on federal lands and impounded them in a corral. Late that night between eight and ten pickups pulled up to the corral and knocked down the fence. BLM families face social ostracism or angry confrontations in public places. Their children sometimes get beaten up in school. There are stories of a BLM area manager being hanged in effigy, utility companies cutting off the power of BLM employes, and local sheriffs refusing to contract with the BLM for law enforcement services.

At times the federal bureaucracy seems an embattled, timid presence in Nevada. Take the case of John J. Casey, the king of the trespassers, who has made a mockery of the Taylor Grazing Act and fools of the federal government.

Trespassing on federal lands was at the root of the confronta-
tion. About 44 million of the 49.1 million acres administered by
the BLM in Nevada are suitable for grazing. The carrying capacity of this rangeland is 1,836,912 animal unit months (AUM)
for sheep and cattle. An AUM is the amount of forage needed for
one cow or five sheep, or their equivalents, for one month. In
1972 the carrying capacity was exceeded by 116,326 AUMs.
This excessive use by livestock was at the expense of forage for
wild horses and wildlife. These figures were cited in a controversial 1974 BLM report on the condition of the Nevada range. It
went on to state, "Many areas have suffered drastically, and abuse
is continuing."

The above figures did not include the number of cattle in trespass—the BLM's polite word for cattle either accidentally or purposely grazing on public lands when they are not supposed to be
there—in other words, illegal grazing.

Nevada leads the nation with such violations, and Casey is the
most consistent trespasser on BLM lands. In 1975 there were
one hundred trespass violations detected in Nevada—about one-
quarter of those nationwide. Curt Berklund, then the national
director of the BLM, warned Nevada ranchers that "unauthorized
grazing use has been a serious problem in Nevada and elsewhere
in the West. It can't continue. It won't." Those were brave words,
indeed.

Last year eighty ranchers were cited and fined $26,400 for
illegal grazing of 20,500 cattle, sheep, and horses on BLM lands
in Nevada. Bureau officials figure this was only a small portion
of the total, since two or three BLM employes can be responsible
for overseeing up to four million acres.

Casey's history of illegal grazing spans twenty years and three
states—Nevada, California, and Montana. This is what scattered
hearing and court records show: In 1956 Casey's grazing permit

in the Carson City, Nevada district was suspended and then re-
voked four years later for repeated violations. Casey then moved
part of his operation to the Susanville district, which spills over
from northeast California to northwest Nevada. Between 1960
and 1971, the BLM logged 89 trespass actions, involving 140
incidents, in the Susanville area. In 1969 Casey's grazing privileges in this area were suspended for five years and permanently
reduced by thirty percent, but his cattle still wandered onto federal lands. The BLM sought injunctive relief through the federal
courts in both Nevada and California and obtained settlements
or consent decrees. Casey went out and leased two new ranches,
thus obtaining additional grazing permits for the area.

While the BLM manager for the Susanville district was vigorously prosecuting Casey, a lenient manager in the adjoining
Winnemucca, Nevada district was issuing Casey grazing permits
right and left. A BLM memo at the time noted, "What makes it
look worse is the fact that by hearing the examiner's decision
California has suspended Casey's privileges for five years and is
going into court for an injunction in an effort to halt repeated
willful trespass, and Nevada is granting concessions over and
above that generally allowed by the regulations."

By 1973 the then national BLM director, Burton Silcock, was
worried about the situation. In a memo to the California state
director, Silcock said, "The credibility of our management
ability is in jeopardy and will be lost if control is not forthcom-
ing." Silcock had another concern: "The manpower required for
range use supervision of Casey's range operation has been so tremendous as to require virtually the full time of personnel assigned to that range unit and others for long periods of time.
This has a significant adverse effect on work accomplished in
many important activities."

In June 1978, an Interior Department administrative law

judge found Casey guilty of further trespass violations in the Susanville area, fined the rancher $5,573.25, and revoked his remaining permits for that area. Casey appealed that decision.

Despite pleadings from E. I. Rowland, the BLM state director in Nevada, Casey has not applied ear tags to his cattle in that state, so they can be monitored more closely. Rowland wrote in March, "It is apparent from these observations and other evidence that Mr. Casey has not made an effort to ear tag, and in addition, substantial trespass exists."

Casey, in his late fifties, was once asked in a hearing by a federal prosecutor, "Do you feel you have a trespass problem, Mr. Casey, in the Susanville grazing district?" To which the rancher-hotelman, who the BLM estimates is worth some twenty million dollars, replied, "I feel I have been and am being picked on."

Since he travels five thousand miles a month between his ranches in the three states, Casey uses a motel he owns in Reno as a mail drop. Frequently, the certified letters the BLM sends to that address are returned unopened. Asked by the prosecutor if he had a problem receiving mail, Casey answered, "I don't have much luck having it forwarded to where I am."

The federal government has spent over one million dollars to prosecute Casey over the years, and he has told federal attorneys he plans to spend a like amount fighting them. When Burton J. Stanley, an attorney for the Department of the Interior, took over the case eight years ago, his predecessor handed him the thick file and said, "You have a massive trespass case up in Susanville. Good luck."

Stanley is now trying to revoke all of Casey's grazing privileges in California and Nevada, but he says of that effort, "My hunch is he can outlast us with the present procedures we have. It is frustrating to me how a government can be so impotent."

Not all Nevada ranchers are as openly intransigent as Casey.

Dean A. Rhoads is the new breed. Polished, articulate, and educated, Rhoads exudes moderation and reason as president of the Public Lands Council, an offshoot of the National Cattlemen's Association. The Nevada legislator and rancher lives near Elko, the administrative center for the BLM's most productive grazing district in the West and a hotbed of organizational activity for national cattlemen's groups. He is one of the founders of the Sagebrush Rebellion.

Rhoads is likely to come on with the "aw shucks, we ranchers aren't used to talking" bit, but this is not true of him or other politically active cattlemen who like to hide their effectiveness behind an Old West image. There is, however, one image Rhoads wants to disassociate his colleagues from, and that is the image of "all of us driving around in white Cadillacs and smoking cigars while we abuse the lands." Most ranchers are simply independent businessmen relying on a herd of cows for their livelihood.

As a Nevada legislator, Rhoads has supported the movement to get the federal government to hand over public lands to the state. These lands would then be passed on to private interests, such as ranchers. A similar movement after World War II led to the first conservationist outcry on grazing matters since passage of the Taylor Grazing Act in the mid-1930s. A series of columns by historian Bernard DeVoto in *Harper's Magazine* alerted conservationists to the threat. "It is the forever recurrent lust to liquidate the West that is so large a part of western history," wrote DeVoto.

≺ ≻

Besides federal bureaucrats, politicians, ranchers, and environmentalists, there is a fifth interest group involved in shaping grazing policy on public lands—the academic community in the western land-grant colleges and universities. This community specializes in rangeland management and has, with few exceptions, been solidly allied with the ranching interests, which in turn have the political power to determine higher education budgets and sometimes serve as regents of the various schools.

Roger Beers, an attorney for the Natural Resources Defense Council, said he canvassed western schools but could find no range specialists who wanted to participate in the lawsuit to require the BLM to file meaningful impact statements. C. Eugene Knoder, director of the Western Environmental Science Program for the National Audubon Society, had a hard time finding an unbiased researcher for a study of Forest Service management of national grasslands. Steve Gallizioli of the Arizona Game and Fish Department says, "The professors are mainly lined up alongside the ranchers, and that makes it tough."

A casual reading of comments submitted on one draft environmental impact statement compiled by the Bureau of Land Management shows the western academic community is touchy about any inferences that overgrazing has contributed to the deterioration of public lands. After all, the graduates of the various natural resource schools and departments are the ranchers and their regulators. Repeatedly, these points were made in the report: There is insufficient baseline data, and other uses of such lands, namely recreation and wildlife, are being favored. A few years ago two range experts at Utah State University, in a report written for the American Farm Bureau, concluded, "The grazing potential of western federal lands could be increased 75 percent through intensive improvement practices."

It would be nice if the western academic community tried to influence Americans to eat less beef. But that is about as likely as western politicians not listening attentively to their rancher constituencies, bureaucrats not trying to enlarge their turf, environmentalists not filing law suits, and ranchers raising fish—a protein-rich substitute for beef.

Meanwhile, those cows keep on munching more and more grass to satisfy such formidable American institutions as the backyard barbecue, the restaurant-bought steak dinner, fast-food chains, and the image of being a virile, red-blooded nation. And the environmental costs keep mounting on western rangelands.

Audubon, January 1979

The Crowding of the West

It was a cool and foggy morning in the 1840s when Joseph Warren Revere, grandson of Paul Revere, rode over the heavily forested hills of the Point Reyes Peninsula and out onto its rolling grasslands. There he spotted a herd of four hundred "superb fat" tule elk, and the slaughter began. The Mexicans and Indians in the party used lassos and lances; the Americans preferred guns.

Revere, a navy lieutenant, had been chasing bandits. But at the invitation of a local rancher, he had given up chasing men for elk on this day. Astride a horse that would not stand still, Revere fired blindly into the thickest part of the herd. "My shot accidently took effect, for when I was able to rein up, I returned to the spot and saw a poor doe lying in a reclining posture, the blood welling rapidly from a frightful wound inflicted by two heavy buckshot cartridges which had taken effect in the animal's shoulder. The unfortunate fixed upon me her large full eye, expressive at once of fright, sorrow, and reproach, and the mournfulness of the scene was heightened by the presence of a half-grown fawn, baaing and bleating around its dying mother." Both were quickly dispatched.

Before leaving, Revere and his party of sixteen, plus some Indians, gorged themselves on the meat and rendered the fat into tallow to be carried in hides back to his host's ranch. On the return ride Revere noted, "The Punta Reyes is a favorite hunting ground, the elk being attracted by the superior quality of the pasture—the land lying so near the sea that the dews are heavy and constant, adding great luxuriance to the wild oats and other grains and grasses. The elk are very abundant at this season and more easily killed than cattle. We passed many places, on our way back, where moldering horns and bones attest the wholesale slaughter which had been made in previous years by the rancheros of the neighborhood."

California was then an exploitative frontier society that could not afford and was not yet aware of the niceties of the conservation ethic. There is not much difference between this tale of slaughter and those of the buffalo and plume birds, except it is less well known.

In the late 1800s the tule elk, *Cervus elaphus nannodes,* was brought to the edge of extinction, there being perhaps one pair of elk remaining in the Central Valley. Once there had been a half million elk in the state. The population, protected for a number of years, has partially rebounded; there are now about eight hundred tule elk, and things are starting to get crowded.

Like other large mammals, the tule elk has strong anthropomorphic qualities that have attracted its own specialized, vocal conservation group—in this case, the Committee for the Preservation of the Tule Elk led by Beula Edmiston. She is a cause-oriented, dedicated woman who knows how to push the right buttons to make politicians and bureaucrats jump in Washington, D.C., and Sacramento, California. The nemesis of this specialized group, and vice versa, is the California Department of Fish and Game.

Both conservationists and bureaucrats have reacted predictably. Tule elk conservationists prefer a laissez-faire, free-roaming condition for the animals. The bureaucrats want to restrict the population, using such management techniques as hunting, culling, and transplanting. At another end of the equation are the economic interests, such as ranchers who feel threatened by the return of the subspecies. Tule elk compete with cattle for grazing and destroy fences. The elk have been shot illegally. It is a classic situation. It comes down to who is entitled to live off the land—humans, an introduced species, or once-native wildlife that have reemerged on the scene.

Within twenty years of Revere's shooting spree, the tule elk were to disappear from Point Reyes, a hook that juts into the Pacific Ocean forty miles north of San Francisco. They were not to return until last March, when ten heavily tranquilized elk were brought by horse trailer to what is now a national seashore administered by the National Park Service, grazed by beef and dairy cattle, and cherished by conservationists and tourists. The only people not happy about the return of the elk were Merv McDonald and his family.

Five generations of McDonalds have lived in western Marin County, where pockets of real ranching country still remain not too far north of the Golden Gate Bridge and west of the affluent suburbs in the eastern portion of the county. Merv McDonald's ancestors arrived in West Marin in 1888, after the tule elk had disappeared from the scene. They first ranched on the east side of Tomales Bay, then moved across to the west side and the Point Reyes Peninsula in 1962. In 1966, McDonald leased the Pierce Point Ranch at the northern tip of Point Reyes National Seashore; he has lived there with his family ever since. This year McDonald was confronted by the return of the natives, and it seemed one or the other would have to go. The ten elk—two bulls and eight cows—arrived at the ranch about the same time as a letter from Howard Chapman, western regional director of the National Park Service.

The letter referred to the unsuccessful five-year search for another ranch in the western states that McDonald could afford to buy, lease, or manage. It backed into the principal message: "With regret that you have not been successful in your endeavor but recognizing that this service, working with other federal agencies having any capacity to assist, has expended much effort and time in assisting you in searching for a substitute property on which to operate, nevertheless, I must request that you cease your business activities on this parcel of land and vacate the subject tract on or before November 1, 1978."

This was not the first eviction notice McDonald had received. In early 1973, shortly after the National Park Service acquired the twenty-five–hundred-acre property, the rancher was sent a much more tersely worded three-month notice. But it seemed that unless a miracle occurs or a court rules otherwise, McDonald will have to go this time. It made one wonder if the diminishing number of ranchers in West Marin are more of an endangered species than the multiplying elk. This certainly was the role in which McDonald's adept lawyer attempted to cast the rancher. But the real significance of Merv McDonald's story is how one man got crowded out, one species got crowded in, and how crowded the whole West is.

The present eight hundred elk throughout the range have sprung from the single pair found in the tule marshes of the southern San Joaquin Valley in 1875. They have outgrown one habitat after another—their moves being dependent on ranchers's complaints. By 1905 the original Buttonwillow herd had reached 145; by 1923 it was 400; then it crashed to 72 at the time the large ranch on which it grazed was subdivided into 40- and 160-acre parcels. One researcher commented, "Probably the small operators applied their own brand of damage control."

Between 1904 and 1934 a number of transplants were made. Most failed. A notable success was the move to the Owens Valley on the eastern side of the Sierra Nevada. This was not native range, but the elk flourished to the point where the ranchers in the early 1940s pressed the Department of Fish and Game for public hunts. A series of hunts were held from 1943 to 1969. At first unsupervised—hunters shot from moving vehicles into the herds, recalling the Point Reyes hunt a century earlier—the hunts subsequently became more tightly controlled, with a resultant reduction in the crippling losses.

Public pressure from conservationists brought an end to the hunts in 1969. Yet the problem of crowding remained. As researcher Dale R. McCullough wrote, "Throughout its known history, the tule elk has displayed a remarkable ability to build up from reduced numbers. This is in marked contrast to typical cases of endangered species in which the populations are dwindling due to failures of reproduction or survival, the causes of which are poorly or not at all understood."

Realizing public hunts were out, at least temporarily, as an acceptable means of managing the Owens Valley herd, bureaucrats formed an interagency task force to search for additional habitat. In 1971 the task force came up with twenty-three possible sites for locating new tule elk herds; four, including Point Reyes National Seashore, were selected. That same year the state legislature passed a bill that set the statewide number of tule elk at 2,000 before there could be renewed hunting. It also set the maximum number of elk for the Owens Valley herd at 490 before they could be relocated. The bill provided, "Department personnel may cull sick or inferior tule elk, but only when this is done for the protection, enhancement, and healthy increase of the species." In 1976 Congress passed a resolution that backed up the state legislation but did not speak to the culling issue. Beula Edmiston was the prime force behind both moves. The elk, it should be noted, is not a threatened or endangered species under either federal or state law.

An aerial census of the Owens Valley herd in 1975 showed 400 elk. In 1976 there were 478—just short of the magic number of 490. With Fish and Game personnel aware of the tule elk's tendency to multiply, it should have come as no great surprise that the August 1977 census turned up 92 "surplus" elk.

The department, having done little to find additional habitat, moved predictably, as did conservationists. The next month the state agency published a notice of intent in several California newspapers that its personnel were going to shoot ninety-two tule elk. A copy of the notice was sent to Edmiston. A public hearing was held in the remote valley. All hell broke loose. The administration of Governor Edmund G. Brown, Jr., pledged to protecting nongame species, was deluged with letters, telegrams, and phone calls. Besides the hysteria and emotion, there was the legal argument that the Owens Valley herd was healthy and thus could not be culled, according to state law. E. C. Fullerton, director of the Department of Fish and Game, argued that if over-population continued, the elk would become unhealthy. And he claimed this gave him the authority to shoot the ninety-two surplus animals. The politically astute Fullerton, pressured by higher-ups, backed down.

The emotionally charged atmosphere created by the culling proposal got the Park Service moving on the 1971 plan to open up the national seashore to elk. The issue was soon to descend upon McDonald's head.

≺ ≻

The compromise whereby there are still ranches in the national seashore has worked quite well. In the early 1960s, when the proposal for the seashore (an oceanside national park) was being considered by Congress, the resident ranchers vigorously protested their pending eviction. The compromise allowed the ranch owners to continue operating during their lifetimes, if running cattle on the land was a compatible use. And, indeed, the pleasant pastoral scenes so close to the urbanized San Francisco area do seem to be compatible, as well as providing a ready source of milk and beef.

As a tenant, and not an owner, Merv McDonald has always been considered a separate case. McDonald's fate was sealed when the Pierce Point Ranch was determined to be suitable tule elk habitat by the interagency task force in 1971, and when the Committee for the Preservation of the Tule Elk began pressing for the animal's reintroduction.

Besides getting McDonald out, a fence had to be built before the elk were brought in and released from their temporary holding pen. The ten-foot-high fence seals off the northern tip of the peninsula and ostensibly will keep the elk confined to the twenty-five–hundred-acre ranch. Park Service and Fish and Game personnel determined the fence was necessary to keep the elk from competing with cattle for feed and knocking down ranchers's fences in the pastoral zone of the national seashore. It was hoped confinement would keep the elk from adding to the depredations already being committed by fallow and axis deer, two exotic species that roam the seashore and periodically are shot by park rangers to keep their numbers at a certain level. (Between 180 and 240 deer are shot annually. While the state wildlife people use the euphemism "cull," the National Park Service prefers "direct herd reduction.")

There are two other arguments for constructing the fence that are a bit hard to follow. It is said the fence will keep elk off the roads. But the numerous deer are the greatest danger to night drivers in West Marin; surely the few elk would not significantly increase animal-vehicle collisions. And, it is argued, the one large fence will do away with the need for a number of small, rustic fences. Clearly, the National Park Service was reaching for justifications.

With little public discussion and analysis of the impact, the fence, a virtual Berlin Wall for animals, was built at a cost of forty-nine thousand dollars for materials alone across two and one-half miles of hilly terrain. Near the road, wooden rails were used for aesthetic purposes, while farther away hog wire was strung on reinforced posts. The fence was located just outside the wilderness area, and that was another problem. If the coming of the elk sealed McDonald's fate, the designation of the ranch as a wilderness area by Congress was surely double jeopardy.

McDonald, in turns, is obstinate and bitter. He feels he has been wronged, but the situation is not that black and white. He has become somewhat of a minor media martyr in this small county and alternately shows signs of enjoying the situation and of seeking to avoid it. At times during the last five years, he has assiduously looked for another ranch throughout the West. McDonald estimates he has put forty thousand miles on his car and spent ten thousand dollars in the search. At other times he has made moves to remain where he is.

John Sansing, superintendent of the national seashore, is the type of administrator who doesn't like to make waves. He saw more waves coming from the vocal conservationists than the ranchers. Before the National Park Service bought the land, Sansing warned McDonald that the plans were to take it over: "I personally told him I could not see any way he could continue ranching in that area," said Sansing.

In February 1973, the National Park Service sent McDonald his first eviction notice. Within the three-month time limit, a search for a replacement ranch was started. Contacts were made by McDonald and the Park Service in Idaho, Nevada, and Montana. It soon became apparent it would take longer than three months to find a ranch that would "pencil out," in the terminology of rancher economics. So the deadline was extended to October 1974. Sansing's superior, Howard Chapman, wrote the rancher that because of the elk and wilderness proposals, "we are becoming firmly committed to possession of the land on the October, 1974, date." When that date neared and no suitable new ranch had been found, the deadline was extended by one year; it was then extended twice more to the final date of October 31, 1978.

◄ ►

As McDonald was caught in a bind, so was the National Park Service, which found itself confronted by a problem symptomatic of the crowding of the West. As McDonald put it, "No cow-man is buying ranches in the West today. They can't afford it." A half million dollars was the most McDonald could raise with his own money and a $300,000 loan. There simply did not seem to be a ranch in the West that could be purchased or leased to support McDonald's operation at an economic level. There were a number of reasons. Land values were inflated beyond the cost of a valid cattle ranch because of development possibilities, ranches being operated at a profit as tax shelters would not make it solely on a working ranch basis, and the necessary grazing permits on public lands were tied up by others.

McDonald and land acquisition agents for the National Park Service found this was the case in Montana, Idaho, Nevada, California, Oregon, Washington, Utah, Arizona, New Mexico, Colorado, Wyoming, and Nebraska.

Last September, Robert Herbst, assistant secretary of the Interior Department, wrote McDonald's congressman: "Mr. McDonald appears to have intensively investigated replacement ranches in the western states. He has made inspections of properties and had discussions with brokers, owners, trustees, and Farmers Home Administration officials. He would lease, but has not found a property or properties to lease. All his investigations appear to support his conclusion that none of the ranches offered for sale are economically feasible to operate as economic units or are priced so high as to preclude them from consideration, or both. . . . Frankly, the Park Service and the Department of the Interior are in a dilemma in that apparently a suitable replacement ranch which is within the financial means of Mr. McDonald is not available."

The National Park Service, required by law to find suitable replacement housing, felt the increasing squeeze as the elk were readied for shipment to Point Reyes and McDonald remained firmly ensconced. Steve Gasper, a realty specialist for ten years with the Park Service, was assigned to find McDonald a new home. In one month Gasper, sometimes accompanied by McDonald, combed Oregon, Idaho, New Mexico, Colorado, Nebraska, Arizona, and Utah. Looking for a ranch that would support one thousand cows at $600 per animal unit for a total outlay of $500,000, the realty specialist came up with a couple of ranches at $1.5 million, or between $1,500 and $2,000 per animal unit.

Nope, said McDonald, maintaining, "We are in the cow business. We don't want to do anything different than we are doing now, and certainly not at a loss."

To Gasper it was frustrating. "I have never run into anything like this before. I have been relocating people and ranches and cows and goats and everything, but I never have run into something like the McDonald situation. Why, I relocated a zoo once and actually made money out of it. The problem is to find a working ranch where the McDonald family can make the payments and a living."

Gasper outlined the problem in the dining room of the Pierce Point Ranch at a meeting with environmentalists called by the rancher's attorney, Albert Bianchi. The lawyer was attempting to use a loose alliance forged recently between ranchers and environmentalists to pressure the National Park Service into letting McDonald remain or to make it financially easier to buy a new ranch. The environmentalists favored the second approach.

Conservation groups throughout the West realize viable ranching is a good way to preserve open space. So, in Marin County they have pushed for higher milk prices and drought relief measures; in California there has been a concerted drive for legislation to protect prime agricultural lands from subdividers; and else-where in the West, environmentalists have worked with ranchers on the issue of grazing public lands. But it became clear around McDonald's dining room table that they were not about to give up tule elk for cows. That some such sacrifices will eventually have to be made in the ever more crowded West seems inevitable.

Audubon, July 1978

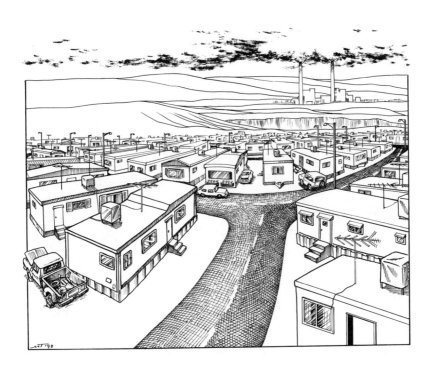

Craig, Colorado, Population Unknown

There are a number of ways to describe the town of Craig, Colorado, population unknown, elevation 6,185 feet above sea level.

First of all, the population is unknown because the town is growing so fast. The 1970 census placed the population at 4,205. Between 1960 and 1970, the population increased 5.5 percent in Craig. Projections place the Craig area's population at over 10,000 for this year, an increase of 140 percent in the last seven years. But nobody is sure of the exact figure, other than to know intuitively that there has been a huge increase. The elevation has remained a constant.

Craig is the kind of town where the Chamber of Commerce

has an "attitude adjustment hour" before a dinner meeting. It is a place where people rise and place their right hands over their hearts and sing when the band plays the "Star Spangled Banner" at the start of a high school basketball game. It is where the Kiwanis Club, to celebrate the coming of spring, puts on an all-male revue at the fairgrounds that gets raunchier as the evening progresses. It is where highway signs are inevitably splattered by bullet holes and traffic is incessant on dusty, ill-repaired streets. On Friday night, after the paychecks have been cashed, there is liable to be a lot of "hootin' and hollerin' "; and there may be some fights in the numerous bars. On Saturday morning people go shopping in their pickup trucks, and Sunday is for rest.

There is not much to say about Craig's aesthetics. They are mostly lacking. The town lies in a valley along the Yampa River, which feeds into the Green River, which feeds into the Colorado River. It is a typical high-country town. The streets are laid out in the four compass directions. There is a main street, Highway 40, that bisects the town. And there is the usual collection of stores to serve the minimal needs of the inhabitants. Craig's western flavor, if it ever existed, has been erased by the pursuit of progress. What exists now is actually more typically western than any hitching posts and false-fronted buildings. The preferred architecture is Safeway and Western Auto Stores moderne. Craig is remote. As the inhabitants say, "We are one mountain pass from everything." That includes the urban areas of Denver, Grand Junction, and Salt Lake City. It is a long way from the northwestern corner of Colorado to anywhere else.

The land surrounding Craig in Moffat County does not vary greatly. Sagebrush dominates the low rolling hills. There is some oak brush and serviceberry on the slopes where the snow remains longest. At the higher elevations there are juniper woodlands and some aspen. Most of the land has been overgrazed. The dominant mammal is the rodent. It is a High Plains climate on a semiarid steppe with an average temperature of forty-two degrees and 13.4 inches of rain in an average year. But the last two years have been far from average, and Craig, like most of the West, is suffering from drought. Open range predominates. There is some dry-land farming, oil production, strip-mining for uranium and coal, and two power plants. More coal mines, railroads, roads, dams, and plants are planned.

Craig is an energy boom town. This does not make it distinctive in the West. It fits right into the pattern established by Rock Springs, Gillette, and Wheatland, all in Wyoming; Colstrip, Montana; Farmington, New Mexico; Moab, Utah; Page, Arizona; and a dozen other communities either targeted for or already experiencing rapid growth because of nearby energy projects.

The West is changing rapidly from a rural, agriculturally oriented area to an urban, energy-producing culture with all the benefits and costs of an industrialized society. Low-sulphur coal is the name of the game, and the lands of northwest Colorado are laced with the nation's most abundant sources of energy. What the production of energy has wrought, and will continue to bring about at an increasing tempo, is the second major land-use revolution in the West—the first being the change from open lands to agricultural use with the invasion of livestock in the latter part of the nineteenth century. Booms and busts are not new, either to Craig or most of the other affected communities. What is new this time is the magnitude and the rapid, irrevocable pace of the transition. In the West, growth goes where the water goes, and water is going for energy these days, not agriculture, which at best is standing still.

In Craig, where the issues are less environmental and more sociological, it is primarily the people, not the land, that will bear the scars. A former mayor of Craig, Doyle Jackson, put it best. In testimony last year to a state legislative committee, the former mayor said, "The highest toll exacted from boom towns is the literal destruction of a community which in the past sustained and nurtured its people. The decline in the quality of life has stolen a community from its people." Jackson later sold his business and left town.

Craig, unlike Rock Springs where organized crime and prostitution took over, is not an exaggerated example of an energy boom town. This is one reason I visited it. The more subtle but no less devastating impacts, such as those described by Jackson, are easier to find when not hidden by gross deformities. But this is not just the story of Craig, Colorado, population unknown. It is an accurate portrayal of the contemporary West during the 1970s.

≺ ≻

The town has been studied to death. Along the way I collected a foot-high stack of documents ranging from the "Final Environmental Statement for Northwest Colorado Coal" to the standard brochure handed out by the Chamber of Commerce ("This is Craig, Colorado, nestled in a peaceful valley along the Yampa River"). There are more documents that I missed collecting. Jim Pankonin, county planning director, points to a stack on a table in his office and says, "All we have now are studies, but that doesn't help." The studies have facts, figures, but no human quotient. They are quickly outdated. Nevertheless, studies are a useful framework and give the illusion of substance. Here are some examples.

In 1974, the Federation of Rocky Mountain States portrayed a hypothetical energy boom town, called "Resource City," in a report. The example fits Craig and similar communities. It states:

Nearly four years have passed since three major companies began in earnest to claim the rich minerals and energy fuels from the land in and near Resource City. Once a small agricultural and mining community isolated 150 miles from the nearest large city, Resource City is now suddenly alive.

Bulldozers, trucks, heavy equipment, plant construction, crowds of people, and trailer camps have transformed Resource City almost overnight. The city has awakened to a whole new range of environmental crises as well as complex social problems.

The population of Resource City has more than doubled since 1970. Unprepared for the environmental and "people" impacts, the city is now faced with critical shortages in housing and public services as well as severe problems related to transportation, public finances, and environmental pollution.

Qualified teachers to staff the inadequate schools and temporary classrooms are scarce and difficult to retain.

Despite high wages and good employment opportunities, the crowded, unpleasant living conditions have caused high job turnover, a fourfold increase in welfare recipients, a 400 percent increase in crime, twice as many probationers as before, and a high number of suicide attempts and mental hospital admissions.

"We just got more than we bargained for," the mayor of Resource City says. Impact studies and projections by the new Resource City industries and state and local planners have often underestimated the impact and proportions of the boom. Resource City is overshadowed with constant uncertainty.

Industry and government officials alike are struggling with their dilemma, but current institutional arrangements have combined to block possible solutions. They are trying to shorten the inevitable lag between the time any boom begins and the time the tax base increases enough for the government to provide adequate public services.

Both groups, working together, have been frustrated again and

again by the complex pattern of interrelated governmental jurisdictions and by the lack of coordinating mechanisms.

One of the best ways to describe an area is by using its own
words, and this is what has been done in the "Moffat County/
Craig Capital Improvement and Development Program." This is
what the town's leaders think of themselves:

> The Craig community and its citizens can best be characterized
> by terms such as self-reliant, thrifty, proud, independent, forth-
> right, and practical. These values were forged out of the common
> experiences of early Craig and Moffat County settlers. Isolated
> from major support systems, the citizens of this area of the state
> learned to be dependent on themselves, if for no other reason than
> just to survive.

Then there is the viewpoint of the developer. In this case the
Colorado-Ute Electric Association was proposing to build the
Yampa project, a power plant now under construction south of
town. The Rural Electrification Administration put together an
environmental impact statement on the project which declared:

> The quality of life as measured materially will, however, im-
> prove as a result of the Yampa project. City and county residents
> alike will benefit from improved schools, hospitals, and services.
> A greater variety of retail service establishments will be available,
> and new employment opportunities will cover a much broader
> range than is presently the case.

A historical study of northwest Colorado by the Bureau of
Land Management (BLM) puts the present boom in perspective.
It reads:

> This region's history was one of constant 'booms' that never
> worked out. From fur to mining, cattle to oil, coal to oil shale
> and back to coal, the northwest corner of Colorado showed great

promise, but for various reasons it has never been able to fulfill the dream that seemed so real.

In addition, sheep, uranium mining, building of Highway 40, and construction of the railroad all caused their own booms. Land sales in the early part of the century promoted by the *Denver Post* brought thousands of settlers into the region. In 1929 there were about forty one-room schools in the county. Today there are two.

The boom-bust cycle caused a somewhat cheery golden jubilee publication to remark, "It has been said of the Craig community that just when its economic life looked bleakest something always happened to start it rolling again, and its history bears out the statement." A somewhat different view was elicited by a public opinion poll sponsored by W. R. Grace & Company, which was proposing a coal strip mine.

> The erratic nature of mineral-related development has left residents skeptical regarding growth. . . . Although economic growth is seen as beneficial to the area, there is the fear that mineral-related growth is temporary and that after a limited period of expansion the economy once more will experience a decline.

Not surprisingly, the survey found that those people who favored growth expected to make money from it. They were in such categories as merchants, business people, doctors, attorneys, and land owners. Those opposed tended to be in lower-income groups, which "seem to sense instinctively that the benefits of growth do not trickle down to them, that they do not share significantly in the community's increased wealth, and that, in many cases, they may be hurt most by growth." Those surveyed in 1974 would be unhappy with the way growth has now occurred in Craig. Only twenty-five percent wanted a community larger than ten thousand inhabitants, and eighty percent wanted steady growth. Benefits cited were increased employment, greater income, and shopping facilities. Costs were overcrowded schools, loss of small-town atmosphere, and increased crime. Forty-five percent thought the benefits would be greater than the costs, twenty-three percent thought the opposite would be true, nineteen percent thought benefits and costs would be equal, and thirteen percent were unsure.

The "Final Environmental Statement for Northwest Colorado Coal," written by the Bureau of Land Management, outlined the impacts on the area by 1990 from fourteen mines, three power plants, 86 miles of new railroads, 90 miles of new roads, and 350 miles of new power lines. The population in the Craig area by 1990 would be around twenty-four thousand, air quality would be degraded, 26,010 acres would be disturbed, and the rapid growth would create "social disorders."

So much for studies. This is what they were talking about that week in Craig, Colorado.

Friday: The Moffat County High School basketball team, nicknamed the "Bulldogs," had nine wins and no defeats in league play. It also had a superstar by the name of Brett Winder, of whom one awed spectator of his athletic achievements said, "He has more than four letters." Actually Brett is less than a four-letter athlete, but the aura he projects is one of natural athletic prowess. Brett, a senior, had scored fifty-one points in a previous game and was looking for an athletic scholarship to college. He also played quarterback on the football team.

In small western towns, high school sports play a large role in community life. The local newspaper had printed an editorial urging the team on to victory against its archrival, Rangely. The crowded gym that Friday night had many more adult than student faces. They were uniformly white, short-haired, and clean-shaven. Many of the adult faces in the stands were older versions of the class pictures lining the wall of the corridor that runs at right angles to the gym. There was a sense of continuity.

Before the game Brett moved easily among the milling crowd, accepting with regal grace the wishes of good luck from adults and students. He was last into the locker room to suit up and last out on the court. Brett knew his role as hometown hero and played it with bravado, which irked the few rooters for the scrappy Rangely High School team. One woman yelled, "We know you're God, Winder."

A Rangely cheer was "Beat Triple A," referring to the fact that Moffat was still playing in the Double A league although increased enrollment owing to energy projects had recently put it into the next higher league. The game was accompanied by a great deal of pomp and circumstance furnished by pom-pom girls, cheerleaders, and the band, which beat out such tunes as the Notre Dame fight song and "Rock Around the Clock." The obvious closeness of the team and its supporters gave me a sense of nostalgia for earlier, simpler days, or at least how they were depicted. It was a scene out of a Norman Rockwell cover for the *Saturday Evening Post*.

The team had played together since junior high school, which was unusual considering the large number of new students in the last few years. Some said the coach favored local boys. Winder said the kids of construction workers did not get on athletic teams "because they move around so much." Craig won its tenth league game that night, 85 to 83, after three overtimes. Winder had twenty-eight points. The crowd was ecstatic.

Earlier that same day a weekly ritual had taken place outside the Rancho Deluxe, nicknamed the "Raunchy Rancho" by local residents. The Rancho was unabashedly built to service the con-

struction workers on the Yampa power plant project. The prefabricated, squat, brown building on the road from the construction site looked more like a warehouse than a bar. The solid
wooden bar, which ran almost the entire length of the west wall,
was made for heavy drinking. The hotpants-clad waitresses were
quite efficient. There was also dancing, but that was strictly a
sideline.

The sign outside read, "Now appearing, Whiskey River. Ladies Nite." Shortly after 3 P.M. a man dressed in a sleeveless
down jacket and carrying an aluminum stepladder came out of
the dark recesses of the bar, set the stepladder down, and climbed
up to change the lettering from "Ladies Nite" to "Payroll Checks
Cashed." And another raucous Friday night was about to begin
in Craig's numerous bars.

Saturday: Things start slowly on Saturday mornings, what
with Friday night and the previous week to recover from. But
they build to a crescendo of slowly moving traffic up and down
the town's streets in the late morning hours as the week's shopping begins with whatever was left over from the previous day's
paychecks. At a shoe store in the Country Mall—touted as the
only covered mall in northwest Colorado—there is a special on
boots. With practically no snow this winter, boots have not sold
too well. Says the owner, "The men at the plant say they don't
feel comfortable coming in here and tracking dirt all around, but
I say it's good, clean, honest work dirt."

Out at Shadow Mountain Village, Saturday morning is a time
to work on the family car or do odd jobs around the mobile
home. Shadow Mountain is a mobile-home community built by
Colorado-Ute for its construction workers. It has all the amenities and far outshines the numerous other mobile-home parks
that surround the outskirts of Craig. There is a handsome, nine-
thousand-square-foot clubhouse with a heated indoor swimming

pool, saunas, hydromassage pool, volleyball courts, pool room, playgrounds, lounge, and meeting room. But Shadow Mountain is a golden ghetto. Separated by a low ridge from the rest of town, it is another world. Old-time residents envy the indoor swimming pool, from which they are barred. Construction workers feel the town is unfriendly.

Jack McCalister, originally from Oklahoma City, was working on his car that frigid morning. It was parked in front of his mobile home; space 561, Shadow Mountain Village, is the address. McCalister is an ironworker who was to start work at the Yampa project again after being laid off earlier that winter. He represents a new type of western gypsy, a construction worker who has followed his trade to various military and energy-related projects.

McCalister had this to say about Craig and his way of life:

> The town is a ripoff. The prices are really high. The townspeople notice it, and they blame the construction workers for the high prices. But it is not really us. It is the business people who are to blame. I like traveling around to different jobs. This climate is really wonderful in the summertime. We don't miss Oklahoma at all. There is a lot of deer and elk hunting, and I got an antelope last season. And the fishing is good down at the Green River. We keep to ourselves out here, and our friends are other plant workers. We go into town to shop or go to one of the bars. What my daughter doesn't like about the high school is the different cliques—the locals and plant kids. She played on the girls' basketball team for a while but gave it up. We started a church out here last week, meeting in a trailer for prayer meetings and Bible study. We went to church in town, but it seemed more like it was a social gathering, so we quit going. Besides, the pastor wasn't friendly. He wouldn't speak to us. We pay $69 a month for our space. The sewer and water are free. We pay for electricity

and gas. This is cheap compared to what the places in town cost. We couldn't touch a home around here. The same house in Oklahoma City would cost half as much.

Later that day I bumped into Mrs. McCalister in the clubhouse. Margie McCalister had this to say: "I feel we kind of invaded their privacy in Craig. I feel more comfortable out here with people I have something in common with. Besides, Marilyn, our daughter, just isn't very excited about the reception she got in town."

Mrs. McCalister said a Women's Club had been organized at Shadow Mountain. At the last luncheon meeting—a salad pot luck—Judy Dunn won the door prize, which was a cream sachet. There was $9.10 collected from donations. This will go toward purchasing flatwear for the clubhouse kitchen. Lois Wise spoke to the women about T.O.P.S. (Take Off Pounds Sensibly). Another weightwatchers' group has been organized at Shadow Mountain. It is called K.O.P.S. (Keep Off Pounds Sensibly) and is aimed at maintaining proper weight. The Craig mental health clinic has started holding rap sessions at Shadow Mountain.

Sunday: Besides being a day of rest, Sunday might also be called a day for recreation. Because of the rolling, open terrain, snowmobiles are popular in Craig. One count places the number at six hundred. In the winter some people go ice fishing. On this warm, virtually snowless day both activities were hard to find, but a few people were making a stab at it in the higher elevations. This is big fishing and hunting country. "Guns and Tackle" read the signs on sporting goods stores. And ranchers don't take kindly to trespassing, whether real or imagined, on public lands they regard as their own. There have been some ugly incidents. One rancher near Steamboat Springs shot thirty-three dogs in two years. He said the dogs were harassing his sheep.

At the eastern end of the region, closer to the urban area of Denver, one starts running into more modish styles of life. Steamboat Springs was promoted into the big leagues of skiing in the early 1970s by an aerospace firm using a hip western image. That image did for Steamboat Springs what the Marlboro Country ads do for the cigarette. The public relations campaigns are masculine and sexual, portray beautiful country, evoke earlier times, and are inaccurate as far as the realities of life in the new West are concerned. A more appropriate image would be a spotless four-wheel-drive pickup truck replete with gun rack, outsized snow-and-mud tires, citizens band radio, stereo tape deck, and large mud flaps over the rear wheels emblazoned with "Colorful Colorado." It would be unlikely that this vehicle had ever seen a day of ranch work, but it would be ideal for a Sunday drive.

Monday: The most visible symbol of the new West is the mobile home. Whether on a ranch or in town, mobile homes are omnipresent. Older log, wood, and brick structures are falling into disrepair. People are just not building new homes out of those traditional materials. The typical mobile home on the range is made of sharply rectangular, off-white-colored metal. It cannot help but be intrusive. It is also economical. And it can be moved. One survey found that more mobile-home units were planned in Craig than apartments and traditional homes combined.

To understand this phenomenon I went to the local mobile-home dealer. Bob Kriewald, a salesman, launched into an immediate sales pitch. It went this way:

> I bought my house in 1967. It was built in the 1950s during the previous oil boom. It had been on the market for five or six years. They wanted $22,000. I offered $17,000. It was a ridiculous offer, but they took it. Last year I was offered $65,000 for

it. It is not Nob Hill [in San Francisco], but it is the best section of town. I had the Ford dealership in town and sold it last year for a nice profit. I wanted to get out because I had to change my way of doing business. Credit and checks were getting to be a problem. Everything was getting more complicated. Any number of people sold their businesses. They were getting good prices and had seen ups and downs. Why wait for another down and in the meantime have to do business differently?

Kriewald then got around to mobile homes.

To buy land for a home costs a minimum of $10,000. Sewer and water hookup is another $1,000. A house will cost around $40,000, so the total will be near $55,000 after you add up everything. The payments will be over $400 a month, plus you have to put more money down. There are very few used homes on the market. Now a furnished mobile home will cost $14,000 to $15,000. That is for three bedrooms, a bath and three-quarters, kitchen, and living room. The payments will be about half of those for a new house. It is paid off quicker. Plus it is movable. It is a hell of a buy for the money. But the workmanship is not that great.

Kriewald then got off the topic of mobile homes and recalled what it was like in Craig during the late 1960s and early 1970s when he and other businessmen were having difficulties. "We didn't care if we had four feet of soot here, as long as we could eat. So what if it sooted up, it was no worse than the dust."

Monday is the day the county commissioners meet in the courthouse. Although there are probably more newcomers than natives now living in Craig, political power remains in the hands of the older residents on the county commission, city council, and school board. There is no question the spoils get handed out unevenly. Craig is still very much a small town; "smaller than a small town in terms of attitude" is what one astute resident said.

There are interlocking ties among those who wield power. This is no different than in a large city, only more openly accepted. The energy developments are in county territory, although most of the growth impact is within city limits. Two of the three county commissioners have close ties to energy companies. Before becoming a county commissioner, Ora Harris helped Utah International get options on coal lands because he was on the board of the utility that was seeking to build the Yampa project. Utah International will supply Colorado-Ute with coal. Harris said he was not paid by Utah International for his services. One of the biggest thrills of Harris's life was when he shook the hand of the president of Utah International at a stockholders's meeting in San Francisco. Don Beckett, the second county commissioner, receives payments from W. R. Grace & Company, which has an option for coal on his land. For some landowners such payments can amount to ten thousand dollars a month.

Bob Sweeney, publisher and editor of the local newspaper, used to be mayor. There were jokes about his going editorially soft on city government at the time. But, people say, the real decisions that shape the area are made by a select group that plays poker and golf together. And the county commissioners are as apt to make a decision around the luncheon table in the Cosgriff Motor Hotel as in the commission's public sessions.

The county commissioners sit at a long table on a raised dais, and the atmosphere is relaxed and clubby. The commissioners talk to each other, take phone calls, shuffle papers, and walk in and out. A little sign on the table before Chairman Chester Watson reads, "Chairman of the Bored." But Watson, a retired rancher and businessman, is not bored. He led the two newcomers to the commission carefully through the day's deliberations. That evening a delegation of residents from Dinosaur, a small settlement at the western end of the county near Dinosaur National Monument, requested a resident deputy sheriff because of the influx of energy workers. Watson, with an eye on the budget and a number of jokes about penny pinching, astutely guided the discussion to a point of no commitment.

Earlier that day the suspender-clad Watson had bitterly complained, "The impact is here, and we can see it. It is disgusting that we have to fight it out with the state for money."

The commissioners do not act in the best interests of the energy companies all the time. When Colorado-Ute was judged to be uncooperative, the commissioners simply ceased to issue any more permits. This stopped construction. "That moratorium sure brought them out of the sagebrush and got them to talk to us again," recalls Watson.

Tuesday: This was the day to tour the mines with personnel from the Bureau of Land Management. Like Commissioner Harris, who was greatly impressed by the monied people he had met at the San Francisco stockholders's meeting, the supposed regulators are awed by the money behind energy companies—seen most immediately in the form of large capital outlays for gigantic pieces of machinery. On this day, at the mine of Energy Fuels Corporation, the sight of the massive dragline, the largest in Colorado, brought out the cameras and questions of the BLM employes.

The dragline, immaculately painted red and white, is quite impressive. Costing $10 million, it took eighty-three train cars to transport the parts to the mine where it was assembled. Operating the dragline costs eight thousand dollars monthly in electricity. The shovel at the end of the 325-foot boom strips away the overburden and exposes the coal seam.

Later, BLM officials passed a poster in the mine office labeled, "The Last Great Act of Defiance." It depicted a small mouse squatting with its back to the viewer. The mouse was making an obscene gesture to a huge, hovering eagle labeled "Department of Interior." The BLM is a branch of that department and is responsible for leasing federal coal lands. There was no comment.

Most of the mine's 290 employes are part-time ranchers. A company brochure describes one: "Perry Hoffman, heavy equipment operator and part-time cattleman, enjoys hunting and fishing in Routt County, where he has resided for 17 years. Horseback riding and snowmobiling are other activities on his busy schedule that includes the presidency of United Mine Workers Local 1344." The opening up of energy projects in the Craig area is robbing the ranchers of a labor supply. With farm laborers getting $3.00 an hour, a $7.50 an hour job sweeping floors at the mine is a great deal more attractive.

In commenting on the environmental impact statement for the mine, the Colorado Department of Agriculture stated, "The resulting farm labor shortage intensifies the trend toward increased mechanization of agriculture, which is often difficult to justify economically. According to a Routt County farmer, he recently bought $100,000 worth of machinery to put up $15,000 worth of hay." Often, to keep a ranch operating, a husband and sometimes the wife will get salaried jobs. Energy companies buy some ranchlands for coal rights, others are purchased for railroad and transmission line rights of way. Nearby developments raise the value of farmlands, resulting in higher taxes and an increased loan value. A ranch can become a liability or a nest egg. But eventually ranchlands seem to be headed for other uses. The department's comments noted, "A sale at significantly increased prices can usually be justified only if the buyer has a nonagricultural use for the land in mind." Remarked one rancher, "One of these days they are going to wake up and find that we are an endangered species." Moffat County raises more sheep than any other county in the state, and its wheat, which has a high protein content, is highly desirable for baking bread. So the loss would be noted.

On the night I went to the Craig City Council meeting, the items first discussed on the agenda were all growth related. A developer asked the council for a letter of intent to serve a sixteen-acre industrial subdivision with sewer and water. His pitch was that small businesses, like welding, could not afford to pay twenty-five thousand dollars an acre for the more desirable sites. His development would sell such sites for thirty-one hundred dollars an acre. Another developer offered to swap a piece of property he bought on speculation for the present City Hall site. His site, the developer stressed, was out of the downtown area and would not contribute to already bad traffic congestion.

A city employe asked the council to raise the mileage allowance for private vehicles from fifteen cents to eighteen or twenty cents, "what with all the prices going up around here."

Police Chief Roger Clausen said his men would like an increase from the twelve cents per mile they were being paid. The matter was rather pressing he said, since the department was short of official cars. They had use of one 1964 Ford with a blanket over the front seat and a citizens band radio. All the other police cars were broken down, and the new ones had not yet arrived. One councilman joked, "They use horses in New York, don't they?" The situation was particularly desperate, the chief said, since there had been a sixty-four percent increase in calls in January over the corresponding period in 1976.

The council then launched into an interminable discussion on whether the police should investigate crimes, such as auto thefts, instigated in the city but resolved elsewhere. The chief, who does not get along with Sheriff Robert Kelly, pointed out to the council that it was his department that had cracked an interstate auto theft ring, although the sheriff made the arrest in county territory and got the credit in the newspaper. (The sheriff tells me that prostitution occurs within city limits. The chief says drugs come from the power plant in county territory. The sheriff is a deeply religious man who has a sign on his desk, "All knowledge is from God," while the chief, newly arrived from Colorado Springs, flies an airplane and is dressed in the style of a Los Angeles police detective, as portrayed in television serials.) The council closely questioned the four-hundred-dollar phone bill Clausen ran up while investigating the auto theft ring. The debate prompted Clausen to go out and get drunk that night.

Wednesday: I met the chief, who was suffering from a hangover, late the next morning at the three-room mobile home behind the City Hall that serves as the police station. He was going out to pick up breakfast at a drive-in in his flashy pickup truck with a box full of stereo tapes on the front seat and a flashing red light mounted on the dash. "The city council is ignorant about law enforcement," he snapped.

Settling down at his desk with a greasy hamburger that had been wrapped to go, the chief launched into his problems. "We are a boom town, and all our problems relate to that. Everyone is half-broke when he comes here. This causes stress and trauma. Then you get things like child abuse, wife beating, and barroom fights. I've got a redneck town. They have very little respect for themselves, let alone anyone else. The town was unchecked before I got here." (Previous to Clausen's arrival, Sheriff Kelly was responsible for law enforcement in the city and the county.) "I pose a psychological threat to that."

Chief Clausen, 6 feet 7 inches tall and weighing 220 pounds, said of his recent run-in with Tom Shockley, the pugnacious owner of the Rancho Deluxe who allegedly pushed Clausen during a melee at the bar: "I know how to fight. I don't like fighting. I once taught self-defense. When I first came here I could have bumped some heads. But you can't win. It is like getting into a pissing contest with a lot of skunks. One of these days I am going to take Shockley out behind his bar and beat the shit out of him." When I was in Craig the fracas was one of the prime topics of conversation. The town seemed evenly divided. It was newcomer Clausen against local boy Shockley and proper law enforcement versus the traditional laissez-faire tolerance about what goes on in bars.

In the meantime, the chief has other problems to deal with. Last year, according to Clausen, the town had twenty-four suicides. And, as one might expect in the high country, most used guns. Clausen said the number of suicides is two hundred percent above what should be normal for a town of Craig's size. All other crimes are way up. Said Clausen, "We are running four times above any standard ever established for towns of this size." Drug use is out of control, and Sheriff Kelly estimates that eighty percent of all arrests are linked to alcohol. The sheriff runs the crowded county jail. "We have a tremendous increase in mental patients. We put them right in a regular cell. There is no padded cell or any way to keep watch on them until they can be transported to the state hospital at Pueblo."

To put all this unrest and crime in perspective, I walked from the police station to the homey office of the Craig branch of the Colorado West Regional Mental Health Center. There Anne Angerman and Charles Holmgren, the clinic's psychiatric social worker and pastoral counselor, told me their stories.

It wasn't too long ago that someone with long hair who came into town would get a friendly but forceful offer to have his hair cut with sheep shears. Now long hair is tolerated and almost *de rigueur* among construction workers. Modern trends have come to Craig later than elsewhere, but now they are coming faster than they used to. The pace of life has quickened. This leads to denial by the old-timers that significant changes are taking place. It is easier to deal with the pretense that there are no changes. For the newcomers, who have not developed the ability to entertain themselves, there are few options for spending free time. This leads to family problems, alcohol, and drugs. Holmgren said, "What we see in families is that one person is dissatisfied with Craig. A job brought them here, and there is little else to sustain them. What they say is that Craig is a hard place to get to know people."

The therapist portrayed this picture of family life at Shadow Mountain Village: "The couple married young. They are in their mid-thirties when their children are adolescents. The kids are not under control. The father is chasing after younger women, and the mother doesn't know how to cope with the situation. The father works, but the mother stays home and gets depressed and bitchy. What is good about Shadow Mountain is that there is a lot of support from others. But they are isolated from the rest of their families."

Angerman, who comes from a large midwestern city, organized an assertiveness training group for women in town as well as the Moffat County Women's Council. The council began to tackle such topical subjects as allowing the girls' basketball team to practice in the main gym that is normally reserved for the boys' teams. Angerman found Craig "very much a man's town," and the women in the assertiveness group began to pull back rather than confront male attitudes. "The threat of change was an overwhelming concern. The women outside the group did not want to change. So the group lowered its sights, and now we just have a support group for ourselves." Angerman's efforts to establish no smoking areas also failed. "They just don't care. They smoke if there is a sign or not."

The Reverend Gene Hutchins, minister of the Episcopal

Church, echoes many of the findings of the two counselors. He added, "There is a lot of crisis ministry here. The construction workers and their families move and bring their problems with them. Then there are the other people who have always been here. They feel threatened by these new people's problems. But they are really hardy people and strong willed. A problem is not to be discussed. It is dealt with in private."

Thursday: This was my last day in Craig, and I wanted to tie up some loose ends.

I decided to test the finding of the public opinion survey that the "haves" favor the energy boom while the "have nots" feel threatened by it. I sought out F. R. (Bob) Montgomery, president of the Moffat County State Bank. But first of all, I had to cash a traveler's check. I must say that in all my travels, I have never gone through a more careful scrutiny to get cash for what is supposed to be considered cash. There was a check to see if the traveler's check was stolen, a request for two pieces of identification, a local address, and more.

I mentioned this to Montgomery. He said, "We have taken some losses on checks. We require a little bit more identification now." When the boom started to hit Craig, Montgomery contacted fellow bankers in Rock Springs and found they had a lot of defaults on loans to transients. "We require them to be here nine months before we talk to them about a loan. Unless they are permanently established here, we just don't mess with them." Montgomery, who started as a teller and bookkeeper in the bank thirty years ago, said, "Our loan value has increased tremendously as have our deposits." Another bank has opened in town, but Montgomery doesn't mind the competition. "This kind of growth is good. You can't stop progress. We will have a more modern community when it's over."

The owner of the Galveston Restaurant, Hans Jacobson, sees

competition as a threat. Jacobson, a resident of Craig for eleven years, dropped live music in his bar because of fights and now caters to the juvenile trade with pool tables and football games. The franchised food chains like Kentucky Fried Chicken and Pizza Hut, recently opened in town, are playing havoc with Jacobson's business.

Sitting in the Galveston that day, drinking a morning cup of coffee, was Sherry Mondragon, who earns $2.75 an hour making pizza at the VFW (Veterans of Foreign Wars) Club. "Craig used to be a friendly place. But now the people say, 'The neighbors never speak to me anymore.' We never leave the house without locking the door. Last Christmas my mother was taking a nap. When she woke up, there was a man standing over her. He was taking the Christmas presents. When we were kids we walked to the show and football games. Now my sister is 15, and we won't let her walk after dark. A lot of women are getting assaulted."

So much for my quick test.

I stopped at the Chamber of Commerce for what I thought would be the standard line of the merchant interests. It started out that way with the secretary-manager, Alice Robinson, explaining to me why there was no boom in Craig but just normal, steady growth. Then it changed. "Sure we had people living in tents last year. There was housing, but they wanted to live out in the open and throw their garbage in the river. They threw their slop water right out there. In fact we had a camping place in the city park, but it had to be stopped. You couldn't believe the way they were living in that park. Clothes were hanging on trees. Dogs were running around. They had a good thing and had to abuse it. One family was even camped in a culvert. What if a flash flood had come through there?"

I decided to check on the school situation and went to see Superintendent Marv Grimm. His office is in a classroom on the second floor of a fifty-year-old building that had once been an elementary school. The building was closed when enrollment dropped and now holds overflow classes from the high school in addition to administrative offices. Parents had told me about the unusual amount of fighting—new versus old students—but Grimm, in the best tradition of school superintendents, skirted this controversial issue. He was more interested in telling me one elementary school had to write for the records of 145 new students and dispatched eighty-five records for students who were going to transfer away. Grimm admitted this turnover played havoc with classes. In the last five years there had been a forty-five percent increase in enrollment, but two school bond issues for new buildings had failed. There was a brochure explaining how to buy, lease, or rent modular classrooms on Grimm's desk.

To find out how an energy company regarded its responsibility toward the community, I talked to John Ward, manager of employe and government relations for W. R. Grace & Company's Colowyo mine. His answer was "Housing! So we don't put up crummy housing. We don't favor a company town, so we are going to put up a development west of town. There will be a 30-day option for mine employes, then it will be open for anyone else. We are not going to limit it only to our employes. We want a mix of interests. It is just a gut feeling that tells us this approach is right." The development will contain lots, single-family homes, apartments, and mobile-home spaces. Although the coal mine was going to start operations on a limited basis on March 1, ground had not yet been broken for the housing development.

And what other responsibilities do you feel toward the community? Ward replied, "We are doing $147,000 worth of work on bridges to strengthen them." Until the firm completes a railway to its mine, trucks will haul the coal over the county road on which the bridge work is being done. "We gave $10,000 to the expansion fund for the hospital, and we pay local property taxes. We will pay a severance tax if the legislature passes that bill." Ward admitted the coal industry was less than enthusiastic about the severance tax bill. Anything else? "We feel there has to be a governmental solution to these problems."

That evening, my last in Craig, I went to a dinner party on "Snob Hill," as the nice part of town located on the heights to the north is called. We talked through a dinner of local lamb about skiing, California, music, the hospital's problems, and whether it was best to remain in Craig forever or to see the outside world. The hostess was afraid her two high school–aged daughters would get trapped in the small-town syndrome of marrying young. A local guest said there was no need to know about any wider world than "cowboying, hunting, and fishing." The host unexpectedly turned to me and asked, "Well, what do you think after one week in Craig?"

I thought quickly. All my time up to that moment had been spent recording. There had not been time for reflection. Furthermore, my words might carry a lot of weight with these folks. Here was the stranger who in one week had cut across all segments of the town's social and economic strata. His presence and purpose since the first day had been known. But I had no special handle on their problems.

I answered that Craig was not the sort of place I would seek to live in. My preference was the coast. I had spent the last few years recording the swelling of the West, and I was ready to escape the bubble. I related the story of my search for land near Telluride in southwestern Colorado. The first forty-acre parcel I desired had subdivision pennants flying near it when I returned two days later. The second had geothermal drilling rights leased to an oil company and a one-hundred-foot right of way smack through the middle of it that was reserved for a Bureau of Reclamation dam project.

My drive at present, I explained, was to seek a growth-proof place. I told them I thought I had found it on the West Coast. The area was on the ocean and surrounded by lands administered by the National Park Service and the California Department of Parks and Recreation. It had the most comprehensive land-use control laws in the nation. The people who lived there did not want growth. I said I realized they were moving in the opposite direction—toward growth. If this was what they wanted, then they would have to make their own personal adjustments. If not, then they should move, as some had already done.

I said it was my experience that you could not have it both ways. I wished them good luck and left, but not before having a nightcap at the Raunchy Rancho.

Audubon, July 1977

Crazy Jake & Company

One of the most bizarre episodes in the West, one that is rife with the myths that have historically driven humans in this arid region, is now unfolding in the Superstition Mountains of Arizona, the supposed location of the Lost Dutchman Mine and buried Spanish treasure.

Whether the mine, which was reputed to have been fabulously rich, ever existed is extremely doubtful. What is known is that the Spaniards first mined the area but were massacred by the Apaches in 1848. Jacob Waltz, the Dutchman, claimed to have found a rich mine in the Superstitions, but he died in 1891 without revealing its whereabouts. Since then treasure hunters and miners have combed the mountains searching for gold and silver. None has found any, and fifty lives have been lost in the process while countless others have been maimed and scarred.

Some of the violence has been documented, such as the killing of Robert St. Marie in 1959. The following is the testimony at the coroner's inquest in Apache Junction:

Question—What did you say to him?

Ed Piper—I don't remember just exactly the words, but I asked him if he was going someplace or looking for something.

Q—What did he respond or what did he answer to that?

Piper—That is when he throwed that jacket off his gun. He said, "I will talk with this."

Q—And what did you do then after he pointed the gun at you?

Piper—I dropped and drawed at the same time and started shooting. I fired three times as fast as I could pull the trigger.

Q—And what did he say when he fell?

Piper—That she [Celeste Marie Jones] had hired him to come out and kill me.

Q—Now then, what did you do, Mr. Piper.

Piper—I stood there and talked with him a minute or two.

Q—And what did you talk about?

Piper—Well, I asked him if he was with Mrs. Jones and he said he was.

Q—And what else did you talk about?

Piper—Well, oh, didn't talk much of anything. He was wanting water and I didn't have any water. He had a canteen on him. He got it around to his mouth.

Q—And what did you do, Mr. Piper?

Piper—Well, I stood there and watched him awhile. Then I walked off and left him when he quit breathing.

Q—How did he get this 46 feet [from where St. Marie was shot to where he died]?

Piper—He worked himself down the hill. He kept throwing himself.

Q—And you were talking to him as he was going down the hill?

Piper—Yes, sir.

Like many things about the Superstition Mountains, Ed Piper's testimony seems unreal. It is too classic, too posed. At the time he supposedly shot the twenty-one-year-old Robert St. Marie, who had him covered with a pistol, Piper was sixty-five years old. The seventy-dollar-a-month pensioner had been in the mountains six years looking for the Lost Dutchman Mine.

The corner's jury ruled that Piper shot St. Marie in self-defense. The old man had a few years left before he died of cancer in the eight-man ward of Pinal County Hospital and was buried in a Potter's field. Some in the crossroads community of Apache Junction will tell you now that one of Piper's young workers shot St. Marie; and the old man took the blame, knowing that he would die soon.

The quick-draw shooting was one more legend to pile on top of others. The Superstition Mountains, an indistinct mass of cooled lava, seem to invite such stories and the violence that spawns them. There is little the human mind can hold onto—just a progression of rock spires, bluffs, steep cliffs, and treeless, chaparral-covered slopes, all shimmering in the crackling heat.

One exception to this mirage is The Needle, a solid, volcanic extrusion around which most of the activity takes place. There are a few other realities. Almost everyone wears a gun in the Superstition Mountains. A gun is a hard, cold fact. So is water, when it can be found. All else, like the 1959 shooting incident, glitters under the relentless sun.

Q—Do you know the reason why Mr. St. Marie took the walk?

Celeste Marie Jones—He said he wanted to look over the country because that was the first time he had been out there and it was so beautiful that he wanted to go up and sit on a boulder and take the little binoculars [opera glasses] and overlook the territory.

Q—Do you know why he took his revolver if he was just going for a walk?

Mrs. Jones—Well, he feared for our lives because . . . I think he said that he wanted to take the pistol just for protection.

Q—Protection against what, Mrs. Jones?

Mrs. Jones—Maybe some animals.

Forty-five miles east of the urban sprawl of Phoenix the rocks are crawling with rattlesnakes, javelina, and armed miners. There are no roads into the 125,000 acres of the Superstition Wilderness Area of the Tonto National Forest and no mechanized equipment is allowed into the wilderness area. Most travel is by horse, mule, or foot.

However, the wilderness area is far from being pristine. Cattle grazing and mining are permitted uses. Tin cans litter the trails, and miners have built semipermanent residences in the mountains. The miners also use helicopters to land supplies behind the Forest Service's back.

On a spring morning, just as it was beginning to heat up, I accompanied a Forest Service ranger into the mountains on an inspection trip. We traveled by horse. Neither of us was armed.

A short distance up the trail from First Water Ranch, one entry point into the wilderness area, a man with a pistol on one hip and a canteen on the other popped out from behind a rock.

"Howdy, my name is Smith. I work for Van Suitt. Just come

down the trail to straighten up a claim marker or two," said Smith.

The grizzled Smith moved on without another word. We continued up the trail.

A diamondback rattlesnake, hurrying across the trail, raised its head as if to strike and issued its telltale warning. Three rocks hurled by the ranger and me killed the snake. We did not hesitate to kill in this environment.

Violence was everywhere. A rusting car body was riddled with bullet holes, as was every tin can visible from the trail. Rocks on mountainsides were blasted apart with dynamite for no apparent reason. I had just returned from Vietnam. The difference was the lack of vegetation.

It didn't startle me that a young miner scrambled down from his diggings with gun in hand as we rode through his camp. He put the weapon aside when he saw the ranger's badge and picked up a puppy and fondled it. We rode on and made camp for the night.

Harry Van Suitt's first camp was located just below Palomino Mountain. He had ten workers and two other camps located deeper in the mountains. His was the largest operation in the wilderness. Van Suitt's claim stakes were everywhere. They were painted white and were not easy to miss. He had laid claim to about ten thousand acres since September and aimed to claim another twenty thousand.

There had been trouble in his camps. A few weeks ago Van Suitt shot one of his workers in both wrists with his .32-caliber automatic. Van Suitt said the worker had him and three other men covered with a .357-caliber magnum, but Van Suitt outdrew him. Others say the shooting occurred during an argument. After being shot, the worker was reported to have said, "If he had shot me once more, I would have quit." He was later fired.

A freelance photographer visited Van Suitt's camp after the incident and wouldn't stop taking pictures when Van Suitt asked him to halt. Van Suitt smashed his camera, twisted the lanyard around the photographer's neck, and began to choke him. A Forest Service ranger pulled Van Suitt off the photographer. The two saw Van Suitt go for his gun, then think better of it. Van Suitt was charged with aggravated assault.

> Q—Did you hire him, Mrs. Jones, to kill Mr. Piper?
> Mrs. Jones—No sir, no. I only hired him to help these workers to do the work on top of the peak there, that is all. I never hired anybody to do any dirty work or anything, because I am a Christian woman and I don't believe in no such thing as that. But this man [Piper] has given me hell since I have been over there.

Van Suitt was a heavy-set man. He had red hair and a red beard. His trademark in the scorched mountains was a fur-lined cap with ear flaps. He constantly cracked his knuckles. His eyes were green and steady, so steady that the impression was that what he saw was either far inside his head or very distant. I noted his features and wrote them down in my notebook later, in order to avoid the photographer's fate.

He came from Los Angeles where his family at one time owned West Coast Trade Schools. Van Suitt, who was thirty-four years old, estimated he had spent thirty thousand dollars on his quest for the Lost Dutchman Mine. He told me he didn't want any publicity now. "Come back in six or eight weeks and I will have a real story for you," he said.

He then abruptly changed his mind, and the words rushed out

in a monotone while he continued to crack his knuckles. I took out my notebook.

"I have found all the Peralta [old Spanish] mines and the Dutchman. I have found them and they are on my claims. I found them as the result of good, sound information. This is Twentieth Century information they don't teach in schools. This comes through the study of geothermal geology. Those rods are the heart of the story. If I told you about it I would have every witcher in the business up here looking for those holes. It is so simple; other people have missed it. That is the secret."

He rocked back on the heels of his boots, then leaned forward and confided:

"I enjoy living. I love life. I would like to live to be a fat, happy, old man like Herbert Hoover. But a lot of attempts have been made on my life. Sometime between February 15th and 17th someone left a note on the windshield of my car. There was a black skull painted on it with red blood coming from the head. Written in that same red color was, 'Van Suitt, you will die soon.' I know who that man is who wrote the note. There is another bunch now in Apache Junction who are organizing to knock off my pack train. They aren't spying on anyone else's camp. Just my camps."

Van Suitt noticed the unsettling effect of the mountains.

"You know what it does? There is a rare earth deposit running through here which gives off static electricity. This affects your mentality and sexual desires, just like in the South Seas. Apache Junction is just like a little Peyton Place. Very few wives there have not stepped out on their husbands. They are nuts, crazy."

Q—I believe, Mrs. Jones, that a month or so ago you saw four Russian pilots or Russian soldiers come into the Superstition Mountains, is that right?

Mrs. Jones—That is right, yes.

Q—How did they come in there?

Mrs. Jones—Well, they come in with green fatigues on and they had beards just as these same men [the miners]. They had USSR pins on their lapels.

Al Morrow had lived in the Superstition Mountains for twenty-one years, far longer than anyone else. His camp was in Needle Canyon. Morrow, who was fifty-four, did not carry a gun. When asked why not, he said, "If you bring fear and greed into the mountains, you will not take any gold out." He repeated this later. It was his mantra.

There was a gentleness in Morrow that was not evident in the other miners. Perhaps this was because he was the only miner who had spent most of his life prospecting, the others having abandoned more mundane livelihoods to pursue a myth. To keep his mind busy, Morrow had twice copied the Old Testament onto lined notebook paper, changing the wording of the Gideon Bible into the vernacular.

"People want to know why I don't go crazy here," he said. "People go crazy in town. They haven't learned to sit at home and think. I have always felt at ease up here. I have found out that if you don't carry a gun you find a lot of friends. A lot of people who come up here with guns are jumpy. The last time I got shot at was two years ago, just below this camp. I was sitting on the east side of that hill for some twenty minutes just thinking and wondering. I went to get up and a bullet hit six inches from my left foot. He was shooting low and to the left with a rifle. I must have startled him. I ran behind some rocks and waited. He left."

Morrow pondered, then added, "Now, Phil Thomas said he had a gun that shot low and to the left; and it was stolen from his camp a few months earlier. I had to sit it out when various parties were in here, like when Piper and that Jones woman had their gangs in here and were shooting at each other."

Q—Did she tell you how to do it?

W. A. Herron—She [Mrs. Jones] just said, "Shoot him. Make sure that he didn't use a knife because he was dangerous with his knife."

Q—And what did you tell her?

Herron—I told her I wouldn't do it.

Q—What happened then?

Herron—Well, then she tried to get Mr. Hammel to do it. He said he would bring Mr. Piper into her camp, but he would not kill him.

Q—And then what happened?

Herron—And she said, "Well, that would be fine." And we said, "Well, let's see some money." And she didn't come up with any money. So we laughed it off and forgot about it.

Morrow became more intense when he talked about what the mountains did to a person.

"There were eight people I know of who left these mountains and are too afraid to come back. If you ask them why they are scared, they can't explain. There was a Britisher and a Canadian in here a few years ago helping me dig. One day the Britisher stepped up on a ledge and looked over into a hole. What he felt made him swear he would not go up there again. He said he got a feeling that he was scared stiff. It was just so he could scream. That's the only way he could explain it. Now, all the fellows who were scared like that were working along one certain fault which runs north and south from The Needle. If you are on that fault, a walkie-talkie will not work. But it will work if you step ten feet off. Some boys have heard music coming from that fault; and when I have been on it with my transistor radio, well, I have heard telephone conversations on that radio nobody would want to hear."

Morrow motioned me to come closer and lowered his voice. "Just between us, Jake's got his eye on this claim. If there is any treasure on my claim, I will find it eventually. Treasure is a will of the wisp."

≺ ≻

I sought out Jake (formally known as Robert S. Jacobs and informally known as Crazy Jake) where he was resting in town after an extended sojourn in the mountains. He was writing a book entitled *The Ghosts on My Shoulder by Crazy Jake*. It was slow going. Nearly eighty thousand words had been painstakingly typed in triplicate with one finger. The manuscript was as neat as Morrow's handwritten version of the Bible.

Concerning Morrow, Crazy Jake said, "I know what he's got up there, and he is the only other guy who has got anything. Some people think he is nuts. But he has got some of the best info. The drawing of the map I saw the other day is super-fantastic. I think he got it from Mexico."

Jacobs wanted to be known as Crazy Jake. "Call me Crazy Jake," he said. It was his trademark, along with a hair-trigger temper, a sawed-off shotgun, and a .44-caliber revolver that was loaded with dum-dum bullets. Someone attempted to bushwhack Crazy Jake awhile back at his fortified mountain camp, and he returned the fire vigorously. "From that day on, nobody messes with me. They do something out there I don't like, they stop it," he said.

No one tangled with Crazy Jake. Forest Service rangers were wary of him. He once threatened to shoot them when they tried to stop his horses from grazing without a permit. Crazy Jake and Van Suitt were enemies, but so far their quarrels had been confined to feuding with their mouths. They told tales on each other behind the back of the other. One accused the other of growing marijuana in the wilderness. The other said his competitor was being financed by the Teamsters.

Crazy Jake laughed at Van Suitt's using two metal rods to witch for gold. Jake's information came from a careful study of twenty-two maps and inscriptions on two stone tablets. From these facts, if they were that, Crazy Jake constructed a labyrinthine theory. He declared, "The Dutchman is found. It is no longer lost. It is ours. We will show it in June when the rest of the idiots clear out."

When not in the mountains, Crazy Jake could be found at his home on El Yermo Street. The neat house—actually two shacks joined together—had boards over the windows for greater security and because he ran out of money for glass. His four seemingly healthy children, whose ages ranged from two to thirteen, sometimes were reduced to eating macaroni, potatoes, or the rabbits their father shot. Mrs. Jacobs allowed, "It is a hard life sometimes."

Crazy Jake sat at the head of the kitchen table. He was thin, partly bald, and toothless. He was a chain smoker and drank coffee incessantly. His two-year-old daughter, a blonde with blue eyes, was giggling at the pictures in a book at the other end of the table from where the .44-caliber pistol rested within easy reach of Jake. His eyes had the same near-far glaze as Van Suitt's. I took notes, gingerly.

Crazy Jake said, "I never shot anybody. All I have to do is look them in the eyes and I scare them to death." I believed him. Earlier he had told me that he had once been a master sergeant in the Air Force and a soldier of fortune. "Let's put it this way. I am a peace-loving person. The FBI figured I killed thirty people." I was not about to question that paradox.

He had been searching six years for the mine. "The odds are a billion to one. You have to be nuts. The average person couldn't cut it. They want security. You never know where the next grub-stake will come from out here."

Crazy Jake's intensity shot up a notch or two. I was nervous but tried not to show it.

"The mountains are a strange place. They will drive you nuts. They close in on you after a while. To be a Dutchman hunter you have to live it all the time—24 hours a day, 365 days a year, year after year. The only thing to do to remain sane is to get away from it. The mountains drive you stark, raving cuckoo. You just go mountain happy."

He escorted me to the door, gave me directions to Phoenix, and I departed.

As I drove back into the urban sprawl of that desert city, it occurred to me that Piper and St. Marie were dead. Mrs. Jones, a large black woman who said she was an opera singer, was in the Arizona State Hospital in Phoenix. Morrow was the prophet and Van Suitt and Crazy Jake were now the main protagonists in the Superstition Mountains—that is, besides the mountains themselves.

Los Angeles Times, May 1970

≺   ≻

Epilogue

I. ALASKA

Lituya Bay

Lituya Bay has changed but little since I visited it in 1980. Instead of a national monument, it now lies within an enlarged national park. The land that surrounds the bay has been designated a wilderness. Oil companies scoured the continental shelf off the bay for oil; but all of the holes proved dry, and they packed up and departed.

A few mountaineers and a few kayakers visit the bay; and that's about it, except for the fishermen who still enter the bay and risk the waves. Every several years a boat is lost at the entrance. There have been no earthquakes of any great magnitude and no giant waves since 1958. The granite that was washed clean by the last wave is overgrown with a thick stand of alders. The odds are increasing for a repeat of such a phenomenon, since giant waves have historically occurred at intervals of approximately twenty-five years. It has been thirty-four years since the last wave.

Given the natural hazards of the place, the Park Service has decided not to locate a permanent ranger station there; and rangers camp for short periods of time on Cenotaph Island during the summer months. A plastic plaque on Cenotaph that commemorated the death of the French sailors lasted but a few seasons in

259

that abrasive climate. It was replaced with a bronze plaque, the only visible human reminder of the hidden power of that place.

War on the Refuge

Attu remains a forlorn military base that spans the years. The Coast Guard detachment still mans its facility. Video cassette recorders (VCRs) have virtually replaced the sixteen-millimeter movie projector as the main source of entertainment. There has been some cleanup of World War II artifacts around Murder Bay; but elsewhere mines still present a danger, should a hiker put a foot in the wrong place. A bronze plaque was erected on Engineer Hill by the Japanese government to commemorate the soldiers of both nations who died in that forgotten battle.

The wildlife refuge remains such in name only, as no refuge work has been done on the island. The depredations of foxes, an Alaskan wildlife biologist recently told me, have been far more detrimental to bird life on Attu than any battle or oil spill. The Japanese dominance of the economy of the Aleutian Islands has increased.

The First Pipeline

Another armed conflict was the cause for a call for renewed oil production in the Arctic. As the Persian Gulf crisis heated up, the Bush administration made noises about drilling for oil in the Arctic National Wildlife Refuge in northeastern Alaska. This time the impetus came from the Department of Interior, which issued a report in 1987 stating that oil from the refuge was "the nation's single opportunity to increase significantly domestic oil production." Given the highest estimate, only four percent of the total national demand could be met from this source of oil.

Since the finds at Prudhoe Bay a quarter century earlier, Alaska had not proved to be as fruitful a source of energy as thought. One congressman commented, "The history of Alaska oil exploration is replete with multi-million dollar dry holes." Still, the Reagan and Bush administrations persisted.

When Iraq invaded Kuwait, Interior Secretary Manuel Lujan, Jr. said that exploration for oil on the coastal strip of the refuge should get underway. Production of oil on the North Slope was peaking; and this new oil, it was argued, would take up the slack. A short pipeline would be needed to transport the oil from the refuge to the existing trans-Alaska oil pipeline that ran to the port of Valdez. Environmentalists tied the proposal up in court; and Congress remained skeptical on the need for the additional oil. Visible, neutral fact-finding procedures were in place for this latest proposal to move Arctic oil south on the pretext of "national security."

Valdez Foretold

Shortly after midnight on March 24, 1989 the *Exxon Valdez* struck a reef off the entrance to Valdez; and Captain Joseph L. Hazelwood announced laconically over the radio, "Evidently we're leaking some oil and we're going to be here for quite a while." The resulting spill of eleven million gallons of oil was history.

I wish that I had foretold something more pleasant. The National Audubon Society put out a press release that called attention to my 1977 story. My former employer, *The Los Angeles Times,* published a story under the headline, "12-Year-Old Audubon Article Warned of Danger of Valdez." The story identified me as a science writer.

The cozy relationship between government and industry continued. Humorist Calvin Trillin noted a year after the oil spill that the president of Exxon's shipping subsidiary had been appointed chairman of the industry's standards-setting organization for oil tankers not long after two Exxon ships had spilled oil off the coast of New Jersey and a federal grand jury in Alaska had indicted Exxon. "This guy sounds like he has such a predilection for spilling oil that he might be considered a menace in a self-service filling station," wrote Trillin.

Also in 1990, a Coast Guard study, that had to be pried out of the agency by a Freedom of Information Act request, showed that there was inadequate inspection of oil tankers by Coast Guard personnel. Coast Guard inspectors were pressured to be quick about their jobs by tanker skippers who were on tight schedules. Exxon wanted to limit material about the oil spill that was to be placed in a public repository. A committee was appointed. Conoco became the first oil company to announce that it was building tankers with double hulls. And biologists were divided on whether the effects of the oil spill would be short lived or last into the next century.

Southeast

The ghost of Heintzleman returned with a vengeance during the last decade to haunt southeastern Alaska. As rain forests all over the world came into vogue, the Tongass National Forest became the cynosure of heated debate over the treatment of such lands in this country. There were studies, law suits, congressional hearings, and newspaper and magazine articles galore. Some examples of the latter were: "Paradise in Peril," *Life;* "Ending the Rape of the Tongass," *The New York Times;* "The Forest Service Follies," *Sports Illustrated;* "The Uncommitted Crime," *The New*

Yorker; and, somewhat more explicitly titled than my story, "Trashing the Tongass," *Audubon.*

The issues were: the two fifty-year contracts that favored two pulp mills, one of which was owned by Japanese interests; the Forest Service paying out far more money for the preparation of timber sales than it was receiving in income; the need for more wilderness; the need for jobs; Alaskan native corporations increasing their logging activities; and everything else that had been part of the stew during the previous decade.

Most of the heat was directed at the Forest Service, and the associate chief of that agency admitted at a congressional hearing, "The economics of operating Tongass timber was poor, much poorer than had been anticipated." A compromise bill was passed by Congress in 1990. "Half a rain forest is better than no rain forest at all," said the president of the Wilderness Society. The governor of Alaska thought the bill would not harm the timber industry.

Sitka-area Indians had begun logging on Admiralty Island, and a mine was being developed at the north end of the island. The Forest Service had easily won out over the Park Service and was administering the island's national monument lands.

In Angoon, it seemed that little had changed. A *New Yorker* writer described the village in a 1990 article much as I had experienced the place a dozen years earlier. Angoon was still dry; and there still was no restaurant, bank, bar, or café. A number of anthropologists, archaeologists, representatives of government agencies, and journalists continued to visit the island.

A Summer With Alex

No other story or book that I have written ever got the response that this article received when it was published or when it was reprinted shortly thereafter in an airline flight magazine. I should mention that no other piece of writing was so easy to produce. It just unrolled from my typewriter in a natural manner.

I got telephone calls and letters from all over the country. A resident of Hawaii wrote a particularly touching postcard stating that he had a similar experience with his son while hiking in the Sierra Nevada that summer. I tacked that card to the wall. A doctor in Florida, mistaking the intent of my article, asked if I would serve on the board of an organization that he was forming for men who had been done in by their former wives. I declined. Some single mothers wrote, expressing interest in meeting me. No rendezvous resulted.

Alex, now married, is about to graduate from architecture school. That trip is our fondest memory, and we frequently ask each other, "Do you remember . . . ?" He now outhikes me.

I should mention that in the next year or two grizzly bears mauled and killed people who were camping in some of the same places that we did at Glacier Bay National Monument. We had the luck that summer.

II. THE WEST

The Fall from Grace

Two years later legislation was passed by Congress relocating the many Navajo and few Hopi families on their respective reservations. It was a wrenching experience for the more numerous Navajos who faced a move onto strange lands. By the 1986 deadline, most of the families had been voluntarily relocated into other housing either on or off the reservation. It was their choice. It was possible to receive a new house and up to five thousand dollars in bonus payments.

However, the legislation did not create a perfect program. Shysters took advantage of some Indians off the reservation, and the government botched the housing in a few instances on the reservation. Those who stayed on the reservation fared better. Life estates were given to a few old Navajos in order to allow them to remain where they had lived for years. White activists tried to muddy the waters, claiming it was all a ruse to benefit the energy companies that were mining coal in the area; but eventually the Hopi received their land back. Energy developments, overgrazing, overpopulation, diseases, tribal corruption, and the appropriation of water continued to plague the Indians.

Also in 1974, the Havasupai expanded their land base by 185,000 acres, in addition to which 93,500 acres in an enlarged Grand Canyon National Park were designated "a traditional use area for the Havasupai Indians." Approximately fifteen thousand hikers visited the reservation each year. There was a new school, tourist lodge, café, grocery store, post office, and tribal headquarters. Sight-seeing planes were almost constantly overhead. A private postal service delivered packages by helicopter. Satellite dishes brought television to the remote reservation. The tribe could not agree on how to balance traditional values with life as it was depicted on television screens.

A few years ago I hiked into the Canyon de Chelly. I saw a woman in a dark-blue, velveteen dress herding her sheep from an enclosure near a traditional hogan to the opposite side of the canyon. I felt, again, that at least there still was this one reminder of the uncorrupted lifestyle of American Indians.

A Coastal Journey

Since I wrote this book, coastal commissions that regulate development along a narrow strip of the shoreline were voted, first, into temporary existence by the electorate in 1972 and then given permanent status by the state legislature in 1976. One of the reasons I left journalism and took a high-level job in state government was to put into public policy what I had been writing about, that being the need to consider the wider, public interest amidst the rush to wall off the coastline to all but a privileged few.

In the administration of Governor Jerry Brown, as in newspaper reporting, we weren't supposed to have any hidden agendas. But I had at least one. I wanted those commissions to have permanent, effective status. I was put in charge of a State Resource Agency task force that was to determine how the coastal commissions would operate vis-á-vis such existing agencies under our jurisdiction as state lands, forestry, fish and game, parks, water resources et al.

Their objections were all turf related. How ridiculous, I thought. But my boss, Claire Dedrick, the secretary for resources, sympathized with the existing agencies. I decided to play the faithful fool and accurately represent their interests. The result, as I had hoped, was that no one took us seriously. The objections were easily waved aside by legislative committees and within the higher ranks of the administration. When the governor decided that he needed to endorse the legislation in order to make a favorable showing in the Oregon primary for the presidency that year, the objections were ruled moot; and I felt that I could safely leave government.

I recently retraced a portion of the coastal journey that I had taken in 1972, and was pleasantly surprised. There were changes, and some seemed detrimental; but the sum of what had transpired in those twenty years was nowhere near what the greatly increased population would have unleashed had there been no restraints. The coastal commissions, seriously hobbled for eight years by a hostile governor, had managed to function effectively.

The Dimming of the Range of Light

Officially designated wilderness areas have increased, but so have the population and the regulations. From Maine to California, limits are in place for hiking trails, campgrounds, river runs, canoe trails, and mountain-bike trails. Not all the limits are observed, because state and federal cutbacks in funding have lessened staffing and eroded enforcement. I know. I sometimes cheat. Restrictions seem antithetical to a wilderness experience, but without them wilderness areas would resemble a cat's litter box. My excuse is that the natural state of humans is inconsistency. As wilderness historian Roderick Nash said recently, "It's ironic. By making wilderness popular, we now have to save it from its friends." Not much, except the scale of use and regulation, has changed in twenty years.

Living With Fire

The cost of homes had increased greatly; but the weather was the same. It was hot and dry and a strong wind was blowing. A small patch of grass caught on fire, and in five minutes it was a raging inferno. In the last days of June 1990, fire again ravaged the hills behind Santa Barbara, this time killing one person, injuring forty others, destroying 567 homes, blackening four thousand acres, and causing $190 million in damages in some of the same areas destroyed by the 1977 and earlier fires.

People immediately began to rebuild in the same place. Their comments once again gave me a sense of déjà vu. They said:

> This is the best place in the world to live. Where else would you go? There are tornadoes in the Midwest and hurricanes in the East. We live with the idea of fire. Risk is part of life in California.

The actions of government and private institutions were similar. Another governor toured the area. Institutional pressure was to rebuild. Nature was also repetitive. It was another year of drought.

A greater inferno arose in the hills behind Berkeley and Oakland, also affluent neighborhoods, on October 20, 1991. It killed twenty-five persons, destroyed 2,153 buildings, and caused upwards of $1.5 billion in damages. Fire was also no stranger to these hills, having consumed combustible vegetation and structures in 1923 and 1940 and 1980. The hammers of construction crews could be heard shortly thereafter in the hills.

And, yes, I checked my insurance and cleared the brush from around the house. Still, in 1989 it was destroyed by fire. My wife and I slept poorly after the Santa Barbara and Oakland fires. We have rebuilt on another lot that is closer to the San Andreas Fault.

Living With Drought

John Steinbeck wrote of California some forty years ago in *East of Eden:* "And it never failed that during the dry years the people forgot about the rich years, and during the wet years they lost all memory of the dry years. It was always that way." And, it seems, it will always be that way.

Not long after this article was published the rains came, and they came, and they came. The West was flooded. A dam on the Colorado River almost gave way. The small community in which I lived on the California coast was isolated for days by mudslides. Once again we were profligate with our use of water. And then the rains, like a spectral presence, departed; and the dry years began, and continued, and continued.

As I write these words, California and the West are in their seventh year of drought. The predictions, if anything, are even more dire than they were in 1977; and I have that same gnawing feeling of tenuousness. There are more people, and there is less water now. Four years elapsed before water officials faced the fact that there would be shortages. The governors bicker. The farmers and the urban dwellers are locked in an intense competition for survival. The same pressures, some in different forms, are being felt along the Tuolumne River.

I am reading now from a state document issued during the last drought. It says, "Californians must remember, however, that the conditions of 1976 are not unique; similar, or worse, conditions have occurred before and they will happen again." But we forget.

The Eating of the West

The statistics have changed slightly (the per capita consumption of beef is down to 111 pounds per year), and the names are different; but otherwise the article remains as true today as it was some fifteen years ago. In fact, other publications quote it; and I still get telephone calls from writers, and in one instance a national television network, asking about certain aspects of the story. Cows munching grass remain by far the dominant activity on deteriorating western lands, and the reports on range conditions are just as dire.

In 1979 the contest of wills that I wrote about was between Gary McVicker and the ranchers around Kingman, Arizona. Let me quote from a 1990 *New York Times* story about regulators and ranchers in the Twin Falls, Idaho area:

> Some [forest] rangers and other critics of the Government's policy say the fees are too low, the herds are degrading the national forest land and the restrictions are being routinely ignored by ranchers who use their political influence with Western senators to undercut efforts to enforce the rules.
>
> The cattlemen say that they do as best they can to protect the range, and that when they slip up, they have usually been given the benefit of the doubt [in the past]. Their view is that a few zealous supervisors led by Mr. Oman are threatening their way of life.

The ranchers wanted Donald Oman, a district ranger in the Sawtooth National Forest, removed; and they threatened him with violence. The twenty-six-year veteran of the Forest Service maintained the land in his district was badly overgrazed, and the ranchers had not been following regulations. The ranchers went to their senator. Oman filed a whistle blower's complaint about harassment from his superiors. The publicity (stories in *High Country News, The New York Times, Audubon,* and *People*) got Oman an unexpected ally—President George Bush.

But, no matter. The names changed again. The spotlight swung to focus on a forest supervisor in Nevada and Wayne Hage, who had replaced John Casey as the king of the trespassers in that state. The periodic national attention on the issue diminished, but the people who depended on cows to make a living remained.

The Crowding of the West

The original herd of ten elk has multiplied to 183. Two of the original elk died, and there were some abnormalities among births. The elk herd, as had the cattle before them, suffered from a deficiency of copper in its natural feed and had to be fed a supplementary diet for a time.

There are problems with overcrowding. Coyote bush is beginning to invade the range and cut down on the grasslands that are rated as being in only fair to good condition. The carrying capacity for the herd on the twenty-five hundred acres is between 100 and 150. The herd is in good, not excellent, condition. A federal report stated, "Since these elk cannot be relocated due to the presence of Johne's disease, any herd reduction will be by lethal removal." Johne's disease resembles tuberculosis and is not curable. The Park Service has not yet bit that particular bullet. The situation was the same statewide, where the number of elk greatly exceeded the two thousand limit; and the hunting of elk has begun on a limited scale.

Eventually Merv McDonald did find another ranch, one that was across Tomales Bay from Pierce Point. It was not equivalent. It was one-half the size and had one-third the carrying capacity of the Pierce Point Ranch. Income and responsibilities were reduced. The family broke up. One son and his family moved elsewhere. The exterior of the ranch buildings at Pierce Point were renovated, but the Park Service was unable to lease them. Park Service employes live in the ranch house, while the outbuildings remain vacant. There is a self-guided tour: "This is the school house," "this is the milking barn," etc.

Elsewhere, the gentrification of the interior West was making it extremely difficult for ranchers to earn a living by running cattle alone; and family members were being forced to take other jobs or sell their land to subdividers or wealthy outsiders.

Craig, Colorado, Population Unknown

I passed through Craig two or three times in the last decade. It seemed like a town that had invited a lot of people to a party, and only a few chose to attend. There was a feeling of vacancy, but that may be because I remembered it as bursting at the seams. Most probably it is just a normal place now.

The population of Craig never reached the projection of 24,000 for 1990. It peaked at 12,300 early in the last decade and dropped to 10,000 in 1990, a victim of the energy boom gone bust because of more plentiful and cheaper Middle East oil. Craig had gone through booms and busts before, and it will again. This is the destiny of Craig, as well as the remainder of the interior West. Gold mining returned recently to alter certain parts of the West once again. Who knows what is next. There certainly will be another energy crisis, and history will repeat itself.

Crazy Jake & Company

A photograph of Al Morrow, showing him working at transcribing the Bible at a table on which a box of Quaker Oats was sitting, was published along with the article. The Quaker Oats people called me and asked where they could send him a carton of the cereal. I told them general delivery, Apache Junction, Arizona. I hope Al got that gift. It was not long after I left the Superstition Mountains that one of his tunnels collapsed on him, and he was crushed to death by a boulder while attempting to dig his way out.

Van Suitt visited me a few months after this story appeared and made quite a stir with the security guards and my colleagues at the Times when he strode about in his buckskin-fringed clothing with a large knife attached to his belt. His mining claims are inactive, and he hasn't been seen around the mountains for some time. Crazy Jake went to prison after pleading guilty to fraud charges in connection with soliciting Texas investors in his mine scheme, and now he is out.

The Superstition Wilderness Area is a lot safer and saner than when I visited it. A few miners manage to sneak in with a little dynamite to do some blasting, but for the most part the Forest Service has got control of the situation. The Lost Dutchman Mine still has its believers, one of whom is former Arizona attorney general Bob Corbin, who has been looking for the mine since 1957. "I think there's a mine," he says, "and it's very rich." It was Corbin who prosecuted Crazy Jake. Jake maintained that the attorney general, who had gotten hold of his voluminous records, was trying to get rid of the competition.